Real
Wales

For Sue

Real
Wales

Peter Finch

seren

Seren is the book imprint of
Poetry Wales Press Ltd
Nolton Street, Bridgend, Wales
www.seren-books.com

ISBN 978-1-85411-483-9

A CIP record for this title is available from
the British Library

The publisher works with the financial assistance
of the Welsh Books Council

Printed by Bell & Bain, Glasgow
Cover Photograph: 'Morfa Bychan beach' by Aled Rhys Hughes

Also in the Real Wales series
Editor: Peter Finch:

Real Aberystwyth – Niall Griffiths
Real Cardiff – Peter Finch
Real Cardiff Two – Peter Finch
Real Newport – Anne Drysdale
Real Swansea – Nigel Jenkins
Real Wrexham – Grahame Davies
Real Merthyr – Mario Basini

Coming Soon:
Real Liverpool – Niall Griffiths
Real Pembroke – Tony Curtis
Real Cardiff Three – Peter Finch

CONTENTS

NORTH EAST

NORTH WEST

MORE

POEMS

INTRODUCTION

So what is this place? Grey crags and green miasma in the western British mists. A place like poetry, where nothing happens. A place of sheep and hairy men. Where is this land? Most of the world do not know. And if they do then they can rarely point us out. Wales, I never heard of that place[1]. Wales, the invisible, the lost. Wales, the real Cantre'r Gwaelod. A small island in the Hebrides. A rock off the west coast of Ireland. A hummock out there in the stormy ocean. Wales, Grassholm writ just that little bit larger. A floating land, full of birds.

The great historian Gwyn Alf Williams said the people of this place had "for a millennium and a half lived in the two western peninsulas of Britain as a Welsh people, (and) are now nothing but naked under an acid rain." The tourist trade sells us as a place of endless singing, long yellow beaches, rugby rugby and folk in stovepipe hats. Business promotion says we are a global centre, a land of opportunity, a place to relocate to, perfect transport, weather like Bermuda. The government says we have the highest incidence of heart disease in Europe. We smoke too much. We don't climb enough of our hills. Wales, a fake place made by Woolworth, cellotaped to the west of the midlands, useful for car rallies, and as a butt of English jokes. You are a country. You can't mean that.

Everyone looks for Wales and so many do not find it. Either like R.S. Thomas they search for a Wales which does not exist, moving ever westward, in hope. Or like the academics find a new Wales right in front of them, constructed from the past's framework, a place that changes and doesn't simultaneously. A land of magic. Wave your diving rod. Follow your ley.

Defining Wales is rather like defining verse. For every rule someone comes up with there will be an exception which breaks it. Ultimately poems become what they are because the poet says so. Wales is like this. The bit you think of as real probably is. The Feathers in Llanystumdwy. The Greyhound on High Street in Newport. Barafundle. The power station at Connah's Quay. Splott. The Millennium Coastal Park at Llanelli. The Spar at Flint. The writers gathered at the Vulcan in Adamsdown. The street of subscribers to *Taliesin* in Pwllheli. The coach spotters at Swansea bus station. Brecon Cathedral. The cairn at the far end of Golden Road. The Urdd Welsh classes for adults. The sewage works at Aberystwyth. The place up near Dyfi Junction where there's no platform but the trains still stop. Pete Davis' Chicken Shed at Brynamman. The left bank of the river Lugg near Bleddfa. The Codfather of Sole chipshop on Barry Island seafront. The place where Dafydd Elis Thomas parks his car near the Senedd. The steps of the National Museum and the pillars behind which John Tripp once hid his bicycle clips. The jetty at Mostyn from where the Airbus wings set sail. The bridge over the lost Roath rail branch on Penylan Hill. All as real as each other.

In a country the size of ours it should be possible to visit everywhere – some claim to have – but there are still towns and villages appearing on the nightly BBC Wales weather maps that I have never been through. And on occasions there is one of which I've never heard.

Some people never bother. Cardiffians – and some of them can be the worst – live and die inside the capital. The Wales beyond is an alien land. Full of workless pits and mountains. No Asda. No Lidl. I am not going there. Why should I? What would I get out of it? I have also met a well-known north Wales novelist who claimed never to have visited Pembrokeshire. The south. Not Welsh enough. Noncompliance as a political act. For him there are three countries: Y Fro Cymraeg, Welsh Wales, an arc of land in the western reaches; Wales that might as well be England, including the capital and the north east and the southern coasts; and Y Fro Efallai where desire and actuality mix, where reality comes in like a short wave signal – Myddfai, Banwen, Merthyr, Pontcanna, Aber out of term time. Trefdraeth when the sun shines. Who is to say that his Wales is any better than mine?   Or that mine is more real?

This book is about this country. A place where some imagine that no one has raised a sword in anger since Glyndŵr's rebellion went down in 1409 and the Welsh were banned from ever owning anything outside their borders. A place where others know, for certain, that the real Wales is waiting, just round the political corner, and a new day will come. Minorities rise. Nation states fragment. It's the post-modern way.

The real Wales may well be a place of people, a land of human intervention, of despoliation in the search for minerals, of pipelines and power grids, and roads that mesh the green like fishnet, but it is not an urban country. The city life of disenfranchisement, dislocation and alienation is not ours. Wales, land of communities, where decisions reach the surface through compromise and conciliation. Wales where power frightens and underdogs are prized. Wales where time slows and life is longer. Wales where the past actually is important and historians are honoured. Wales where highrise is feared and there is no navy. The real Wales is where people always talk about who they are, strive after roots, want fields rather than mansions, although generally have neither. The real Wales is the one I've gone looking for. Not sure I've found it all yet.

When I wrote *Real Cardiff*, back in 2002, I determined to write about the land as I saw it. No considered history nor topographical guide, no socio-economic handbook, nor fictional prose. As I observed it the world kept changing. The past slid from me. Those guarding it seemed to want to usher it away. What we were went underground to stay hidden or to be dug up by the disinterested, and burned. Few seemed to care. The land also seemed to be secret. Full of self-contained, excluding epi-centres, places where you could only gain access if you had a key. The Cardiff of Geraint Jarman's Welsh reggae, of Philip Dunleavy's Castle, of Callaghan's slum clearance, the Cardiff of Geoffrey Inkin's Barrage and Bay. These innovations were making us a completely new Welsh city, a post-industrial capital for an incoming millennium, something out there was happening. It had to be tracked and written down.

Real Wales adopts the same approach for the whole country. The *Real Cardiff* books (volumes one and two already bestsellers and a third out there in the hazy, not-yet-completed wings) spawned a series. *Real Swansea. Real Merthyr. Real Newport. Real Wrexham. Real Aberystwyth.* And more. Written by experts, to the Real formula. Series edited by Peter Finch. The present volume is my look at my country. Didn't know it was mine until I grew and went out there to see. There are many like me. Lights go on. We need to find out just who we really are.

I've used classic *Real Cardiff* techniques here. Visited places by accident, simply because they sounded interesting, or because I found myself nearby. Places determined by their importance to Wales. Places that had to be rediscovered. Places where things existed. Places where, apparently, they did not. I went on tour, doing poetry readings. I visited alone, with my partner, in the company of local experts, literateurs, oddballs, historians, novelists. I used old maps and new ones. I read local histories and national overviews. I travelled by car and train and on foot. Much of the distance on foot, for often there were only unpaved tracks.

I discovered a lot. The sheep are many. The rain is often. The light is brilliant. The skies can be huge. The past can be picked up because it is often so near the surface. The past can also never be found again

because of what we have done to it. Broken it, built on it, lost it,
thrown it away. And there is also the matter of the mysteries, that stuff
of Wales which makes things happen, or seem to happen, of which
I've found no evidence anywhere else. Kings sleeping below rocks.
Blood in trees. Wonder in the grass. Future in the air.

Notes

1. Conversation between the author and some picnicking black Americans on the coast of
    South Carolina.

SOUTH EAST

CYFARTHFA

Above China, the once riotous and sewer-poor centre of industrial Merthyr, stands Cyfarthfa. Seventy-two rooms, three hundred and sixty-five windows. Built in 1825 by the iron master William Crawshay. A castle of stone, grey dark and desperate in its Victorian bulk. Merthyr, town of Tydfil the martyr, most populous place in Wales for much of the indus- trial revolution, centre for iron making like no other. Just thirty miles up the valleys from the port of Cardiff and another world.

The myths of Merthyr: no one is more than five-feet tall; highest heart attack rate for anywhere in Western Europe; most people who work here don't live here; most popular dog is the greyhound; rain- fall highest for south Wales; never snows; curry staple; ferocious alco- hol consumption, not changed since the Chartists riots; the elaborate cast-iron Robert and Lucy Thomas Memorial Fountain at the foot of Lower High Street has never run with water. Sir William Thomas Lewis and Williams Thomas Rees, of Aberdare but natives of Merthyr, who ordered this splendour from Walter MacFarlane in Glasgow, never knew.

Harri Webb lived here in the 70s, at Garth Newydd, a rambling Victorian now-demolished crumble on the hillside, home of singers, poets, pamphleteers and nationalists. The Lamb, the local pub, would not serve women. There were riots on the streets at closing time. Hurling left hooks that spun and missed, head hammers that didn't. In a curry house, half way through a first-generation British vindaloo and chips, popodoms not available, the police arrived. They locked the doors lest anyone should attempt escape without paying, nodded good evening to Mr Webb, and proceeded to arrest at least ten diners for things they'd done elsewhere. There was little violence. Two extra bowls of curry sauce spilled. One chair knocked over. My Bombay Duck crumbled beneath my nervous fingers. Don't concern yourself, said Harri, they don't want you, you're too posh. Saved by my station in life once again.

When Crawshay dominated this place and the fires of hell lit the night skies things were little different. The streets were unpaved. The population looked more ragged. But the drinking was just as intense. The Canaan of gorging sewers and cholera may have now been wiped but the oblivion of alcohol still dominates, making the world bearable.

Glyn Jones, king of Anglo-Welsh lit's second flowering, was born here in 1905. Clare Street, featureless terrace, painted white now, fewer parked cars than any comparable street in the Western world. We're here for the Glyn Jones day school being held at Cyfarthfa. When the Crawshays gave up in the early twentieth century the Castle was sold to Merthyr Tydfil Corporation. Robert Thompson Crawshay, the ironmaster most-hated, died in 1879. He lies in the churchyard at nearby Vaynor under an immense eleven-ton granite slab surrounded by low Victorian iron railings. On a plate in its centre are the words "God Forgive Me". Just those.

Glyn actually attended school at the Castle. When William Crawshay the fourth left Merthyr in 1889 the Corporation purchased the buildings and grounds, converting the north western end into a grammar school. This opened in 1910. It is still a school today, heavy stone, milk smelling, worn corridors, doors that are chipped with their cracked glass panels half boarded with ply. The Day School, celebrating the work of one of Merthyr's greatest sons, is in the ancient gymnasium. Left along a green tile lined corridor, past the leaking boys' toilets and the place where, when they wore them, they would hang their coats, their mackintoshes and their caps.

The gym itself is huge with wall bars, beams, horses and sets of hanging climbing ropes all still largely intact. Piecemeal conversion has added a black curtained, stained and highly scuffed stage, rack-mounted spotlights and piles of stacking chairs. There's a table with three tea urns on it and a smiling local dispensing. The attendees, a disparate bunch of mainly older writers, historians, and locals, cluster, warming their hands on mugs of Typhoo and cups of instant coffee.

We get lectures. Meic Stephens, who knew Glyn well and is

now his literary executor, enormously entertaining on Glyn's writing and personal history. The late Mercer Simpson, almost eighty years old at this point and looking like a renegade from Dad's Army, tracking the same territory. Glyn emerges as a writer with Wales in his blood who taught, hating it, simply to keep the wolf from the door. Mike Jenkins, the celebrator of local culture and an author totally at home in Merthyr's valleyed-up south-east Wales Welsh accent[1], reads a few of Glyn's pellucid poems. "It is Glyn Jones's gift, of heart as well as mind, that he has always known how to make of the blemished and unlovable an unexplainable song"[2]. In poor light Mike makes Glyn's poetry shine.

With John Pik[3] in charge the whole company then sets off for a zoom around Glyn's Merthyr. The actual place. We get our feet dirty. The charabanc is courtesy of Williams Coaches. It drives our assemblage of the aged and the keen straight and swiftly to the bottom of High Street where we disembark near the waterless Memorial Fountain before plunging up through the roaring open market. We are in search of the 1840s Woollen Mill near Tram Road, inspiration for much of Glyn's most well-known novel, *The Island of Apples*. The market sells everything – cabbages, trousers, pirate CDs, huge bras, stacks of hammers from China, badly printed batteries, fake Gucci handbags, cake, remaindered romances, pencils, plastic flower pots, bagged coal, facsimile games for Play Station, yellow perfume, iron gate posts, soap, knickers, apples. John is like a small firework, sparking ahead at high speed through Merthyr's cumulus Saturday crowds. As the tour passes Wetherspoons's Y Dic Penderyn three stragglers divert for research purposes. They are not seen again until the end of the afternoon. There is a brief detour to visit Soar Chapel where Glyn and his family worshipped, still extant and a centre for the Merthyr Welsh (siop llyfrau, dysgu cymraeg, mouldering paintwork). At the top of the market, breathing hard up the incline, the group, whisked past the four-storey and enormously impressive crumbled red-brick Young Men's Christian Association building with no comment, find the Woollen Mill, now Merthyr Upholstery. The small square in front of it, inspiration to the young Glyn for his life's best book. We gather close to listen to our tour leader. The gullied Morlais Brook roars beyond us, thick with darkness.

John Pik's recounting of this place as Brewery Square in Glyn's book, of Dragon Mills, Dewi Davies and his parents, of Jack and Carrie, who sell hats, boots, suits and costumes and the Nant, a tributary of the Ystrad, black with coal dust, is enormously engaging.

Tour followers are entranced. Pik smiles and sings through his lecture. Literature should be dull but worthy. This exposition is full of light.

On our ramble back down to the parked coach, John Pik vanished into the distance, Meic Stephens relates slices of Merthyr's real history, the politics, the places where our world began and where industrial revolution fermented. The late Gwyn Alf Williams had once taken a literary group on a similar trail, recounting the town's past with typical humour. What we'd learned on that trip, however, had been limited by Gwyn's propensity to lose himself in anecdote and the need to frequently stop and greet people he knew. This appeared to be at least half the local population. Meic is more circumspect but none the less entertaining.

Back at Cyfarthfa, beyond the steam railway, the lake with its bird islands and the dried up paddling pool, Tony Brown lectures us on Glyn and the nebulous. Glyn the man lover, the great Christian, the Anglo-Welsh king with a deep uncertainty principle. Could Tony be right or was this academic bluff? In the seeping dusk Glyn's Merthyr ghost, clean hands, lemon yellow tie, smiles, avoids the issue.

From the Cyfarthfa car park with Merthyr below me in twilight the lights make it look like just any other valley community. Famous once, like Spain, like Stanley Matthews, like Bill Halley. Now not. But this neighbourhood has more past than most. So much that if it were not for the fact that generations of corporate redevelopment had wiped the place clean the past would certainly overwhelm the present.

HAY

Offa's Dyke runs right along the side of Hay. It would if it were still there, red dotted line on the Landranger map. The Dyke, an Anglo-Saxon version of the great wall of China built by King Offa of Mercia in the dark of 757 to keep the Welsh out, has never been visible from space. On occasions it is barely visible even when you are standing on its top. The Dyke comes down from Knighton along the side of Wye, and then, missing the castle, heads south through Cusop along the ridge towards Chepstow. Not that there's much still extant in Hay: built on, gardened across, run with sheep. The Dyke, all 168 miles of it, is still more or less the Welsh border. Local Government boundary rearrangements down the years have chipped and added but at Hay the line is pretty precise. Hay-on-Wye, mostly in Wales but with streets in England. Welsh water but some drains in the English marches. Doctors with leeks but a few with red roses filling their front lawns.

In the Welsh language Hay translates as *Y Gelli*, the grove, one of the few places in Wales with a definite article like The Snowdon, The Bala, and The Barry[4]. I plunge down the Broad Street in the Hay past the clock tower to find the Poetry Bookshop, Alan Halsey's all-embracing wrecking yard for the bardic output of the English-speaking world. It's 1989 and technology has not yet made publishing the free-for-all it later will. The process remains expensive. Getting a book out, a slim vol of your poems, still means a lot. Alan's bookshop stacks the rarities and the rejects. Old Fulcrums, Cape Golliards, San Francisco City Lights in their square black and white stripe, small press endlessness from Aquila, Albion Village, Latimer, Ferry Press, Assembling, Six Pack, Transatlantic Review. Visual shrieks from Tlaloc, Poor Old Tired Horse, Coach House. I may have finished with *second aeon* but that part of my past is still around on these shelves. But I am in Hay not to buy but for a reading, and not at the Poetry Bookshop either, that visit was for pleasure. I am here for the Festival. The Hay Literature extravaganza and things have only just begun. Norman[5] is still alive and Peter in his banana yellow linen suit is funding things from the proceeds of a poker game. The star is Arthur Miller who before he got here thought that Hay on Wye was a sort of sandwich. There's a tent in the school yard and no pavilions. The festival runs in bars and restaurants, halls and chapels right across the town.

Hay, of course, is tiny. Population 1450. Castle, motte, market. Ancient taverns. British Legion. Legendary witch Maud Walbee walled up here with her son to starve to death for displeasing the king. In the nineteenth century the preacher Frances Kilvert living in nearby Clyro wrote up the town's doings in the famous diary. Today full of galleries and shops that sell scented candles and tie-dye t-shirts. And bookshops. Hay, the world's first town of books. Dozens of outlets, scores. Ancient and modern, antiquarian and junk, stacked in overkill from east to west. It is all Richard Booth's fault. He went to America and saw just how easy it was to buy old books not by the box but by the container load. He shipped them back here by the hundred thousand. Literature as oil spill, seeping into every corner and staining all the walls. He bought the Hay Fire Station and the Cinema and the Castle and turned them all into Wal-Mart-style book shifting enterprises. Sell cheap and sell lots. Others joined him. The best place in the world to open a new shoe shop is right next door to an existing shoe shop. Your customers will not halve but will multiply. So it was and is with books.

It helped, of course, that Booth was a natural showman. After touring south Wales commercial bookstores with a car full of over-stocks (and in his case everything was an overstock) in a failed attempt to offload his unsaleables he decided that local overkill might be a better approach. He declared himself King of Hay, had his photo taken in robes and cardboard crown sitting outside the Castle, declared Hay independent, issued his own postage stamps and began to sell passports. In the hard winter which followed he looked after his subjects by sending taxi-loads of unwanted dross to pensioners so that for warmth they could burn them on their stoves. The press coverage he got was instant and extensive. Hay the Booktown was born. One bookshop for every thirty-six residents. A million volumes musting on their shelves.

I am here with Horses Mouth, a poetry reading trio consisting of me, Ifor Thomas, and Tôpher Mills. We do a cross between stand-up lit and music hall, poetry as a branch of the entertainment industry, poetry performed to boozing audiences who throw things and heckle. For this year's Hay we are booked to read at the Blue Boar. Tickets cost £25.00 which, until I discovered that the price also included a fine-dining supper, I felt to be the first indication I'd come across of my true worth. Before this the most anyone had ever had to pay to hear me read was £4.25. Horses Mouth dress the part, performing in dinner suits, bow-ties, and wearing shiny black shoes. For this early Hay Festival Florence had found himself unable to run to a dressing room and we'd had to mange in the open. I'd chosen to change between my car and a sheep transporting pantechnicon parked in the large car park which sloped gently to the south. I'd got the white shirt on but not the trousers when the parked lorry drove off. This left me like Brian Rix, facing several dozen middle-aged tourists and Hay book shoppers loading their purchases into the backs of their Astras. Who cares?

The supper club was long and thin with a small stage at the front end. The diners drank and slumbered. A centre-piece of my act at this time was a piece about smoking written in newspeak. *Ex-Smokes Man Writes Epic.* "Breath in. Place hot end in mouth. Close lips tightly. Blow. Smoke pours out through filter. - Brown fingertips, nicotine traces. This is the mark of a man." To add impact I give the audience a spiel about how I've decided to give up fags on the way here. I hunt my dj pockets, find the twenty embassy stashed there and throw this at random into the listening crowd. I actually throw it to one of my two fellow Horses Mouthers who then make their way to the stage, opening the packet and lighting up as they go. As my poem proceeds the pair light the entire packet and stand there with ten glowing red tips apiece. Laughter. Smoke everywhere. Underlines my point.

The problem on this occasion was what to do with the twenty burning tubes once the poem was done and I was onto my next. Ifor chose to dump his ten into a Bakelite ashtray on a nearby table. Tôpher followed suit. What they failed do was to stub correctly. Smoke continued, in bulk. A pissed diner from the front row took objection and stepped forward to dowse the smoulder with his drink. There was a sizzle and a great escaping plume of smoke. For a second or two silence hung in the air. Then the fire alarm went off and we were all rushed out into the dark car park, stumbling and shouting, drinks sloshed, dinners ruined, Ifor not performed yet, cold, drizzle.

We didn't get paid. No roses. A Hay tradition was born, the former rather than the latter. Read at Hay today on the new site in one of the new great flapping pavilions and you'll be given some champagne and a long stemmed rose. Financial recompense, if available at all, is down to your publisher.

But Hay is a great place. Eccentrically wound with record shops, galleries, bookstalls, old map sellers, shops retailing country gear, trendy dresses, flowers, zinc watercans, bails of garden twine. Hay Bluff and the Black Mountains lie behind it, England beyond. The English find Hay not full of barbarians and the mouths of locals speak to them in accents they can understand. The town roads twist and turn in an arbitrary manner never seen in cities. Alley ways. Narrowings. The place is old. King John, son of Henry, the man who signed the Magna Carta fought Llewelyn the Great here. Both sides sacked the castle. In 1977 the place caught fire again. But it's still there, repaired (ish) and insulated from the real world with printed bound volumes. Near it stands Hay's Honesty Bookshop, pick up a water-stained pulpy title and pay whatever you want. Stuff your money into a wall mounted slot. Or don't. How many more books do you need? House agents will tell you that shelves of books do not sell a property. Books say must and age and dust. Keep them in boxes or resell. Horses Mouth planned a book but broke up shortly after the Hay debacle. Just as well.

BARRY ISLAND

The problem with Barry Island, marina development apart, is sheer familiarity. There's no obvious literary connection, no series of readings that have drawn me. Creative antecedents are weak. Dai Smith lives in Redbrink Crescent, Deirdre Beddoe is at the Knapp. Tony Curtis, Prof of Poetry, still has an Edwardian semi up at the top of town. This is a place I've been coming to since I was a child. The Island at Barry, nearest stretch of clear sand to the industrial smog of Cardiff. Half an hour on the train from Queen Street and the grit and dark would vanish to be replaced by white topped waves and acres of sky. This place was big. Through the eyes of a child the sands went on forever.

Y Barri, Westbarry, sub-enfeoffed[6] to the de Barri family in Norman times (it was they who built the castle), was little more than a village and a haunt for smugglers and pirates until the industrial revolution arrived. The Island was a rabbit warren. It is shown on Evans Mouse's 1622 map of Barry Manor as the island of Cold Knappe "invironed with the sea of all partes". All was to change in 1884 when David Davies of Llandinam, Davies the Ocean, took on

the great Butes of Cardiff and dug his coal dock here. The four villages scattered along the coast – Cadoxton, Holton, Merthyr Dyfan and Barry itself – merged as the boom filled the spaces between them with workers housing, railtracks, yards and warehouses. The course of the Cadoxton River was diverted to the Bendricks. Two great dams were laid to end the island's isolation and join it to the mainland. Ruination no more.

Barry exploded in a fury of Victorian infrastructure and trucks of anthracite steam. The badly drained marshlands were rapidly built on. Heavy immigration from the West country, Ireland and Scotland turned the boom town into an English monoglot melange. There was no planning, things went up where they were needed. Slums staggered along the sides of waterways. Roads slushed with sliding mud. For a time the docks held the largest stretches of contained water anywhere in the world. The Barry Railway brought in valley coal along sixty eight miles of track crossing three great viaducts – Porthkerry, Llanbradach and the Walnut Tree at Taffs Well.

The town still bears the scars of this shambolic development. For the large part today it's a broken and busted place. Storefronts are closed, things are not painted, buildings on ill matched spaces lean into each other. On Broad Street green algae grows across the illuminated sign advertising the still open working men's club. By the sea light plays in along water-facing ferro-concrete retainers. This is no longer the land of the working men, work has largely gone. The docks are quiet, Barry Chemicals, a great industrial complex on the Cadoxton Moors is the only remaining salvation. Smearing the sky out beyond Jenner Park it just about keeps the wolf from the door.

The Victorian transformation of the island farm into a peninsula was salvation, of a sort. In 1909 Whitmore Bay Grounds were acquired by the council and by 1922 the sea wall and the promenade had been built. The famous shelters, the east and west concrete becolumned repositories for stacked deckchairs, tea huts and lost children were added in the nineteen twenties. The scene for the establish-

ment of south Wales' first great seaside playground was set. Collins opened their fairground in 1924. They built a great figure eight and then, just before the Second World War, replaced it with the famous scenic railway – a sort of papier-mâché, wire frame and lunatic tunnel assemblage, painted brown and grey in representation of real rocky mountains, tall enough to be seen for miles. It lasted thirty years until wear and weather caused it to be demolished in 1973. Caravans arrived, and following them train loads of working men and their families all looking for leisure time by the sea with sand and candyfloss in their hair. A Welsh Blackpool. Donkeys, buckets, rock pools, rented deck chairs, knotted handkerchiefs, spades. On a sunny summer day in the 1950s at the resort's height the beach was so full that the sand could not be seen.

I came here with my great extended family, encamped at the border between the hard wet and the soft dry sand at Whitmore Bay's eastern end. To use this place you first looked for the number, painted on the sea wall behind you. We always camped by the number four. Later when you emerged from the lifeguardless and heaving surf you ran, wind borne grit slashing your legs, towards your great whitewashed chosen number, only way to get back home. Tea came on a tray in mugs with a silver pot and extra hot water. Deposit returned when you took the empties back. Paste sandwiches. Slices of Swiss roll. Walls ice cream, unwrapped and stuck between two wafers, now and then. No fruit no crisps. Chips and burgers had yet to arrive.

The days were endless and the sun almost always shone. My father read the Daily Sketch. My mother knitted. My aunts were in one-piece ruched waffle nylon swimsuits, zip up the back, corset-like finishing cut straight across the top of the leg. They had matching bathing caps, ate cashews, choc brazils, smoked. My trunks were blue, knitted, held the Barry sea water cold on me for hours. My parents never noticed. I never cared.

The route back up to the train home was like climbing a mountain, done in barefeet, aching with drying sand. The funfair between the sea and the station was Shangri-la. Dodgem cars, waltzer, rocket ride, ghost train, penny in the slot where I won a cigarette, Players Gold Flake, just one, kept it hidden, never won a thing on that crane which moved and grabbed and slipped across a glass case of wonders. The fun house had moving floors, distorting mirrors and vertical slides. There was a cake walk across the front where gusts of air blew

up the 1950s bell skirts just like Marilyn Monroe.

The train had leather-strap controlled slide windows on its com-partment doors and black and white pictures of Hastings and Aberystwyth on its walls. You hung your head out of the window, lost your cap and got smut in your eyes. The tracks rolled back to Cardiff around the great curved sweep of West Pond through Barry Town, Barry Docks, Cadoxton, on to Cardiff Central and finally Queen Street, where we got off, leaving the heaving train to continue its jour-ney all the way to Treorchy and then Blaenrhondda.

Steam ended in 1958. There were no more whistles. Dai Woodham, dock porter turned scrapman, rented from Associated British Ports the sweep of land reclaimed from the sea by the build-ing of the Barry Island dams. He and his brother then bought, from a rapidly dieseling British Rail, several hundred scrap locomotives and quite a few thousand wagons. Over the years which followed the Woodham Brothers scrap yard became the Mecca for rail enthusiasts and for rail preservation companies looking for engines to rebuild. Thousands of rusting steel locos went through the Woodhams' hands. Many were cut up for scrap, hundreds more were not. It was the wag-ons that saved the locos. They arrived in greater number and were much cheaper to dismantle. Realising their scrap value was a much swifter process. The locos were stored in dark rusting ranks on Woodham's sidings to wait for later. And by the time later arrived their value to collectors had been recognised and Dai Woodham had become a hero. King of engines. Saviour of steam. Over the ensuing decades hundreds of locomotives were rescued, rebuilt, regeared, repainted, coaled and watered and set to steam on preserved lines right across the UK. Woodham died in 1994. The Vale of Glamorgan Steam Railway Centre overlooking his former yard is a decent memo-rial. 2861 4115 80150 92245 51919 Class 108 DMU DMBS[7]. Anoraks will know what that sentence really means.

In 2007 there is still sun. The Council have paid to repave the promenade, had it tiled, installed celebratory mosaics. There are shops selling cockles, prawns, mussels, whelks, crabstix. At Boofys, the Codfather of Sole, you can get a Bacon Roll £1.70, a Small Hot Dog for only £1.00. There are gift shops doing mother and nana sen-timent plates ("God made many lovely things, sunsets, flowers and trees, He gave another gift more rare, a wonderful person most fair, A mother dear as you" – WERE £2.50 NOW 70p), ice cream, donuts, sweets, kebabs. There are kids with sand in buckets, parents laden with prams and bags. The Barry Island Pleasure Park offers unlimited rides for £15. There's a Haunted Mine, a chair spinning Terminator, a water flume. When I walk through it the amplified music, amazingly, is still 1950s Bobby Vee. The beach, no longer crammed as it was forty years ago, still has a fair scattering of deckchairs and sun lounger encampments. Handball pitches are marked out. Kites. Frisbees. Cricket sets. It is full today with Asian extended families, kids digging castles, playing football. No donkeys, no handkerchiefs on heads but lots of brightly coloured saris flowing in the breeze.

ABERGAVENNY

"You can see it on the roadsigns on the way in. They're calling this place *Y Fenni*. It makes it more Welsh than it already is. Abergavenny, that's the real name. A *Welsh* name. It means mouth of the Gavenni. Obvious, isn't it?" This may be a visitor talking but he's right. Abergavenny, a town built where the River Gavenny enters the Usk, surrounded by south Wales mountains, almost in England, but not quite. Sun outside, streets full of people. We are in Ottakar's, the booksellers, where all Welsh titles are stacked in a thin section labelled Local Books. Guides to the meaning of place names, so we can check, cannot be found. We are surrounded by bilingualism. *Fuglen / Fiction. Chwaraeon / Sport. Llyfrau Lleol / Local Books. New Books / Llyfrau Newydd.* Ottakar's have a couple of recent ones, John Williams, Niall Griffiths, John Davies' *History of Wales*, a reprint set of Alexander Cordell. I remonstrate. "These aren't local. They're Welsh. Where would you stock…" I try to think of somewhere on the other side of the country, "…books on Anglesey?" The riposte is swift. "British Tourist Guides – up there on the left." It is how it is in Abergavenny, Monmouthshire. This is where the wreckage of the industrial revolution sprawls over the hills to the Welsh west and the soft green farms of monied gentry lie to the English east.

Abergavenny is famous for lots of things – blue cheese, strong ale, the invention of the pot noodle – no, actually, none of those. The Romans built a fort here on the mound that was centuries later developed by the Normans into a castle made of stone. The town was walled. You can see the remains of the wall's ditch where the town faces the Usk across a water meadow. The Black Death hit hard in the 1340s. Owain Glyndŵr came through in 1404 and, with full expression of his burnt earth policy, laid the town flat. But it recovered. There

was a tannery and flannel
weaving and a sheep and cattle
market. Town names testify –
Butchers Row, Chicken Street,
Rother Street[8], The Bull Inn,
The Cow Inn, The Hen and
Chickens. Rudolf Hess was
kept in the town's mental asy-
lum during the Second World
War. Rumour says he was
taken for local walks and drank
Welsh beer in a local pub. Sir
Harry Llewelyn exercised his
Olympic gold-winning horse

Foxhunter across the nearby hills. American crime writer Ethel Lina
White was born here. Catherine Merriman's novel *State of Desire* is
thick with Abergavenny references, although she calls the place
Abercwm. Jeff Nuttall, king of the British beats managed his final literary revival here in the 1990s reading across the buckled floor
upstairs at the Hen & Chicks.

In the castle, focus of the town, the medieval remains (which are
substantial and, despite what the guides say, quite atmospheric) have
been topped with the addition of a totally incongruous Victorian keep
(1819) loosely modelled on the kind of thing that appears in chicken
wire and plaster form at funfairs across the country. The town itself
has an air of being out of time, more old than new, development slow,
no high rise, no apartments, no glass, no blonde wood. The rest of
the world has sped on into the future. Abergavenny still lolls in the
past, hanging around the fractured and worn-paint arms of Charles
II high on the side of the Kings Arms inn. "Good quartering forever…1817. 15th Huzzars" says a Napoleonic graffito over the fireplace. Who needs the modern world.

Standing below the Castle in the car park by the bus station where
one of the best-stocked and largest tourist information centres I've
seen anywhere in Wales stays open even on Sundays Abergavenny's
Welsh roots are palpable. There are hills in all directions – the
Fujiyama Sugar Loaf, the whale back Ysgyryd Fawr – the Great
Skirrid, one-time St Michael's Mount, holy mountain, with a chapel
on its north facing cliffs[9], the great cup of the Blorenge (the only word
anywhere that rhymes with orange), which hides the tips and iron
making wreckage of Blaenavon beyond. These are the ranges which

spawned Bruce Chatwin's inbred brothers in his brooding *On The Black Hill* and to which the poet Allen Ginsberg came in 1967 for his acid-aided *Wales Visitation*. He thought he'd reached the heart of the land of the eternal bards, couldn't see the sheep-filled crags that ran further, on and on. The car park, centred on the Oasis Café, is full of bikers, at least a hundred of them. The young ones looking like Power Rangers, the oldsters in all-over leathers, beards, headscarves, helmets, black cigarettes, chubby wives. Wales is a Mecca for bikers. They drift here in the morning, roll on to Aberystwyth later, return via Llandovery. They come on hand-built trikes, Fazers, Silver Lehmans, fatboys, buggies, dozens of Yamahas, Hondas, Moto Guzzis, Tuono Fighters. You do this in border country where there are long, bendy, open roads to roar on. No congestion. Can't do that in cities.

In an attempt to re-invent itself for the modern age Abergavenny has become the foodie capital for a whole new generation of diners. They come from the warm flatlands of middle England and from the overspill of once-industrial south Wales. The principle vehicle is the blossoming annual Food Festival, doing for cuisine what Hay-on-Wye has done for literature, bringing in experts, producers, farmers, writers, grocers, innovators, cooks, café proprietors, restaurateurs, growers, dinners, eaters. 2006 is the eighth year and, for two days, the town fills with stalls and demonstrations, cooks with headphone mics, afternoons of tasting, masterclasses in food preparation. Smoked, marinated, bottled, packed, boxed, tinned, bagged, salted, dried, packeted and otherwise new branded Welsh foodstuffs are sold hand to hand, samples free. There are huge queues at the beer and cider tents and lots of singing on the Castle green. Everywhere are the fat in jeans, doing well pale people, cravats, walking poles, country cords, hippie hair. Women laden with bags of bright red apples, men with fish and cheese, kids with ice cream made from sheep's milk and crushed blueberry. Cider in profusion. Steel bands on the streets. Men stagger by with muddy carrots as big as marrows. Women with cook books from River Cottage. Bags of sunflower seeds

smoked with oak. Cases of salt from the Welsh sea.

Beyond the bustle of venison burger wielding middle-aged owners of Honda Civics we escape to an organised walk around Upper Red House Farm at Llanfihangel-Ystern-Llewern, (more genuflection to St Michael[10]), where, just beyond the paintball woods, Teona Dorien-Smith talks and walks us through her environmentally friendly acres. Teona, a landscape architect by training, came here from the Scilly Isles. She and her partner, Edward Branson, were simply looking for a place in the country. The one they ended up buying had farming acres attached. They kept them on. Upper Red House dates from 1650, early brick and beamed, restored with grant aid from CADW and has a basement full of lesser-horseshoe bats. "We can't go down there now," says Teona. "They are a protected species". Bats One, People Nil. She reads the assembled group an obligatory Health And Safety Executive risk assessment: You can get your feet stuck in holes. You can catch your clothes on gates. You can get stung by wild bees. It might rain. None of these things happen.

Her 117 acres are farmed entirely according to organic principles. Field grass is unimproved to encourage insects and wildlife, sewn with chicory and yarrow to bring up trace elements from the subsoil, cut and composted. Let to others for sheep and cattle grazing. In a field full of excited cows, clustering us as if we were cattle television, she patiently explains the difference between steers, heifers, and bulls. "Steers are castrated, kept for meat. Heifers to grow teats for milk. Bulls to keep the cattle world alive." The hedges here are being restored, hawthorn cut and bent to grow at 45°, the old way. "You always used to lay what you cut off along the edges to keep the stock from eating your new barrier," she tells us. "But this no longer works. Stock densities have increased. The animals trample and eat the grow-ing shoots. You have to put in stock proof wire fencing either side, a meter out, to protect your supposedly stock-proof hedge. And then you have to build your wildlife corridors to keep the animal kingdom in touch with itself. It's hard work." This is all done with the support of the government's Tir Gofal scheme which is aimed at managing land in a way that does not destroy everything in sight in the name of profit. Will it work? Eventually. If climate change doesn't render the whole system irrelevant. Already, Teona tell us, she is experiencing hotter summers and drier seasons than the publicly available computer mod-els have predicted. It's happening far faster than most of us realise. Where is all this going? Low land flood, olive groves and refugees.

Upper Red House Farm is crossed by permitted paths, walked by our group of fifteen, most of whom actually wanted to go on the Food Festival's mushroom walk but that was full. The cake and tea and Teona's intelligent and data-rich introduction to green-world farming, however, has won us over. We pass the heaped spill from deep boring. "We had a diviner up here during last year's drought to help us locate new water sources." "Was he any good?" "Not really. He turned out to only have one leg and his crutch kept sinking into the soil. So he sent his son round with the twitching hazel twigs." "Did they find anything?" "No".

In the low September sun the tilting fields are dry and so enviously peaceful. We cross Morris Dingle and make back through Red House Wood to emerge alongside the orchards – crab apples, perry pears, sloes, cob nuts, elderberries, dragonfly, ponies – and the mini bus back to the mono-cultural food extravaganza. In the Lake District things like these had been closed on the grounds that they'd done nothing to broaden their appeal to recent incomers. In Abergavenny the incomers are the English hoards. Welsh speakers reduced to a mere 7% as early as the fourteenth century. Wasn't this farm once called by a Welsh name, I ask Teona? Ty Coch Uchaf. But that was way back. The language again runs out as it falteringly approaches the border. Who are we here? What we think we are. For now.

Back at the bus station those on the mushroomers walk have not yet returned. Panners for edible gold with their woven baskets and gloves. Only seven from the hundreds of fungi types that grow here can kill you. Low risk. On the public toilet wall is a map showing recent motor cycle crash sites. Hundreds of those. A foodie passes, street-eating pie, ketchup and chips from Charlie's Fish Shop. Nothing, ultimately, is sacred.

WYE

Can we see it? We can't. The Wye followed by thousands of cars coming down from the English midlands, reaching Wales through Hereford and Ross, chasing the river down through Monmouth to Chepstow. Welcome to Wales. The sylvan river, sleek with slow grandeur, hidden behind trees. From the A466 it is only a rumour, blue glimpses from the roaring saloon, water below leaf, a beauty talked of but rarely seen. This river, in its greater rush for a final fifty miles before it empties into the tidal Severn, is where Wales runs out. To the west are Porthcasseg, Gaer Hill, Fedw Wood, Pwllmeyric,

Fedw Fawr, Coed Beddick, Penallt. On the east of the river Broadrock, High Wood, Triangle, Woodcroft, Wyegate Hill, Great Dunkilns, Sedbury. The language doesn't even fade, it simply crosses the water and changes station. Turn the dial, the old tongue gone.

From the topography we can sense that this is a region of shifting allegiances, of uncertain geography, always has been. The political boundary between England and Wales bends and snakes and shifts as if it were in a dance. No straight furrow made easily by a court administrator but an irregular edge formed, as if by chance, by the erosion and accretion of moving water, by centuries of political and military manoeuvring, by the ebb and flow of man. Marcel Duchamp once took a few metres of thread up a flight of stairs and threw them into the well to create bending, irregular lines that he then used more times than once in his revolutionary art[11]. Wales ends and starts like this. And it has few bridges. You cannot seep across, put your feet simultaneously in two countries. You need to make a decision, move a bit, seek a crossing. Offa's dyke runs along this line, a wall from sea to sea, from Chepstow to Wrexham. Ditch, rampart, ditch on the Welsh facing side, wall to stand behind with your sword on the English. The sections that remain visible today, and there are many, are sited just to the east of the Wye, now forever in their kingdom and not the principality. Owain Glynŵr came through here in 1405 to fight the English at Grosmont. The Romans and the Normans and the Marcher Lords and the English all fought the Welsh here. Centuries of skirmish. Castles on every outcrop. But the lush Wye forests heal the scars, the waters roll slow below them.

Historically the river also marks the start of the great wildness, the place where civilisation ends and barberosity begins. For centuries the English view of the west was that the world ended somewhere beyond Bath. Travel on and you would encounter falling water, fire and dragons, pestilence, great rocks, paths that climbed without mercy, huge mountains, scarred and illiterate ruffians with swords at their peaks. Wales, land of demons, place of bastard biliousness, where there were no books and white robed druids would wail at you through never ending mist. You travelled here if you needed to. Giraldus said that the Welsh were "constant only in acts of incon-stancy. They pay no respect to oaths, faith, or truth"[12]. The land that supported these people was not easy. For centuries Wales was North Korea or medieval Japan, dark and locked. Visitors kept away.

The Welsh view, of course, was that everything to the east may have been green and golden but was in reality riddled by tax and pomposity, ached under a Saxon yolk, was bastard French, ignorant and irrelevant, full of high opinion and sneer. Cross border traffic was slow. Until the tourists arrived, that is.

Mass visiting of the Wye was an outgrowth of the seventeenth century Grand Tour which took the English wealthy on a rites of passage trail through the remains of antiquity and the society of the European aristocracy. They rode from Dover to Paris to Rome, to Pompeii and Herculaneum, to Munich and Flanders and then rode back. By the eighteenth century, with the industrial revolution turning the world dark with steel and steam, and with war across Europe, the rich turned from the desperate east to look at the unknown west. In 1745 Dr John Egerton began to take friends down river from his rectory in Ross-on-Wye. In 1770 the Rev William Gilpin pioneered the notion of the picturesque, landscape to be experienced for its peculiar beauty. In 1771 he wrote and published *Observations on the River Wye*, the world's first tourist book. Thomas Gray toured in 1770, sailed along the river, "its banks are a succession of nameless beauties," he wrote. Painters and poets followed: William Wordsworth, Coleridge, Turner, Thackeray. They took boats from the Herefordshire lowlands to the Wye gorge and on down below the brooding cliffs to the castle and then the sea at Chepstow. They imagined themselves in the wild distance where nature had wrested control back from man and returned the world to primitive state. Castles here were all in ruins, ivy overgrowing them. Wilton, Goodrich, Chepstow. The visitors reveled in what they saw. They withstood the storms and the rains and the deprivations of their fifty miles trips. They reported back in rapture to the wider world. To civilized England. Of course.

The tour was mapped, described, graded. Viewpoints were selected for their splendour, classed according to whether they were from or of the river. Upper Wyndcliff, Yat Rock, Capler Camp. All still in place.

In 1736 slave owner, Valentine Morris, bought Piercefield House, a mansion at the north end of what is now Chepstow Racecourse, and developed its great estate into a seventeenth century precursor to Disneyland. His landscaping of the parks and woodland which rolled up to the Wyecliffe's edge and then tumbled down into the winding river set a standard for Victorian greenfield follies. He built grottos, ponds, dams, cascades, lost temples, rock wonders and climbs and endless terraces. He installed a complex network of paths which led to carefully constructed viewpoints from which the revealed landscape could be viewed: the Octagonal Seat, Lover's Leap, the Druid's

Temple, the Chinese Seat, the Platform, the Alcove. From these high-spots, reached by single-file walking, early Victorian giggling, and much handkerchief to nose and mouth, could be seen the breadth of the Wye, the Severn and then Devon, Somerset and Gloucestershire beyond.

Visiting artists used the Claude Glass, a slightly convex, oval, tinted mirror which could capture and frame the sylvan view. The devices were named after the French seventeenth century landscape painter Claude Lorrain. Their sepia tinting and the way they could contain the apparent wildness of the view made them enormously popular. How do you control nature? On your mobile today, taking the shots at least at 3 megapixles. Early tourists would turn their backs on the view and try to hold what they'd glimpsed in something not much bigger than a Sony Ericsson K750i.

North of the estate and connected by further moss rocked walkways are the 365 steps. A haul up Wyndcliff from the water's edge to the Eagle's Seat, a high viewpoint with wooden rails and benches for the heavy breathing tourists. Coleridge climbed here. Saw the whole romantic world stretched out below. There used to be a tea shop at the steps base, gone. There's a sign that warns visitors of the risk of loose boulder and mossy wet stone, shot up by Chepstow youth staggering around here with their midnight lager. Crushed cans in the woods. Wordsworth would have been unimpressed.

A few miles north is Tintern, the great ruined Abbey, visited by almost everyone in the UK, and beyond. A highspot of the walking tour, the boat tour, the motor tour, the trip by coach. Kept in repointed, grass-trimmed shape by CADW, Welsh for *keep*, the Welsh ancient monuments board. Tintern is east of the River but somehow still in Wales. 1131. Cistercian. Fell apart after the Reformation. Lost until Turner painted it and Wordsworth wrote his famous poem and the railways brought even more visitors after 1876. We're on our way there in 1987 with Broadribb at the helm. This is at the invitation of CADW who, in one of their less well organised gestures towards the arts have invited a bunch of poets from Cardiff to read. Chris Broadribb[13] is in red shoes and carries a case full of flares. In the same car are Ifor Thomas and Betty Lane. Thomas has already established himself as a poet unafraid of props. Broadribb has also booked Dannie Abse who will meet us there. But somehow or other Broadribb has not posted the letter. Dannie does not show.

We will read within the great walls below a roof of sky. When we get there CADW try to charge us to go in. But we are the act. We're performing here. The uniformed attendant has no idea what we are talking about. There's an argument at the gatehouse. We win. There are no posters announcing our event anywhere. Broadribb had talked about doing a mail shot but somehow it never happened. I ask the attendant in the ticket hut if she knows where the audience are. She shrugs. There's a dog. It looks like rain.

Broadribb sets up flares on sticks at the four corners of the grass-filled space he has chosen. Avant garde. Lights them. There is smoke. He asks me to read. No one to read to. Not even a passer by passes. I do 'Welsh Wordscape'[14]. The rain keeps off. To earn their fees the others recite a desultory verse or two. Broadribb himself doesn't contribute. Keeps his book shut. Stays silent. Doesn't introduce us either. The dog vanishes. We give up. Where's the money? Didn't fill the form in. Sorry.

The Wye vanishes again as we drive back. It takes so little for it to slide back behind its cover of leaf and branch. Went to Jacobs Market, south of the railway in Cardiff. Hunted the stalls for a Claude Glass. Couldn't find one. Twenty years later thought about it all again and checked on eBay. Nothing.

Wye Valley Visitors

RS (Austin Healey)
Bob Cobbing (van)
Wm Wordsworth (rapture)
Coleridge
Jeff Nuttall
Glyn Dŵr (upset)
Bill Clinton
Broadribb (flares)
William Gilpin
Mills
Dame Barbara Hepworth
Lord Nelson
Thomas Gray (boat)
Louisa Anne Twamley (toils & tumbles)
Wyndham (excellent)
Claude Glass
Michael O'Leary
Joseph Mallord William Turner
Kingsley Amis (beer)

PENRHYS

The Rhondda starts at Pontypridd. The big one, the Rhondda Fawr, bangs on straight to Blaenrhondda. While the lesser, the Rhondda Fach, takes in the snaking terraces of Ynyshir, and the perched crayon-black rows of Pontygwaith, the heights of Tylorstown, and the fastness of Ferndale, to end at the last place in the red Welsh world, Maerdy. Cwm Maerdy. Home of generation on generation of coal black miners. But now the coal has gone.

Do I need to come here? Can't I read the guides and watch the films and then imagine I've done it? *How Green Was My Valley. Blue Scar. The Proud Valley. The Angry Earth. Giro City. The Englishman Who Went Up A Hill But Came Down A Mountain.* Have I to breath the actual air and climb the steep valley sides? Get caught up in the minutia of road grit and cold air, of passing pantechnicons and mothers on pavements with pushchairs and Asda carriers, of how long it takes to get petrol and the headlines on the newspapers in the plastic sales bin outside? All this. It takes the focus away from what I might have come for. The essence. Others can do this for me. Experience the detail, leave me the spirit. Sit in my chair on my terrace and take in south America, the islands of Andaman, Cape Verde, and the whole of Wales. I can use the time I've saved by not going there for more rewarding pursuits. Whatever they may be. Read the paper. Clean the house. Form many opinions on the world and its ways and the machination of its politicians by watching the news on TV. Experience the world through surface traces brought to me by others. It's so warm in here. Out there in the real world, god it's cold.

But I have to come. Nothing is ever as you expect it, nor even as you once remembered it. It only takes the sun to come out from behind cloud or for rain to fall for the vista to alter. How the world is when you are in it. That's actually all there is. The one pointed moment of experience, your own. The past is as smoke, the future an illusion. Stay with the out breath. Sitting here, in the car's driving seat, hauling up past the first and last pit, red rust headgear, at Trehafod, past the roadworks at Porth, over the grit twisting roads, kids with snotty noses sprawling across abandoned cars, soccer in the tiny streets, tiny girls with tiny prams. This is a world built when coal was oil, when the universe ran on steam, made its fortune off the backs of the poor, when the lost of the world arrived in south Wales, economic migrants seeking salvation, and when the only ones to gain were the owners. The already poor moved here, for more than a hundred years worked till they dropped, and for decades more stayed poor. Now the work has gone their descendants cling on. And still no one here has any money.

These are the deprived valleys. They all have shoes now, bread to eat, televisions. But measure them against the new criteria. Check against child mortality, incidence of heart attack, frequency of travel, percentage in work, addiction, reported car theft, crime against person, break-ins, arson, graffiti, views from windows, litter in streets, extraneous sound, cost of delivery from central depots, attitude, chest infection, tattoos, lost animals, population per local doctor, NHS dentistry, number of poets, alcohol consumption, distance to supermarket, rainfall. Measure against these and the place falls a million miles behind. Europe save me, the local council can't.

Merthyr Tydfil, up there beyond the valley's head, and Blaenau Gwent, in the valleys to the east, both made it to the top three of the worst places to live in Britain, 2006. No one came to check these mile wide lost Rhondda places. No longer sexy. Lewis Jones and Gwyn Thomas dead. Manics in another place. Tom Jones' Rolls never reached this far.

On the valley top between Llwynypia and Tylorstown, 1100 feet up, nineteen sixties state-fuelled social conscience put 951 dwellings. Radburn principle, houses set around cul-de-sacs, kitchens and services at the back where there's road access, lots of grass. Give those who need the light the vista. Let them see the wider world. Get them the high winds and the driving rain. Let them watch the graveyards and the well-to-do walking the greens of Rhondda Golf Club. Let them gaze east and west and in both directions see valleys they'd rather live in. Give them communal heating run from a central boiler house[15]. Let the works never be hot enough, let them constantly break down. Penrhys, with its white render and mono-slope roofs, its closed stores and burnt out garages, and its angular complex of maisonettes looking more like the brackets which hold loads onto car roofs than the future of Welsh habitation, was the loving result.

From the outset things did not go well. Sink sunk. Wreckage. An amphitheatre built from sleepers into the hillside to engender community spirit. Set on fire. Houses wrecked and boarded then demolished. Community shrunk and still shrinking. 951 houses built in 1966 only 300 still occupied today. Heavy drug use. Much graffiti. No work. Community spirit failing but not lost. There are road signs directing you to Canolfan Rhys Community Arts Centre from the road which leaps over from Fawr to Fach. The new project is Crazy Alien Chicks, children's animation. But when I get there the centre is closed.

Around me are the demolished remains of several maisonette complexes. Hard-core fenced off and not yet removed from site. There are huge stacks of combustibles in tepee shape. Doors, branches, and planks, dot the green spaces. It's October. Bonfires will burn soon. I ask a small girl carrying a loaf of white bread why she thought they knocked the houses down. "They were haunted," she says. What else? At the Penrhys, the pub, the drinkers in their check shirts are loading lager. In the car park are white vans and pick-ups. The village, for that is what this place is, is just large enough to drive across. Heol Pendyrus goes right round it like a race track. The boy racers in their Peugeots and hoodies spin. Same here as anywhere where they earn less than Madonna, anywhere west of Richmond or the posh terraces of Bath. Everyone talks as if they've just stepped off the set of Torchwood, valleys Welsh, the accent the media imagine we all have, no matter where we come from in Wales. But it's real in Penrhys.

In the early nineties the local authority woke up to the fact that this sink estate was on the verge of black holing. A writing project was established for the Penrhys disaffected – thirty year old grandmothers who wanted to read things about people who spoke with valley accents, who lived lives like theirs were, spending their days in contemporary Penrhys, Tylorstown and Porth. Amongst all the world's literature there was nothing. So they created some, made their own.

Local population 98.1 white. 1.9 mixed origin.

Community integrated. Community centre often vandalised. Community partnership store operating behind steel shutters. Needles in the grass. Our Lady with her face to heaven. Mostly left alone.

Before the estate there was a smallpox hospital here as well as Penrhys Isaf and Penrhys Uchaf farms. The site was chosen for its isolation. Who came up this mountain? Built in 1906 it lasted until 1971 by which time smallpox was in world-wide retreat. To ensure that it stayed that way demolition was by masked and helmeted firemen who razed the place to the ground. No disease here since, must have worked.

Penrhys (lit the *head of Rhys*) may have got its name from the beheading of Prince Rhys ap Tewdwr here by the Norman-supported Iestyn ap Gwrgant. It happened on the hilltop say the early legends. Some historians disagree. The past is so flexible. Squirms like a snake. Just like the present it is often impossible to hold down.

The place's undisputed claim to historical fame remains the well. This pagan outpouring of water, set just down the western slope from the estate's entrance roundabout, has offered cures for rheumatism, king's evil, head pain, bad blood, inability to see, scabies and consumption since pre-christian times. A carving of the Virgin Mary[16] "nursing Jesus for a kiss" appeared in a tree, a gift from heaven, almost a thousand years ago. The statue and the chapel built to house it and the holy waters then stood unmolested for five hundred years until the reformation when the carving was removed in 1538. It was taken to London, thrown out of the west window of St Paul's by Bishop Latimer in a fit of protestant fury and, like the great heap of world literature in Ray Bradbury's *Fahrenheit 451*, burned. Fire will cure anything. So history says.

The well is still there, seeping, inside a small stone building with a slab and mortar roof. Clear water in a trough, bent pins rusting as evidence of supplication. This place is still on the pilgrim's route[17]. 25,000 came when it was rededicated in 1953 and a new statue of Our Lady erected on the hilltop above. When I visited there were lit candles and flowers by the statue and at the well itself photographs of those in need of help cellotaped to the railings outside. Do you just get a blessing by coming or does the cure still operate? I entered a gap in the railings, scrambled in through the small doorway with its concrete lintel bearing the words "Little Church" to test the latent powers. I did this at Ffynnon Llandenis in Cardiff. Both sites of great and long veneration. Shut my eyes. Hoped. But again, nothing. Eyes did not improve. Skin stayed bad. Maybe I need a Damascus Road moment. It's not come yet.

Outside, nearby, is a twenty-foot pole with a metal millennium beacon basket on top. Lit in 2000, dark since. The views down into Llwynypia, Blaenclydach and Clydach Vale are free from industrial smoke. Hilltop tips green. Memory sinks. I can hear the chimes of an ice cream van working the distant street. We'll keep a welcome in the hillsides. Really. That's what it plays.

DINAS POWYS

My aunt lived in the fifties. She'd also been around in the thirties and the forties and the sixties and the seventies and some of the eighties but it was in the fifties that she lived. I had no idea this was the case. And at the age I was, compared to hers, I had no way of judging. She was a sister of my father's and had no children. The world was full, instead, of gin and orange and card games and Kensitas filter cigarettes. In her front room was a Regentone radiogram in a walnut cabinet, full of valves and dust and with an internal rack that held fifty tweve inch LPs. She and my Uncle Bob (who hardly said more to me in his entire life than the toilet is out the back. He'd travelled in something. No one in the family was sure quite what. Cutlery. Headache powders. Undergarments. He had thick black hair and always wore a blazer. It had a badge. Something to do with tennis although they never seemed to play) listened to albums of rumbas from Cuba, waltzes from Vienna and flamenco from Spain. Tapping their feet. Patting their hands. The albums had bright coloured covers showing female dancers with their breasts spilling from their dresses. The house had lots of china but no books. And ash trays. There were ash trays everywhere.

They lived in Dinas Powys. So far from Cardiff complained my mother. We caught the Barry train from Queen Street, alighted at dismal Dinas instead of carrying on to the glittering sea. Dinas Powys today still feels more like the fifties than the new century. If you avoid the main Cardiff Road and walk back to the village centre time will move with you. The streets are unstraightened, the shops irregular and of a kind now vanished from larger towns – post office, baker, barber – and there are pubs[18], clusters of them hanging together for drunken warmth. My aunt would have been as at home here today with her glass of sherry and her strings of pearls as she was when she lived. Unchallenged on Pen-y-Turnpike Road, moving through her English air from trumps and tricks at the house of the Colonel to tea and sandwiches with Mrs Norbert-Smith. She would have missed Dinas' new layer of green and total Welshness, the density of the bilingualism on the public notice board and the Plaid dominance of the Community Council. Communities do this, live differing and emulsified lives that spin and pour together but never actually mix.

They pass each other in the shops but they rarely speak. They imagine other groups not to exist somehow, or to be imaginary or visiting. To own nothing, to breathe different air. They pass on the pavement as if the pavements ran through an airport terminal where there are so many people that you notice none individually, just the pressing and anonymous mass. Nothing registers. You occupy your own slice of the space-time continuum with its own local individual and never-shared facilities. Beth yw cam nesaf? Establish a nursery for the children, keep them in the community, let them feed on our values, osmosis through contact with like minds and like skin. The world is like this, increasing stretches of it, a place where blindness is an admirable quality and selective compassion a thing that keeps one alive.

I've come here today, in the new millennium, to look again for Dinas Powys castle. It's on the maps, stuck between brave new Eastbrook and the ancient village core. Castle (remains of). But I've never got to it. On my last attempt I found myself big booted on the golf links being shouted at by men in Pringle sweaters and women with ferociously permed hair. I had a guide book then. Useless. Threw it into the Wrinstone Brook[19]. This time I've been convinced by Mario that the castell is really there. Mario Fiorillo is half-Italian, half-Portuguese, used to be in the Italian Navy, escaped to Cardiff for peace and luck. He's a scribbler from my performance writing past. Publishing was going nowhere so we abandoned it. Took poetry to the stage, made it once again sing. Mario is a painter now and a repairer of stiles and country pathways, clearing ditches, coppicing hedges, relining gullies, replacing stepping stones. He's had his painted landscapes hung at a Cardiff gallery and sells slowly on the internet. More convincing than his poetry although somehow lacking that verse's Italiano-English rush at love, life and smoking. It often takes an outsider's eyes to tell you how you really are.

Today Mario's complexion resembles horse chestnut. Being Mediterranean he's swarthy anyway but his work out of doors has lent his complexion a deep and glowing orange brown. There's a

Welsh dragon sewn on onto the back of his rucksack. This ancient daysack seems to have come from Army Surplus. He locks his bike to a lamppost alongside St Peter's Church on Letton Way and we set out. The way to the castle is up a steep and unmarked path to the side of an electricity booster station. It's early December and leaves have fallen, those that are going to, but the growth of beech and knotweed is still pretty dense.

At the top of the rise is a wall, hidden almost entirely by ivy leaf and thick creeper. This is Dinas Powys castle, what's left of it. The curtain wall is at least twenty feet high and encloses a substantial ward. At the north end are the ruins of a square keep. Stone has been filched by generations of local builders for their cottages and cow sheds. Inside are brambles and wood undergrowth that have been left to expand as if they were a protected species. Mario has cut his own path through their centre. He produces a pair of secateurs from his pack and proceeds to do some extra trimming. Never travel without them. Dinas Powys castle is a Norman creation, built in the twelfth century on the top of earlier stonework, derelict by the fifteenth. The Arthurian King Ynwyl reigned from here. Did he? The de Sumeri family owned the castle until the last De Sumeri died in 1321. "al in ruine" said Leland in 1536. Bust and buggered for more of its life than it was ever real. Mario, whose take on history bends like a Virginia creeper, reckons that this was the home of the great Welsh King Caradoc and would remain in ruins until his bones were returned from where they lay. And where might that be? No one knows. "The Coliseum is in better condition than this," Mario complains, cutting ivy from the postern gate. Maybe the Romans were here but the stonework looks wrong. Who owns it? The local civic trust, it turns out, who took the place over in 1982. It's been downhill ever since.

We scramble down the revetment beyond the lost north tower, through dense undergrowth and mounds of sliding leaves to emerge at the bottom end of Cwm George Woods. North of here is Cwm George Camp, a lost palisaded hillfort, earth ditches that date from centuries before the Romans, but which was still occupied in the sixth.

Mario sees the wooden now rotted-to-nothing hillfort as a centre of local Welshness with the ruins of the stone castle a place built by invading Saxons or Cymraeg-hating Normans. Or maybe it was even a home for the Romans with their body armour and battle engines and buckets of boiling oil. History spins. The camp is impressive. Four ditches with substantial earth ridges remaining. Leslie Alcock[20] excavated here and found pottery fragments bearing animal ornamentation and fifth century bone hair combs owned by the "petty rulers and tyrants" who controlled the isles of Ynys Prydain after the Romans went. Nature has grown back thickly to cover the scars.

Beyond the camp the land flattens into the valley formed by the twin streams of the Wrinstone and the Bullcroft which meet to form the aspirationally-named River Cadoxton, known locally as the Mill Brook. These are the Casehill Meadows which stretch out between Dinas Powys and its satellite, the tiny, lost and very exclusive Michaelstone-le-Pit with its grand houses at Cwrt-yr-Ala. At the north end, unexpectedly, are the Wrinstone salmon leaps and weirs. They climb into a tiny and high-sided valley which runs towards the transmitting station at Wenvoe. In here the peace seems immeasurable. Mario reckons this valley to be a Rhondda in miniature. A seventeenth century Rhondda, as it might have been before the coal. The wind blows through leafless beech high on the ridge top but down here nothing moves. We are no more than a mile and half as the crow flies from Caerau, Ely, civilisation of a different, twenty-first kind. But no one has wrecked a car here, yet. The Wrinstone is too hard to reach. No burned metal carcases, no litter of lager, no Asda bags in the trees.

Back in Dinas the village seems to have been corralled by ever extending new estates and money-making housing developments, turning the hamlet into a town. East of Dinas Powys rail station they've built another, Eastbrook, to serve the estates north east of the road to Cardiff, and then the massed Radburn-style housing of Murch – Spar and security ctv, shutters, Grand Avenue grass – to the south.

Literary famous in Dinas: John Pikoulis (Alun Lewis), Roseanne Reeves (Honno), Robin Reeves (*New Welsh Review*), John Osmond (Wales devolved – lived in Penarth but spent more time in DP than there). Did any of these call their town Dinky Poo? Doubt it.

On Pen-y-Turnpike they've put a district walks map in a public glass case. The scale is hopeless and the colour non-existent. We've done part of the Wenvoe East Walk or maybe we haven't, through the condensation it's hard to tell. Mario hands me a Christmas present, a rock the size of a fist done up in a plastic bag with a piece of paper held to it by a thick rubber band. For me? I am touched. I'll put it under the tree. It turns out to be an example of concretion from the south Wales coal measures. These are bits of organic residue that have found their way into the sediment and over the millennia attracted iron to themselves. Mario found this one on the Lesser Garth and had it investigated by the National Museum of Wales Geology Department. He's thorough if nothing else. The attached paper is their identification report. While the others enjoy their scarves, new iPod shuffles and pairs of slippers I have my two layered red-grey rock. Beyond Cwrt-yr-Ala there are more like this. Dinas Powys dug iron until Bessemer steel production rendered the local ore with its high phosphorus content useless. Are there other places like this one, asks Mario? Plenty of Dinases across Wales, quite a few Powys, but only one where the two words meet. Powis City. Capital of the Vale.

SOUTHERN HILLS

The long walk is up the Ffrwdgrech Road, the trading estate men with vans and oily hands. Past Castle Farm and the hamlet of Ffwrd-grêch, past Pont y Ffwrd-grêch, villagers in their neat houses behind their neat hedges, terylene, dralon, elastine grey black trousers, cata-logue shirts. They've seen all this for as long as there has been living memory, visitors with walking boots and day sacks, now GPS and walk poles, flasks and maps, kids by the dozen in school minibuses from places in flat rich England where they wear maroon uniforms and say sir and think of Wales as a place where the world ends. They've watched it for so long that they now ignore it. We tramp by and their faces don't even flicker. The invisible interlopers. The com-munities of man once again passing though each others hands with-out touching. Ffwrd-grêch becomes Pont rhyd-goch, Cwrt Gilbert, Pont Rhydybetws, and Llwynbedw. The valley of the Nant Cwm

Llwch flowing north from Bannau Brycheiniog over waterfall after waterfall to reach the Afon Tarell at Abergwdi and then flow into the great Afon Wysg, the Usk, just before Christ College in the heart of military Brecon. Barracks, camp, fort, tump, Y Gaer, the *Cicucium* of the Romans. The route from here to Y Pigwn and then Coelbren and Neath.

These slow long-named places take long times to cross, the long road winding south with the great red sandstone scarp of the Beacons' three peaks before us. Only the English in their mighty sweaters and Oxford brogues call these the Brecons. These hills are Beacons. Bannau. Mountains. High enough. The first rise of land since the north. They look so easy and they can be conquered on a fine day. But then weather can turn like a spinning coin. These hills have the highest rainfall in Wales. Great Irish clouds riding in from the Gulf stream to the west, rising, losing their Atlantic volume in a driving gush over the sandstone and the peat. The hills kill as many as Crib Goch, wanderers lost in the falling fog, in the mist that engulfs them and turns the grass to a slippery peril and the rocks to unseen traps for legs and arms. Bodies slump in gullies. Fail for falling temperatures and lack of anything to keep the rain from wearing their skin to pink and swollen pulp. It can be like a crime scene up here but most of the time it's not.

The path rises, steadily, running alongside the Afon Llwch, where travellers camp and visitors pull up in their caravanettes and their four by fours. There's a ford ahead and then the track turns first to stone and then mud, narrowing between long hedges, too narrow for traffic, sheep nosing the grass, staring as if we were television, speaking to us as if they had important things to say.

The Cwm pulls in around us. U-shaped, carved by retreating glaciers 18,000 years ago in the last of this place's hundred ice ages. The snow fell on the peaks which are up ahead. Then snow fell on snow. And snow fell on that again. The whiteness thickened, snow became ice, deepened, 1000 metres of permafrost, dragged itself down the slopes lifting the surface as is went. This tongue of ice, bent from a white sky above Corn Du, Pen y Fan and Y Gribyn, the three distinctive peaks of southern Wales, this glacier, striating rocks, carving a path like an ice cream scoop in a tub of tutti frutti, made the tight narrow vee of the Llwch into a deep glacial trough, a cirque, an ice-age, bowl-ended valley full of lost rocks, glacial erratics, and scree.

It all gets faster as we climb. Names shorten. Cwm LL. Disused military targets. Shooting here. No longer. Wtrfalls. Breath panting. Fff. Land rising. Maybe it wd echo if I shouted. Hello. Nthing. Crow. Sheep. Arthur asleep under rks. He's asleep everywhere, that ancient. Thin grass. Can see the ridge of Crn Du. Silhouette against the southern light. I am near Heavn here. Gabriel. Gd. Jsu. Hear them singing. Angels. Grt Jehov. When the revelation comes.

Nw rk. Obelisk. Shad. I cn s th skyl. Brth n strms. Oo ooo. Wtr. Drp. Cairn. ê. Ll. Grib. Rmn. Grss. Swt swt wpe. Shp gne rded up. Sk lk a gt dome fl lght grey lght whte lght. Ears fl hrt fl lgs fl. Fly. Fly. Fly.

U Uf ff ff uph phphp. M. Breathe. Hmmm. Fff f. There. e e e e e o o o o e e e e e o o o o. We r r r r r r. Ph. F f f f f ff. Pull. Yup.

Suddenly, over the top of a green-faced terminal moraine, a mound of rock and mud at the foot of the great red-grey curving of the Corn Du escarpment with its zig zag rising over it is a stretch of trapped water. The place from where the nant springs. Llyn Cwm Llwch. A glacial tarn like something from a fable, blue grey, overflown by ravens, almost perfectly round. There's a small beach at the northern end, big enough for two deck chairs. The wind ripples the surface. Six cold meters in the centre. Deep dark.

The magic is palpable. This lake once held a floating island, they say, a crannóg. Oak piles interlaced with branches and wattle. A safe place to sleep. Swords have been thrown here. Their blades now lost in rust. Jewels by the hundred. Silver plates. Golden cups. Hoards from life. Men have lost themselves in this place. None of them returned.

Near the northern beach stands a great rock below which runs the passage to the lake's oaken crannóg. Invisible to all until they reached it. The door in the rock opened once a year, on May Day. The land it led to was both bountiful and enchanted. Take nothing, leave nothing behind, these were the instructions to visitors. The rules obeyed in our contemporary wildernesses have been around for a long time. Someone, however, put a flower in his pocket, took it home, showed his partner. Fell ill with delusion. Fractured memory. Perversion. Obsession. Personality coming apart. Died a madman. The rock door

closed never again to open. The crannóg sank, or stayed there won-
derfully kept from sight. No one could tell. Things lost here were
found again, miles distant, on the surface of Llyn Syfaddon. Floating
things, clothes, rings, body parts. In this Beacon's wilderness our
world and others intertwine.

Years later, after the passage of enough time for several kings to
have fallen and for Glyndŵr to have won and then lost and his land
to have been set on fire, Cwm Llwch locals determined to seek that
which had been thrown into their Llyn and, finding the waters impossibly deep and ferociously cold sought to have it drained. They made
a cut through the moraine at the northern lip. Dug through hard
yards of rock and sandstone mud. They created a channel. It's still
there. We come through it today, seeped with slow water, to reach the
gate rock. I knocked on it, felt for movement, listened for echo, for the
sound of anything. But there was nothing.

As the spades dug and hands pulled at rocks the edge of the lake
became ever nearer. Then the trench slowly began to fill with water
and the sky went dark. There was thunder, enormous thunder. Its
sound echoing like the crack of great guns from the sandstone scarp.
The surface of the Llwch rippled and rolled, began to spin and
dance. A hand, a great hand, rose up, weed-encrusted jewels on it.
Then there was a head, huge beyond belief. A three yard beard with
water falling from it and a voice as awful and as loud as the thunder.
Leave this place, it roared. Disturb my peace and I will drown the
Llwch, the Tarell and then the mighty Usk. Nothing can stop me. I
will lay waste that old Roman place you call Brecon. I will do it. I will
begin now[21].

The workmen fled, petrified, work uncompleted. They never went
back. Today the gap that remains between their trench and the lake
seems small enough to push through with your hands. Let's do it.
Won't. Can't.

The zig zag to the ridge takes some sweat but it is exhilarating. The
wind makes conversation impossible, my ears sting, my mild vertigo
makes me grasp the grass and the edge of the red rocks. We rise and
rise and then we are there, in the saddle between Corn Du and Pen y
Fan at the obelisk, the Tommy Jones Memorial, inscription still legible despite a century of driving rain[22].

Last time I'd made it to Tommy Jones' final resting place I'd taken
the route up from the south. There is a well trodden, much repaired,
and pretty wide muddy-puddled slog up from Storey Arms on the
A470. Storey Arms stands isolated, the only building for miles in any

direction, at the very heart of the National Park. It was a tavern, once, for dusty travellers crossing here for whatever god forsaken ancient reason. Sold thin beer. Highest pint in southern Wales. It's an outdoor education centre now. Opposite it is a car park complete with burger van and another selling Walls Cornettos. Cars here bring boots and anoraks. Walkers up for the hour-long wrench up to

the top of the highest peak in the south. Pen y Fan once held cairns and burial pits, jars containing the burned ashes of beaker folk, iron age ancients, older than the Romans. The pots crumble as you lift them. Why do we do this? The dead have only peace for a short time before men with metal detectors and shovels come hunting their remains, or construction workers unearth them and they are lost to trenching, road widening, foundations, tunnelling, the laying of pipelines. History like a faded flag. But the dead don't care really. All they are here for is to vanish. Many succeed. On the top of Pen y Fan there were some who didn't. But gone now, taken off to museums, their space trampled flat by visitation and the setting of a concrete trig point. On a fine day you can see clear to Berlin, eastern China and the Azores. If you are lucky. But the mists usually intervene. Reality fog.

I took blind Dave Reid up here. Clarks shoes, flat sole, no cleats. He wanted to do and did do most of what the rest of us sighted managed. Suggested we walk to the top as if the whole landscape was a braille publication. Braille was his great skill. He could sit and read braille volumes on his lap under a table, below his coat, beneath the bed sheets. Didn't need to look at the page, as I did, of course not. Braille books came in multiple volumes. Resembled ancient accountant's legers. Were delivered in Royal Mail sacks. James Joyce's *Ulysses* came in a stack as high as the mantle shelf. You could build protective walls from his braille library.

Braille had been invented by Frenchman Louis Braille in 1821 when he reduced the alphabet to cells of six dots. Dots could be raised forming up to sixty four different positions. Reid could slide his fingers across them as fast as my eyes could take in ink-printed text. He was also familiar with one of Braille's rivals, Moon, which had been invented by a post-scarlet fever Englishman, William Moon, in 1845. Moon used stylised raised letter shapes. Not much was published in this rather cumbersome rival but Reid had taken an interest. Like me he was intrigued by the ways in which text could be transmitted.

The idea was that we'd climb to Pen y Fan not directly alongside Storey Arms but from the ever-open Powys Council toilets in the overflow car park below the trees, a couple of hundred yards to the south. The route crossed the Blaen Taf Fawr on its slow drip into the Beacons reservoir and then went straight up to join a bit of the gap road at Bwlch Duwynt finishing along a path of scree and loose rock to the mountain's glorious summit. Reid would feel his way as if the surface was a vast Braille text dotted with intervals of Moon. He would interpret and I would write down. The art of landscape. The poetry of the natural world.

Wet start. Reid not clinging to me in blindman style but slipping off the path edge and finding himself in water. Long and slow and then faster. Wind increasing. Sun. We'd brought apples. Ate those. Reid shouted things out as he thought of them. Couldn't hear me because of the wind. This is enormous. Let's run a bit. Had to hold onto him to keep him from streaking off across the peat bog slopes.

Then we got to the gap and Reid became Braille personified. Yeel. Roll. Rall. Rich. Room. Rist. Rumatopid. Torpic. Can. C could. Could. Could. Clod. Could. Ssss. Stimul. Rimstone. Rheinstome. Pig. Carl. Girl. Can. Blood. Blood. Stime. Slime. Sticker. Still. Stoll. Stern. Smm. Mur. Wip. Willy. This stome still style. Mest. Moulder. Brite. Bolling. Brism. Stumphlog. Lear. Lart. Cleat. Can we crim. Bost. Bigh. I. This m. Mish. Reid streaming this to me scribbling and to all fellow walkers who thought he might be mad or in trouble. Offered to assist. Can we help you get him back. Bugger off, Reid shouted. I am climbing. Rhellof. Risttop. Roomering. Sodsol. Smmm. Nadologish.

Miiiis. We did. More noise than you should have in a place of convening with the god of the clear blue sky. Have you written this down, he shouted at me. Novarma. My notepad red-brown with sandstone mud. Grit. At the top he held on the trig and read bits of that. Ripperingwhite. You are inventing this, I accused him. I am not.

We went back down, eventually, with more stumbles and blind shouting than I would have really liked. The whole landscape reduced from green and red grey to wroopsm mmsg hms attakrist boom. The silence a thing I might have remembered if I'd had any head space in which to engage with the act of recalling. My arms aching from holding. But my spirit was flying. Back at the car it wouldn't turn. We had an ice cream. Let the carburettor dry out. Tutti Frutti. Tried again after ten minutes. The world once again slowed down.

VIRTUALLY COELBREN

Coelbren is up beyond the head of the Neath Valley where the coalfield ends and the limestone massif of the Bannau Brycheiniog begins. I had the idea to let Morgan take me to there, to a place that he had talked up incessantly over poker games in back rooms, over pie in Cardiff Bay cafes, over tea in shops on the Penarth headland and in phone calls to my office during which he babbled about the place as if it were where Wales ended and Wales began. And it might have been. Coelbren, Onllwyn, Pant y Ffordd, Duffryn Cellwen, Banwen – these villages once formed an industrial triangle deep in the Dulais Valley. A place carved by ice and the Afon Dulais. Steep, scree-strewn sides that kept the light in the sky. A place so far away that if you ever got there you'd never come back. Did you leave, Morgan? No. He'd like to pretend he was still there.

Morgan Francis, the angel maker, the man who listened for poems in the air. The angels he fashioned from sea-rolled glass fragments washed onto south Wales beaches, stuck with optician's glue to form

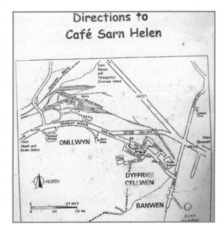

Directions to Café Sarn Helen

shapes from myth and from our hard-believing pasts. The poems he made from elsewhere. We'd sat in the Ship and Pilot once where he'd explained that most of Cold Knap, Sully, Lavernock and pebbled Penarth were now free of glass fragments. He'd vigorously collected for years, combing and recombing, probing bladder wrack and hunting the great drifts of grey pebbles, and now there was little left. They use plastic for their bottles today, cheaper than glass, either that or the tides had changed. Global shift. Sign of the age. He went on to explain that the wooden counter in the soon to disappear dockland beer stop[23] in which we were sitting had been made by men with tools that few now knew how to use. Jack planes, lambstongues, slitting gauges, drawknives, augers, button brace drills, and boxwood gimbletts. The skills had gone along with knowledge of what those names meant. Gimbletts, what do they do? Artefacts now sold as collectables on e-bay. Spoke shave – £46. Brass-back saw – £50. T-augers, "handles have a number of wood worm holes, adds to their charm" – £15.

Coelbren, said Morgan, was a famous conurbation full of pubs. Some of them so huge you could play football inside. He'd been born in Banwen which was not marked on maps. George Brinley Evans came from there. And Ed Thomas. And B.L. Coombes had visited. The choir had sung in America. Down the road was Onllwyn where they made rugby players. Morgan's house had been in Pant y Ffordd. Ystradgynlais was in a distant valley. Cardiff was on the other side of the world.

The literature of these north Neath valley townships, hammered out during the industrial revolution, had been prolific and comprehensively ignored. How Cold It Was In Coelbren. How Cold It Was. Onllwyn Dawn Raiders. The Roundabout At Pant y Ffordd. Outside the House of Banwen. Rape of the Ystradgynlais Country. Falling Hard Under Henrhyd Falls. Be My Baby Banwen. Coelbren in the Rye. Love In The Time of Coelbren. Ystradgynlais Full of Sorrows. Severn Brides for Severn Sisters. The Banwen Manual. The Onllwyn Register of Dentists. Banwen Knew My Father. Banwen In Great Brightness. Banwen Banwen Where Hast Thou Gone. Banwen of the Sunsets. Banwen Bungles. Banwen Bungles Again.

It's Christmas and we are in the Vulcan, back of Cardiff Prison, an old, unreconstructed Brains pub with sawdust on the floor and a clientele of working-class locals, tattooed dart players, battered ancients supping Dark and sniffing roll-ups with brown-edged fingers, photos of the old city on the brown-stained walls, coal in trucks waiting at a ship-filled dock, warehouses, staithes, smoke, no

Millennium anything, dark and dirt, no grass in sight anywhere. Lloyd is back from America where he's been searching for traces of Robert Mitchum. Robert Lewis, who wrote *The Last Llanelli Train* and its brilliant follow-up *Swansea Terminal,* rolls up. Rachel explains that since she won the money only her family have come knocking asking for subs. She's got ready mades. Always be ready. All writers die young. All writers smoke[24]. Grahame Davies is worried about his book on Wrexham. Hard to research. It's much further than Llanelli. And compared to Banwen the other side of the world. John Williams looking like a less-hirsute Jack Kerouac, check shirt and open collar, buys a round. Sean Burke exhales clouds of Drum which for a moment transports me back to the Old Holborn slaked Greyhound at the end of Bridge Street. The scrumpy pub of the down and outs. Gone for thirty years. The tobacco smell was a trigger. Ifor doesn't arrive, stuck in fog. East of England. Morgan talks. About Coelbren. Tells me about Pantyffordd. Doesn't smoke. Doesn't drink. Did once. So he says.

Coelbren, this week, we do not reach. The country is filled with fog like something out of Charles Dickens. Smog which doesn't move. Floats like a blanket. Six miles thick. No planes flying. Headlamps at mid day. Valleys with visibility at feet, a yard off and you are lost.

The choir which toured America and sang with Paul Robeson and then Otis Redding and finally had Ray Charles rock them up on piano had returned, full of James Brown and Jehovah. Their leader, Taliesin Rhagfyr Williams, had retired and passed direction to his brother Daniel Ionawr Williams, a squat man with dark wavy hair, like an Italian. He used his arms much more than his sibling. White gloves. Took the tenors on flights, arms rotating like a Rome traffic policeman, always neat suited but for the boots. Onllwyn mud on his turn-ups. Clack and crap in the eye-holes. Taliesin would sit in the pews behind him. Watched, straight faced, conducting his soaring and loyal singers with the moving of his eyes.

Morgan had done time at the brickworks where they'd gathered the silicate slag waste from the iron making and processed it into moulds to create pastel-shaded rock-sharp Onllwyn bricks. The kiln was hot as Hades and you got extra money when Hades itself caught fire. Most of the valley was built from reconstituted slag, so hard you couldn't take a drill to it. Usually bricks are dug clay, shaped, then fired to orange firmness. They leave clay pit holes in the landscape which fill with water. The Onllwyn variety, by contrast, took industrial waste and reprocessed it into something that might

endure. The brickworks were on the site of an ironworks on the site of the Roman Road from Y Gaer to Nidum, on the site of an iron age track on the route the hunter-gatherers took. The tribes from the age when these hills touched Ireland by landbridge, when the world was cold. Before them this was a nesting place for dinosaurs, when the world was steamy hot.

Coelbren in the thick fog emerging like an idea for a country. Morgan talking about the drifts, the pits that went into the Valley sides horizontally. Onllwyn Number One. Drum[25]. Onllwyn Number Three. Coal waste everywhere. The washery. The waste heaps. Buckets on high wires. Railtracks. All gone now but for the open cast and the few private drifts, run by chancers, knocking the scree out of place, keeping post-industrial regrowth in check. The Carmarthen Fans with their long ridges and stone circles and open emptiness all still there as a backdrop. Morgan talks of coal. Without it the land would have been like the Hebrides. Lost at the edge of empire. A country out there where the signal faded, where transmission ended.

The darts players are dancing, if you can call it that. Tinsel in the women's hair. Sliding to the juke box music. Roy Orbison. Johnny Tillotson[26]. Del Shannon. Those names tell you how old these dancers are.

Morgan has set up a press to publish his poems. Type *Onllwyn* into Google and you get Morgan's face rather than a picture of the distant valley township. *Selected Poems* by Morgan Francis. There's a CD of him reading available too.

We look out the Vulcan window and through the dusk the fog still rolls. The street lights are orange blurs in a grey continuum. If traffic passes we don't hear it. Coelbren Can Wait. Banwen the Bountiful. Banwen After Years Have Passed. Pantyffordd at the Finish. Dulais At The End Of Time.

We don't need to go there, Onllwyn, Coelbren, Pantyffordd. Do we? In the fog we'd see as much as we can see in this bar. Talk about it, Morgan. I'll write it down. They want to know what I'm doing, these writers I'm drinking with, they ask. Someone's new project is always of interest, where are the ideas moving to, where have they come from. You never say, of course, that would be like mentioning the name of the Scottish play. Talk the idea and it will rush away from you faster than you can follow. Keep them deep, keep them yours, open them up in secret. It's just talk, I tell the writers. Morgan has another lemonade. Roy Orbison comes on the jukebox. Soaring tenor passion. Marvellous. Morgan nods. Do you like Roy Orbison? What did he write, Morgan asks?

BLAENRHONDDA

There are other valleys. The Cynon, the Dulais, the Swansea, the Neath, the Taff, the Usk. Many. But none of them as sexy sounding as this one. The Rhondda. Cwm Rhondda. Help me help me O great redeemer. Help me Rhonda. Guitars and soaring voices. The Rhondda a place made entirely of the clanging past. A past that reaches us now through memories turned over so often they've worn thin. Show through. Faces and places coming up in the wrong order. Grainy film and scratched photo. Grey and black. Shots of trucks then dirty faces then pit heads and rail tracks and then more shots of spoil and wrecked hillside. And because of one thing, all of this, coal. Dug right across south Wales but it is the Rhondda that made it all famous. Too famous.

It's all old men talk of. Now it has gone it's celebrated in art and sculpture. You can buy glazed chunks at museum stores, mounted on plaques, turned into jewellery. Fragments cut to resemble lamps. Carved to look like engines. Made into paperweights. The young do not know what to do with it. They have little idea how it can be set on fire. Still less about how it might turn water to steam. Or how any of that worked. We don't need those things now. We don't live that way. These are modern days.

The modern days, of course, have always been coming. Things have always been improving, making our spirits sing, always changing the way we live for the better. Believe that as my father did, god rest his soul, and you'll believe anything.

I'm standing at the top of the Rhondda, as far up as it goes, right there where the road rises and spins onto the common at Hirwaun and the Afon Rhondda Fawr wells up near Carn Foesen at the top of Craig y Llyn[27]. The river that carved a valley, made all this. Looking

south I can see valley and mountain and outcrop and crag, rays of Blakean sunlight slanting in from broken cloud, shadows chasing shadows, wisps of mist evaporating from folds in the forest where the sun has touched. Road lines crossing rock faces, ribbons of blue-white water cutting their endless trough at the valley base. Grey roofs below leafless trees. Field outlines in blocks on cleared valley sides like chalk marks in a playground. Flattened gorse. White winter grass. Grey tumbled rock. But overwhelmingly this place is green in all its shades. Grey green white green dark green winter green slow green but no longer black. There's a wind, too. Something that wakes you up to all this.

There's no coal. Instead there are electric bands: Sugarhouse, Paranola, Azora, Detera, Tomorrow's History, Lost Prophets, Midasuno, Funeral for a Friend, In Me, Stereophonics, the Alarm, Efran Kaye, Richard Gould, Rhondda and the Runestone Cowboys (Iceland), Rhondda Gillespie (pno), Eyes of Blue (left uk), Racing Cars, Seraphim, Juliet, Bullet For My Valentine. Playing in the clubs and the falling apart pubs.

When there was coal here they first scratched it out from small drifts and from shallow pits. You didn't dig in far and you didn't get a huge amount back. The early bituminous black of the lower Rhondda. The big moment came in 1855 when Bute bought Cwmsaebren Farm from William Davies for £11,000. The pit he sank discovered steam coal. Cwm Saebren became Herbert Town named after the historic family long associated with the Butes. Tre Herbert. Population of the entire parish[28] in 1861 – 3857. Ten years later – 17,777. The Bute estate built fifty or so dwellings to house his mine workers. The rest arrived in a Klondike crash.

There's no coal now. Tower Colliery, on the Hirwaun plateau, far side of the Craig-y-Llyn escarpment and the last deep mine in Wales, has finally gone. It was saved from Thatcher's closures in 1994 by 239 members of the workforce using £8000 each from their redundancy money.It reopened under the leadership of larger than life Tyrone

O'Sullivan in 1995. Work, books, fame, blazing media success. Opera written by Alun Hoddinott about Tower's David and Goliath success. By 2007 it was taking over an hour to get to the coalface and the seams were riddled with faults. In 1995 British Coal said Tower would last five years. Tower managed thirteen. The coal ran out on January 25, 2008. Tower's conveyor belt, housed in grey corrugate, runs silent for half a mile across a flat and now largely green landscape, a solitary reminder of how this world once was. 140 years of production finally ceased.

Yet here, a few miles away, at the high end of the big Rhondda, where the valley finishes in a round-ended fork – Blaenrhondda, Tynewydd, Blaencwm, the three village outriders of grand Victorian Treherbert – there's hardly a memory. These compact acres once had four mines – North Dunraven, Fernhill (four pits), Glen Rhondda (two pits), Tydraw (Dunraven Colliery), a rail link to Cardiff on the TVR[29], then the Rhondda and Swansea Bay Railway and its tunnel through the mountain to Blaengwynfi and on down the Afan valley to the great seaside beaches of Aberavon and Porthcawl.

You can see where the pits were, where the spoil tips have been flattened or terraced, greened, worn back by rain and nature, grass with black re-emerging. For a time in the 1970s, to alleviate the loss, there was a wild west theme park here. Ex-miners wearing chaps and double guns in belted holsters, leather waistcoats, collarless shirts from their pits days, broad-brimmed felt hats, small blue scars on their skin, a pulling hard for breath as they swaggered from swing door saloon to coal tip corral. Didn't work. Wild west in the wild west, like taking coals to Newcastle.

At Big Pit in Blaenavon, same coal seams but at the top of a different valley, the theme park is the industry itself. Pithead baths, working wheel house, a shaft you can go down, ex-miners as guides to take their helmeted visitors where the coal once was, deep underground. They tell you there that the world has used almost all of its gas and petroleum and that the coal cutting trade is about to make a grand

return. Economics, see butt, used to cost too much to get what's left of the coal out but things are changing. They've got new ways now. Any day now they'll be sinking new shafts and recruiting men. Number One seam, six inches thick. Number Two nine rising to a foot. We'll cut it like butter, put it in wagons, haul it out.

Wales has 250 million tonnes of workable coal, says Tyrone. But no one yet is rushing back to drag them out. They are economically difficult, distant, dangerous and usually in the wrong place. Rhondda wind park. Fast breeder at Merthyr. Cold fusion at Porth.

After the strike in 1984 proved Thatcher right and Scargill wrong the work in these valleys collapsed and the world changed forever. Compensation packages brought in a trickle of light industry, some assembling, Remploy white goods, ice cream franchises, art factory, pottery workshops, sole ex-miner start-ups carving figurines, burning patterns into bread boards, making house name plaques, trying to keep some dignity and the soul alive. The rest of the world just forgot about the whole thing. Let them get on their bikes. Let the Rhondda take the rain. Let the Rhondda sink and steam.

Most of this history is lost on those who have never been here. The valleys have produced a whole bank of legible literature, fiction, verse, the great Welsh novel, epic poetry about the disaster at Senghenydd, but most of it has today simply sunk down the back of bookshops' shelves. Enter 'Welsh Mining' into Amazon's search box and you'll go directly to a copy of D.H. Lawrence's *Women In Love*. Underground you couldn't see them and now they are invisible again.

I never knew B.L. Coombes, nor Lewis Jones. Both well before my time but their books, poorly plotted and with little glory, told the miner's tale as it certainly was. Richard Llewelyn faked pit life at Gilfach Goch and had a winner on his hands. *How Green Was My Valley*, green again now. Gwyn Thomas, best industrial age writer Wales ever produced, caught the valleys in their battered, bristling and most bravura moments. The mines and their people frozen in aspic. But locals never loved him. A teacher from Barry with a difficult manner. I met him a few times, the risen writer riding his fame. Little time for avant garde poets. I tried to get some fiction out of him for my literary magazine, *second aeon*. He wasn't interested. His widow burned great heaps of his papers after he died.

Ron Berry, born at Blaen Cwm and didn't leave, turned up at some of Cardiff's 70s literary boundary busting events, but wouldn't contribute to the magazine unless I paid him. Couldn't. A former miner his work tracked across the loss of spiritual value in the mining valleys now that comparative prosperity had arrived and the air was safe to breathe. He wrote about valley life as it was just before the Thatcher years, when things were, if not wonderful, at least vaguely improving. The bookstores of the proud Rhondda should have been full of his work but there were no such places. Instead the books sold hand to hand, reached their home readership through a shrinking library service. Reading as a leisure activity has largely left the western world.

Glyn Jones and Rhys Davies both used their industrial south Wales backgrounds in their work. But both had left early. Davies to live and work famously in London. Glyn Jones to become doyen of the Anglo-Welsh revival, much loved and always admired, in Whitchurch, Cardiff. The Rev Rhydwen Williams from Pentre, Rhondda, baptist, twice crowned bard and prolific novelist wrote extensively in Welsh of valley life. He is mostly now unavailable and hardly translated.

Mogg Williams from Ogmore Vale and Robert Morgan from Penrhiwceiber both worked down the pits before turning their experiences into readable verse. Both were self published. You can still find some of Mogg's stuff on bookshelves if you look hard enough. Robert Morgan has vanished from the face of the earth.

That leaves Jack Jones, last of the fictioneers, author of *Bidden To The Feast*, *Off To Philadelphia In The Morning* and the endlessly sought after *Rhondda Roundabout*. In the 1970s the Welsh Arts Council produced a poster of Jones looking like a manicured Hemmingway. Students put it on their walls. The Merthyr born writer had begun life down the pits and had used those experiences to power an enormous stream of novel, autobiography and drama. His trick was to research local history and to then portray, with absolute fidelity, the people and the places he'd read about. Check the bookstores. The best you'll get today is stock still left from a 1967 reprint of *Me and Mine*. Does anyone care[30] about heritage anymore? I met Jack once, aeons ago at a reception for a Welsh literary award. Everyone was wearing suits and drinking wine. Jack stood resplendent in wide braces drinking bottles of brown ale brought in specially. He looked just like his photo.

I've missed a few names here. Harri Webb, Mountain Ash librarian, and the best republican poet Wales ever had. Walter Haydn Davies, raconteur and recorder of day to day minutia. George Brinley Evans who worked Banwen Colliery (see *Virtually Coelbren* page 49). Punk singer from the sink estates John Evans[31] who wrote *How Real Is My Valley*, a multi-media post-industrial experience valley life. Rachael Tresize. Richard John Evans. But these are writers who came well after the coal.

Actually it is Bruce Macdonald who has brought me here. We are standing in the Hendre Mynydd car park, Beware Of Thieves Operating In This Area, burned out information signboard, water-filled public barbeque kit, Power Ranger suited Suzuki rider half hidden in the trees, two lads with a new BMW taking turns to have themselves photographed at its driving wheel, wind whipping north, cold enough for a hat. Retired from BT. Bruce now runs a walking and heritage website[32] for Glamorgan which includes maps and routes to places that get scant mention in regular tourist books. His Blaenrhondda six-mile circuit takes in everything from pre-history (the hut circles of Hen Dre'r Mynydd, fallen rocks that look like either the remains of great Celtic dance halls or more prosaically, cattle enclosures), abandoned rail tunnels, lost pit heads, paths still rich with small coal and spoil, to Pen Pych (the world's only flat-topped, three sided mountain) and the waterfalls of Nant Carnfoesen, Nant Melyn and Nant y Gwair that become the Afon Rhondda when they reach valley bottom.

The trip, done on a dry winter day, takes a good four hours and involves hill climb and an amount of tramping through white grass tussock. Industrial heritage, apart from the obvious black-green scars of the now vanished pit heads, is less than I'd imagined. Some of the trails are along abandoned railways and dismantled tram ways. Coal seams visible. Great pipes in stream beds, lost iron fences, abandoned boilers. But mainly trees, growing again for the first time in two hundred years. During the valley's industrial height these hills were bare – denuded of anything that would burn for fuel, and of anything that could be used as pit prop, house wall, shed side or roof support. Pen Pych in the old photos looks the three sided flat top it actually is. Today it's soft-edged again, blended into the landscape with a curtain of ruffled green.

Back at the car park the BMW photographers and the biker have gone to be replaced by an unshaven oldster with stick and collie sitting in a three-wheeler Reliant Regal, taking the air, best he can. A few hundred yards to the south, alongside the zooming A4061, is something marked as "plastic shrine" on Bruce McDonald's online map. This turns out to be a single-story white painted and nailed-up hut backed by giant many-coloured plastic carnations spread over the steep-rising hill. No signs announce this as a regeneration art project. The slopes here are wired back to prevent rocks from falling onto the road. Bruce reckons that before this safety feature was installed a retired miner lived here, cleared the road of loose scree and fallen boulder and, faced with the impossibility of growing anything decent this high up, planted his patch with a surreal post-industrial crop of fantasy flowers. From here the artificial gardener would have looked straight down at Blaenrhondda's all too real Fernhill pit wheels. He's gone, so are they.

Pits Rhondda once had: Dinas Lower Dinas, Dinas Middle Dinas, Ynyshir / Jones Navigational Ynyshir, Cymmer Porth, Ty Mawr Hopkinstown, Hafod No 1 Trehafod, Hafod No 2 Trehafod, Coedcae Trehafod, Llwyncelyn Porth, Gyfeillion / Great Western Hopkinstown, Tynewydd Porth, Tylecoch Treorchy, Bute Merthyr, Pentre Ystrad, Pontygwaith / Cynllwyn Du / No 8 Tylorstown, Ynysfaio Treherbert, Glamorgan / Scotch Colliery Llwynypia, Ferndale No 1 Blaenllechau, Abergorki Treorchy, Bodringallt Ferndale No 4 Ystrad, Tydraw Treherbert, Maindy Ton Pentre, Dare Cwmparc, Parc Cwmparc, Tynewydd Treherbert , Fernhill No 1 Blaenrhondda, Fernhill No 2 Blaenrhondda, Blaenrhondda Blaenrhondda, Ferndale No 2 Ferndale, Cambrian No 1 Clydach Vale, Fernhill No 3 Blaenrhondda, Fernhill No 4 Blaenrhondda, Fernhill No 5 Blaenrhondda, Penrhys No 6 Tylorstown, Penrhys No 7 Tylorstown, Blaenclydach (Gorki Drift) Clydach Vale, Cambrian No 2 Clydach Vale, Maerdy No 1 Maerdy, Maerdy No 2 Maerdy, Tynybedw Pentre, Ferndale No 4 Ferndale, Gelli Pentre, Lady Margaret Treherbert, Standard No 1 Ynyshir, Eastern Colliery Gelli, Standard No 2 Ynyshir, Naval Penygraig, Bertie / Lewis Merthyr Trehafod, Pwll Mawr / Cwtch / National Wattstown, Pwll Bach / Cwtch / National Wattstown, Trefor / Lewis Merthyr Trehafod, Cambrian No 3 Clydach Vale, Ferndale No 5 Blaenllechau, Ely Penygraig, Ely Tonypandy, Nantgwyn Tonypandy, Maerdy No 3 Maerdy, Penrhys No 9 Tylorstown, Lady Lewis Ynyshir, Anthony Tonypandy, Glenrhondda No 1 Blaencwm, Maerdy No 4 Maerdy, Glenrhondda No 2 Blaencwm, Maerdy No 3, Maerdy No 4. Black gold gone unless the wind farms fail and technology advances like they say it will and small coal works again. Then all this might, as some dream, return. Do the locals want that? Jury's still out.

ACTUALLY BANWEN

Banwen Pyrddin, pit village with today no sign of a pit, turns out to be nothing like Morgan had led me to believe it would be. A couple of streets centred on Roman Road, a terrace of sixty four houses, so badly maintained by the NCB when they were in charge that one fell down so now there's sixty three. I'm driving round with George Brinley Evans, former collier, author and eighty-two year old local celebrity, strung about with cameras to record my visit, and top coats to keep out the driving rain. We're in Norman Burns' battered Nissan. The springs are squashed by our combined weight. Norman is the secretary of the local history society and can tell you the past of almost every stone. Morgan, delighted the fog has lifted and who has got me up here to show me the places of his childhood, turns out to be known locally as Brian. We reach the top of the village. It's taken us about five seconds. End house is boarded up, the one next to it has a large and dopy Alsatian spread out on the inside window ledge like a cat. Midday. Upstairs a vision in pink tracksuit, fag in hand, has just got up. A man in a cowboy hat comes out to start a car, fails, then immediately gives up. The rain comes in along Roman Road like an army of legionnaires. This was once Sarn Helen, clattering into Banwen from the fort at Coelbren then roaring out, up over Hirfynydd to the rest of the civilised world. Except that in those days there was no Banwen, nothing. Almost like now, not even a scrape in the ground.

We've been up on the mountain at Clwdi Banwen to see the famous fake rocks, the Gnoll Stones[33], high in the rained-on forestry. The fakes are of a fifth century memorial pillar stone marking the burial of Macaritinus son of Bericius[34] and of a pre-Norman wheel cross showing a man in a kilt[35]. The originals are now in the Swansea Museum. The fakes have been perfectly replicated by Terry Briers from Carmarthen. Norman reckons that if you extend the fragment of wheel that remains and then imagine legs below that then the cross would have originally been three metres high. Not tall. But bigger than us. We were going to have a compass added, Norman tells me, showing what you can see from here. Fan Gyhirych, Fan Fawr. But the forestry have planted so many lovely trees that now you can't see a thing. Bloody greenness. We stare out into the rain drenched gloom.

Down in the valley, although I have to say that as valleys go the Dulais and its juniors are disappointingly flat, the landscape undulates and the air is always full of light. Down here is another stone, put up two years ago with its metal memorial plate already shot up by the local lost. The stone celebrates the fact that St Patrick, who was an Onllwyn boy through and through, was taken from here by marauding Irish when he was sixteen[36]. George has us cluster so he can take a video of his visitors observing the local sites. Patrick wasn't like

David, he explains, speaking as if he knew them both well. In fact speaking as if he'd just left them both at the greengrocers down the road. Patrick always referred to the Irish as foreigners, right up to the end. He was easy to get on with. Liked a joke and a drink. Now David, he was much more distant, not the same at all. Wanted us to abstain from overindulgence and pray all the time. Things like that. Not an easy man. Should saints be easy then, I ask? George smiles.

The cluster of towns here run into each other. And they are hardly towns more like villages: Banwen, Duffryn Cellwen, Coelbren, Onllwyn, Pant y Ffordd, Aberpergwm, and beyond them, Seven Sisters. Birthplace of the poet Ruth Bidgood. But of her there's little mark. Industry has largely left too. Deep coal mining is over. The opencast[37], however, with its reliance on huge machines and a tiny workforce, still drags up the black stuff and sends it to the washery at Coelbren. There's a railway here, trucks with coal in them strung out across the landscape. Yellow dumper trucks and floodlit yards. But the landscape stays green. No tips, no smoke. We pass the site of the once famous Halfway Inn, the Slope as it was called locally, the pub for the pits which had one wall of its cellar right in the middle of the eight foot seam. Barrels along three walls, coal on the fourth. Gone, not a brick left. In Coelbren itself Morgan's brother-in-law, retired collier Moelwyn Evans, shows me the far northern reach of the coal-field, a ridge, a change in the colour of vegetation, that runs along the end of his garden. We look out over the leafless winter landscape towards the slow rise of the Beacons. This vista doubled as the Transvaal when they were year filming *Young Winston*. They blew up a train right over there. Terrible bang it was. In his garage Moelwyn has two ton of anthracite stacked neatly in green plastic boxes and a mountain of chipboard off cuts from the Remploy factory. Up here the temperature is at least one pullover colder than the rest of Wales.

There is one shop in Coelbren, the Co-op, and none in Onllwyn. We take a photograph of the bungalow on Wembley Avenue, birthplace of Hywel Francis, MP for Port Talbot. We pass an iron shale waste tip, behind which was once a sixty-foot quarry. Filled in and now allot-ments. To the right is a bright and almost emerald green football pitch hand-excavated over the top of another set of refilled iron workings. In the early 1950s Krishna Menon[38], Indian High Commissioner, came here to the tiny wooden Onllwyn Sports Pavilion to speak to the min-ers and declare his non-violent solidarity with the hoary-handed, hard labouring, Welsh working man. Few of those left here today.

Where Onllwyn becomes Pant y Ffordd the road signs face each other like gunfighters. For Morgan this place is holy ground. To the north rising greenness and the grass-covered top soil mountain from the Nant Helen Opencast. When they're done they'll put it all back and replant. Couple of years and the devastation will be gone. Like nothing had ever happened. So they say. The rail link from the Banwen coal washery parallels the road. Morgan shows me the field where he once played cricket. Not a field, no pitch, a patch of bog and hummock, crossed by the meandering Dulais. The fast bowlers would leap the water as they ran into the invisible crease. Beyond them was Tin Town, a cluster of zinc prefabs erected to house migrant miners and immigrant brick makers. Above was where the Brecon Forest Tramway once ran taking newly-cast iron canon balls to the Swansea canal.

At Tonyfildre Farm the farmer, Byron Jones, loads us into his four by four and takes us roaring and skidding across two wet fields to see the Sequoia, a millennium gift from George's Canadian nephew to the people of Welsh Banwen. It's six years on today and the miserable one-foot sapling that came in a plastic tube is now at least five-foot tall and looks like something you'd put in your house at Christmas. Proudly George has his photo taken standing in front. Below us is the Onllwyn Gaer, a Roman auxiliary fort situated halfway between those at Neath and Brecon. You have to use your imagination here, Norman says. These bumps in the ground are all that's left. Although they did find a single shard of late Iron Age/Romano-British pottery in a molehill on the northern rampart. The rain moves in sideways. Rampart? I can't see a thing. Just blur and grass. There's a marching camp nearby and that's six times the size. Do you want to have a look there? Do I? Anything more to see than wet grass, I ask? Norman shakes his head.

Back in tough Banwen we have a valleys lunch at Caffi Sarn Helen, baguettes, latte, panini, and pizza slices in a building converted from the offices of the National Coal Board Opencast. This is the Dove Centre, a community venture providing computer suite, day nursery, garden, re-education and training facilities and a home for the miners library. Founded by Mair Francis in the teeth of the 1984 strike this is an example of women reclaiming their heritage. The all-women miners support groups hanging on. Agents for change, re-educators, sustainers of life. Lesley Smith and Julie Bibby take me round, laughing, bubbling with enthusiasm for what they do. There's more life here than anywhere else I've seen in the whole Dulais Valley. On the wall are framed jackets from George's books. *Boys of Gold. Where The*

Flying Fishes Play. A living connection with an underground past. During a break in the dampness we go outside for George to show me where the pit head once was. A bumpy green field with a wrecked car in its corner. The line of the Roman road rises beyond, smashed by open cast and forestry planting but still visible, just. Then the rain, friend of reclamation, once more increases and we go back inside.

SOUTHERN BORDER

Wales, land of echoes. Down here, where the border between England and Wales hits the sea it's just like it is in the north. The political boundary snakes down a river, the Wye this time rather than the Dee. The rivers then enter greater waters, this time it's the Severn, to mix and swirl and flood. The place where southern Wales ends and England begins is in water. And once again the military stake their claim. Onshore the Second Battalion The Yorkshire Regiment (Green Howards) and their barracks stand watch. Barbed wire. Search lights. Uniformed female solider in the camp guard post, headphone in her ear.

This is Beachley, in England now but once part of Wales. Beachley Point snake-heads out into the estuary and points itself at Bristol. Before the building of the first Severn Bridge in 1966 the Aust ferry sailed from here. Sixteen cars at a time, one mile trip across a treacherous estuary on the decks of the *Severn Princess*. The ferry has run from Beachley since the start of history. The Normans are recorded as allowing the monks from Tintern to use it in the twelfth century. Daniel Defoe came here in the eighteenth. The Duke of Beaufort built

stone jetties and ran a steam ship operation in the nineteenth. Bob Dylan crossed just before the bridge opened in 1966. There's a shot of him on the cover of the soundtrack CD to Martin Scorsese's *No Direction Home*. He's standing at the Aust landing, spiky hair and shades, looking like the poet John Cooper Clark[39]. The number plate of the car he is to ride in has been digitally altered to read 1235 RD, a reference to

Rainy Day Women numbers 12 and 35, the Dylan hit of the day. Until a few months ago the wreck of the *Severn Princess* lay on the foreshore a couple of meters east. Rust red but still a boat. Removed now by a preservation society. Or maybe sold for scrap.

Beachley is a village with a church and a pub, a vast army barracks and then the Army Apprentices College where new soldiers learn their trades. Politically this is Gloucestershire although the barrack signs are bilingual. Cars to Enter Camp Sidelights On. Cynllun Gwarchod CCTV. The bridge, the first Severn crossing, flies above. It's high, mighty and surprisingly silent. At the Coast Guard station Pete Bissell tells me that because of the huge tidal range here many people get stranded. Ramblers on the Severn rocks, kids, city dwellers looking for crabs, fishermen, amateur sailors. The Coast Guard use their inflatable to rescue them. Usually the station is unmanned but at holiday week-ends like this one they keep someone on duty. Too many idiots. There are a lot of jumpers too. They walk or drive out onto the bridge and then leap the barricades. Do they die? Every time.

This is also J.K. Rowling territory. She was brought up near here, Chepstow, went to school up the road in Sedbury, and spent her teenage years sitting on the Beachley Point rocks, thinking up plots. Or maybe that was just her PR machine's imagination.

The headland, the Point itself, carries woodland, huge super-size electricity pylons, the land-reach for a three metre National Grid cable tunnel, Army barbed-wire, housing for the inshore lifeboats of the Severn Area Rescue Association, signs warning of Danger of Death, car park for visitors, cans, trash, and a touching hand-built memorial to two children drowned when the lightening incoming tide caught them. The rocks here, revealed when the water is out, have names – Hen and Chickens, Leary Rock, Great Ulverstone, Upper Bench. Men in waders fish from them. A Welsh angling club are running a contest when I visit. No one has caught much. Few eels. They crack open lager cans around the weigh-in. The accents are Valley Welsh rather than Gloucester. But move a hundred metres up the road

into the village and everything changes.

Offa who built his dyke as a way of demarking his territory rather than as a defensive bund began the job just up the coast. Late eighth century and the ditch and mound are still there, footpath running 168 miles north along its top. Offa didn't mess with rivers. He left the Wye, both banks, to the Welsh.

notes

1. "I come from-a ewgest 'state in town, / second ewgest maze in Ewrop, they say, / coz planners potched it up, the clowns: / I'd give em a proper lampin / on'y they've all gone away." – from 'Gurnos Boy' in Mike Jenkins' *Graffiti Narratives, Planet* 1994.
2. Entry on Glyn Jones in *The Oxford Companion To The Literature of Wales*, compiled by Meic Stephens, OUP 1986.
3. Dr John Pikoulis, author, critic and Chair of the Welsh Academy.
4. Yr Wyddfa, Y Bala, Y Barri – as opposed to Cardiff, Newport and Carmarthen, indefinite places all.
5. The Hay festival of Literature was founded by Peter and his father Norman Florence in 1988.
6. Given the freehold possession of the land
7. For the pedant the first four numbers relate to steam engines preserved on the Barry railway: 2861 GWR 2-8-0 of 1918 (4) Withdrawn 1963. 4115 GWR 2-6-2T of 1936 (4) Withdrawn 1965. 80150 BR 2-6-4T of 1957 (4) Withdrawn 1965. 92245 BR 9F 2-10-0 of 1958 (4) Withdrawn 1964. 51919 Class 108 DMU DMBS is an early diesel set. DMU – Diesel Multiple Unit. DMBS – Driving Motor Brake Second.
8. Rother-horned cattle
9. St Michael's fame lives on in Welsh with a large number of Abergavenny district churches dedicated to him. Llanfihangel. Llan – holy site, Mihangel – Michael. Take home a scrap of earth from the holy Skirrid's old red sandstone tip, for luck and for faith.
10. The church of St. Michael, Llanfihangel-Ystern-Llewern, restored in 1874-5, dates from 1685. Built on an earlier religious site.
11. *The Three Standard Stoppages*, Paris 1913.
12. Giraldus Cambrensis, *Description of Wales*, 1194.
13. Chris Broadribb later changes his name to Chris Ozzard and moves west to Carmarthen.
14. Peter Finch, 'A Welsh Wordscape', 1968. Collected in *Selected Poems*, Poetry Wales Press, 1987.
15. District Heating by way of central boiler house has never worked anywhere. Breakdowns are endemic. After years of failure the Penrhys Boiler House was closed and redeveloped as a youth centre.
16. This gilded figure of Saint Mary was "crowned, had ruddy cheeks, the holy infant in its arms and a precious stone in the bosom". The poet Gwilym Tew noted that there were human marks on the face of Our Lady of Penrhys. The statue cried.
17. The Cistercian Way – Llantarnam to Penrhys, Penrhys to Margam. Go on to Strata Florida, or back to Tintern.
18. The oldest, The Star, dates from Tudor times and has a dressed-stone doorway and a spiral stair.
19. I got a poem from the experience, *Dinas Powys*, the first of a long series of walking poems.

Adversity is never totally negative. There's always something that can be turned to advantage.

20. Professor Leslie Alcock, 1925-2006, Archaeologist who excavated King Arthur's 'Camelot' and redefined the scholarship of his discipline

21. *The Welsh Fairy Book*, W Jenkyn Thomas (1907). Tale retold. Did it happen? There has to be something in the historical past from the time when islands floated here and men came over these hills bearing swords and spears. Storytellers will retell and embellish, interpret and recast. This is an oral tradition where nothing is ever recorded in writing and history passes from mouth to ear to mouth to roll forward through generation on generation, bending and turning as it goes. How else could there have been giants and doors in rocks which no longer open? Doesn't stop me pushing at the very place, just to be sure.

22. Tommy Jones was a five year old who, in 1900, lost his way while returning home with his father. They were walking from the rail station at Brecon bound for the family farm house at Cwm Llwch. Half way they stopped for tea at a camp made by soldiers. They were joined there by Tommy's grandfather and Tommy's thirteen year old cousin, William. The boys were sent on ahead but part way along the route Tommy took fright for some reason and returned alone to find his father. He never did. Instead he climbed 1300 feet to die, exposed, on the Milan Ridge. At the inquest juror's fees were waived and a collection for a public memorial begun. This stone obelisk marks the spot where Tommy's body, after five days of searching, was eventually found.

23. After doing time with half its letters missing (*hip & lot*) the pub morphed into a restaurant come wine bar, *The Orange Tree* in 2005. By mid 2006 that enterprise had failed and the once down at heel and full of life dockland public house joined the *Mujibs* chain as a Chinese/Indian restaurant. It is now *Mischief's Café Bar*. Morgan and I have yet to experience its contemporary delights.

24. They still do but now *outside* the pub. Last time I visited The Vulcan half the writers were inside smokelessly discussing the work of David Peace while the rest were at a sort of picnic table on the side of the road tapping their ash into the gutter.

25. The Colliery below Mynydd y Drum, first commercial pit in Onllwyn, dug in 1823.

26. The only one of this trio still alive – Tillotson – rose to UK fame with a teen ballad *Poetry In Motion* in 1960. He is still recording.

27. "The main source of the Afon Rhondda Fawr is a spring, Ffynnon-y-Gwalciau, at about 544m OD. The main headwater Nant Carn Moesen then descends rapidly, joining the tributary of Nant Selsig, below Pen Pych." – Glamorgan Gwent Archaeological Trust. (http://www.ggat.org.uk/historic%20landscapes/Rhondda/English/Rhondda_Features.htm)

28. Treherbert, Treorky, Llwynpia, Pen-y-Graig, Pentre, Ystrad, Pandy. (Slater's Commercial Directory 1880. http://www.genuki.org.uk/big/wal/GLA/Ystradyfodwg/slaters.1880.html)

29. TVR: Taff Vale Railway

30. Someone does. With a large slice of Welsh Assembly Government financial support Parthian Books are publishing a series of classic reprints. Under the editorship of historian Prof Dai Smith *The Library of Wales* will reprint eight or so titles annually. Already Ron Berry and Gwyn Thomas have benefited.

31. No 27 in Culturenet Cymru's list of 100 top Welsh Heroes: (http://www.100welshheroes.com/en/top100

32. Glamorgan Walks – http://www.glamorganwalks.com/index.html

33. The Gnoll Stones, originally uprooted and moved to the garden of Gnoll House, Neath by Lord Macworth in 1790

34. MACARITIN- FILI BERIC [-/HIC IACIT (?)] Originally standing close to the line of Sarn Helen near the north-eastern end of Hirfynydd, at a point where the Roman road begins to descend towards the fort at Coelbren.

35. Fragment of a disc-headed slab cross, characteristic of west Glamorgan in the nineth and

tenth centuries. Found near Capel Coelbren.

36. Attested to by American historian Tom Clark – Banwen is the best bet.

37. The area is described by the poet Harri Webb as "The opencast capital of Europe" (The Big Job). "Everything comes to the surface at Banwen," writes George Brinley Evans (letter to the author) "You could pick a bucketful of iron nodules off the bed of the stream that runs through my garden in no time."

38. Krishna Menon 1897-1974. Home rule supporter and enthusiast for the People's Republic of China. Held the record for the longest delivered speech at the United Nations – eight hours in support of India's stance on Kashmir.

39. Probably the other way around. Dylan came first. Dylan is older.

SOUTH WEST

TO THE SUN

There's a push to travel west somewhere deep in most of us. Something about getting the sun on our backs and heading off where it too is going. Being pulled by some magnet out there. A desire to travel until the land gives out, searching for something we can't quite define: love, splendour, fulfilment, gold, sweetmeats, Shangri-la, Atlantis, Mu. The mystic and the marvellous. The perfect and the pure. The great lands of wonder that lie at the edge. The west. Where the Buddha is. Portal to the netherworld. The manifest destiny[1] of water, mist and maize. Place where the sun goes down in red passion. Place of milk and honey where the body can live forever. In a darkened room a blindfold man was spun in circles and then released. He walked west more times than any other direction. If you stand on the border between England and Wales and look west along the snaking M4 corridor it's not that far. 136 miles of slowly sloping land, falling down as the earth curves, the west where the ancient is nearer the surface and the air almost pure. It sparkles, it almost always does. Travel that way and over Pembrokeshire, when you get there, the blue breaks out in Wales' eternal grey skies like a hoard of UFOs.

Passing along the coastal landscape of southern Wales where the smoke of industry is slowly giving itself up to the increasing green glow of field and hedgerow is such an easy activity. The arterial M4 swooping in long open furls. The south Wales mainline unsullied by junction. The ancient pathways, the saints' tracks and the roads of the drovers galloping unhindered along the track of the sun. On my iPod are the right songs:

Santana – Samba Pa Ti
Shadows – Apache
Tornados – Telstar – shower of Joe Meek future
Meic Stevens – Mwg
Muse – Knights of Cydonia – the future doing it
The Chemical Brothers – Do It Again
Canned Heat – Going Up The Country
U2 – Where the Streets Have No Name
The Travelling Wilburys – Heading For The Light
Simon and Garfunkel – America
John Lee Hooker – Travellin' Blues
Blue Travellers – Rockin on the Highway
Johnny Winter – Highway 61 – motoring where Dylan walked

Simon Armitage – O Motorway Motorway Where Have You Bin

When the pilgrims did this route, or something approximating it, they strode in the swirl of place names which surrounded them. Maenclochog, Castell Hendre, Bethesda, Bletherston, Llys y Fran, Treffgarne, Pont yr Hafod, Llandeloy, Caer Farcell, Rhodiad y Brenin. They knew what all these words meant. The place the King walks. Place of the black stone crags. Place of the winter castle. Place of the three great piles of stone. This was the history of where they were.

The theory is that these routes have been used for so long by so many ancient peoples that by a process of slow osmosis parts of the travellers and their spirit have become imprinted in the rocks and the soil. The tracks have acquired an element of their travellers' purpose, some of their strength and part of their needs. Old energy runs along these trackways. A power not dealt with by science. Something not containable by the modern world. A message that moves air and rock and makes compass needles spin. Walk the route taken by many thousands of earlier generations and something of them will surely seep your way. And if they were able to split the sky with a wave of their wands then, if you hang around long enough, then so too will you.

I've got myself up into the three peaked Iron Age fort of Foeldrygarn at the eastern end of the Preseli Mountains. These are not real mountains you understand but rocky outcrops that in their green isolation resemble the wild world in miniature. Golden Road starts here, an ancient track that runs like an arrow to the sea at the end of the Gwaun Valley, just south of Newport, Trefdraeth, and its angel-topped dead volcano, Carn Ingli.

I've found my way up through the winding back roads of rural north Pembrokeshire where the language has hung on with surprising tenacity. I've come through the tractor town of Crymych, to the tiny and so silent village of Mynachlog-ddu, the place where Wales' greatest pacifist and on the strength of his one single book,

Dail Pren, the greatest Welsh poet of the twentieth century, spent his early years. Waldo Williams. Born to an English-speaking mother in Haverfordwest and brought up in these hills by his Welsh-speaking father was Wales' Wordsworth and Wales' Walt Whitman. Waldo was a poet whose work centred on the old ways of living. He used the traditional meters, unseen in English verse. He was loved by everyone who came across him. His pacifism, non payment of income tax as a protest against the Korean War, imprisonment as a peace lover, his Quakerism, his avoidance of fashion, his supporting of the underdog, his love of children and the verse that ran always through his veins have come to symbolise the character of so many Welsh people.

Those who locked themselves to the gates at Brawdy, who sat down on the Welsh Office steps in protest at Polaris, who walked our cities' streets with unfurled anti-Trident banners, who sat down where they wanted to build new atomic power stations, who leafleted, who spoke out on radio phone-ins, who wrote to newspapers, who chained themselves to the fence outside the Atomic Weapons Establishment, who sent rude letters to almost all Welsh Secretaries of State since the dawn of time and now send the same missives to Rhodri Morgan and to Paul Murphy. Who signed their lives away on petition after petition, who wore badges and who shouted slogans. Who sang and who sat and sang again, hauled off by police to paddy wagons and to armoured buses, locked in cells, sent home, fined, bound over, shouted at, finger wagged, complained about darkly by officialdom but who nonetheless and undeterred grew strength, made networks, carried on. They owe, all of them, in their socks and ragged jeans and M&S pullovers, something to the spirit of this man. Waldo the unbelligerant Christian. The freeman who wanted Wales to be pure and peaceful and sparkling and essentially Welsh. Could it be ever? There are thousands who still think so. He'd be proud.

I've gone through the village and on to the rushy ground of the lower hills where, amid the prehistoric standing stones and suggestions of circles, rests the Waldo memorial: Waldo 1904-1971, slate plaque on a pointed granite menhir. "*Mur fy mebyd, foel drigarn carn gyfrwy, tal mynydd wrth fy nghefn ym mhob annibyniaeth barn*"[2]. Stopped the car got out and walked. Wet grass, ringing. Crossed landscape. Climbed up to the ancient three-cairned hillfort remains of Foeldrygarn. A place full of wind where I'd always felt unsettled, as if something were trying to get itself ended here. This is the start of the ley that runs west, full of golden light. The path is clear and open. What ley hunters have called a terrain oblivious line. Where others have walked before and where the spirit should ascend and the putting of one boot in front of the other should take little effort. But it does. Walking here is always tough. Many times I've followed this track – looking for the remains of Arthur or traces of the *Mabinogion* or trying to get my compass to spin madly. Arthur's knights are frozen into the rocks and there's a set of stones in the shape of his boat. Changed by time from wet wood to hard rock and left here like Noah's Ark, high beyond the floodline. Global warming and rising seas have been with us before. Read the great book.

We're on the edge of the Dyfed Triangle, a place of UFO sightings, silver ships in the sky, lights that dart and dive, saucers that spin their way behind the tops of Carn Menyn, Carn Bica and Carn Siân. If there were crops on these hills then they would without a doubt be full of circles. For fifty years UFOs have been seen here. There are tales of silver suited beings prowling the fields. A UFO the size of the Albert Hall is rumoured to have come down in the 1970s and was immediately recovered by the RAF who took it all by camouflaged low-loader to Wales' own Roswell. Still there in a bomb-proof hanger at Brawdy or maybe in the tunnels under Trecwn. Ufologists are not diverted from their theories by the proximity of US Cruise at Brawdy, stealth fighter testing across the dark skies of Cardigan nor the British guided missile range at Aberporth. Here, out west, things stay full of power and mystery. It's what the west is for.

The energies we don't know enough about all mesh here. Ley hunter Paul Devereux set up his Dragon Project to investigate these apparent latent powers. He visited sites and walked routes in the company of photographers, dowsers, psychics and sensitives to look for earth's energy. He measured with all the scientific equipment he could get hold of. Recorded and analysed. Looked for patterns and patterns within patterns. Worked for ten years until 1980 at which time he concluded that there was no such thing as an earth energy. Nothing that actually sparked, nothing that had a measurable flow. The Geiger counters stayed still. There were no new energies to be found. However, and this is the big but, existing energies did show anomalies – local geomagnetism fluctuated, background radioactivity shifted, the air moved more slowly. Something at the edge of measurability was going on. But his devices were not sensitive enough to track it down. He is trying now with dreamers. Sleep at Foeldrygarn and instead of waking a prince or a madman you rise and write down the track of your subconscious meanderings and send it in to be analysed and considered against those of others who have done the same. These lights in the sky down here don't stop.

I try floating west, make the boots lift. See if I can get the mud to unclog. Try transmitting myself by the power of my mind right to the heart of the Pentre Ifan cromlech or even the bar at the Golden Lion. Furrow my brows. Hard. Hard. Hard. Nothing.

Still the sun is breaking through and it's up there ahead of me. Both sides of the path the landscape open, trees in the distance, crags for company. Muscle power. Breath. Best walk in Wales. One of them.

LAUGHARNE

I came to Laugharne for the first time long ago enough not to be able to recall the day or even the year. I wore my green check jacket with the wide lapels and the pocket inside for the writer's notebook that I hardly ever took out. Didn't write much then. Thought about it. Enthused about the work of others. Hoped some of it would cross over by osmosis so I could avoid the grind myself. This was a literary bus trip in the company of thirty or so Anglo-Welsh luminaries, backroom scribblers and ladies of a certain age who would have lunched if, in those days, there had been anywhere in which to eat out. The trip had dawdled, stopped for tea, had poems read en-route through a fuzzy in-coach microphone and pulled in to have the road to Raymond Garlick's house in Llanstephan pointed out by an erudite enthusiast. One of our best, declared Roland Mathias. Outside of the luminaries most of those on the bus had never read a word he'd written.

I'd been asked to play the part of Captain Cat, the gnarled blind

mariner from *Milk Wood* with whom I had no empathy what-soever. I hadn't bothered and the trip organiser had taken offence. The Welsh way, furious and contained, with bright sparks of anger in the eyes. In the queue for tea at the Milk Wood Diner I was last. At the Castle they didn't have a ticket for me. At Brown's Hotel there were no more seats. We were taken on a town walk by John Ackerman, bumping our snake line of unlikelies, literateurs, and ladies on sticks over the foreshore paths from Boat House to car park, rolling Dylan Thomas, his times and his smack black booming black works at us in an inspiring stream. On the trip home I'd sat at the back reading *I Robot* by Isaac Azimov just to get the Welsh literary past out of my system.

Laugharne is a town of only 2942 people and would have been celebrated for not much more than its Welsh princes' castle if first Richard Hughes hadn't settled here and then, of course, Dylan Thomas. Hughes was famous for *A High Wind In Jamaica*, an adventure story of childhood that for many outgunned William Golding's similarly-plotted but more famous *Lord of the Flies*. He lived in grand style at Castle House and pretty much as soon as he'd arrived in Laugharne adopted the younger and much boozier Dylan. Dylan and his new wife Caitlin moved into Hughes' Sea View at the back of the Castle[3]. The Laugharne legend began to form.

The weather is damp and extreme when I arrive again in 2006. It's been a week full of wind driven squalls as if Wales were a south Atlantic ship rounding the Horn. In Cardiff the drain systems had mostly given up, clogged with leaves and flooding roads that usually stayed clear. Climate change clanged the *Echo*, full of erudition. Here there is a stretch of unexpected sun. The globe is warm.

We have arrived in the middle of a run of three festivals none of which is actually happening while we are here. This is pretty much in keeping with the synchronicity I've experienced during visits to other parts of Wales. Never arrive when it's buzzing, always get there when they are either too busy to speak to you for all the preparatory organising or too exhausted because the thing is now done. Laugharne's trail of festivals are amazing. We're staying at a b&b with the organisers of the Annual Local (in aid of the upkeep of the Cors Field Play Area and Park – swings, slides, bright yellow and red plastic adventure structures for kids, well-watered very green grass). Next door lives Jane Tremlett, Chairman of the Official Arts Festival who was responsible for the 2003 fifty-years-since-Dylan-died humdinger. This

year both festivals are planning rival productions of *Under Milk Wood* to be staged in succeeding weeks in August. After this the proposed out-of-town literary biggie will arrive with, we are promised, Hugo Williams, Mr Nice and Patti Smith at its head but no one in Laugharne seems to know much about this yet. Up at the Millennium Hall, the brand new 300-seater community facility of glass and concrete, there's nothing in the diary bar a meeting of the Laugharne Quilters, a surgery with local AM Christine Gwyther[4], the vegetarian minister for agriculture, and the return of the very popular weekly line dancing classes recently postponed due to indisposition on the part of the organiser.

George, Jane's husband, bookdealer and author of a number of celebrated and controversial volumes on Dylan, regales me with tales of their 2003 success – Bob Kingdom as DT in *Return Journey*, the Swansea Little doing Llareggyb, Aeronwy and a Thomas-inspired bop plus a first performance of Ballet Russe's new classical ballet based on the lives of Dylan and Caitlin. How many more interpretations can there be? An earlier stroll along the now stone-slabbed walk taken three decades back with John Ackerman has revealed a Milk Wood anchor chain, pebble and seagull installation made by local youth, a wooden bench with a wavy back embellished with fishes and inscribed with selections from 'Over Sir John's Hill' created by the local school, and an impression of an inordinately slim tie-wearing Dylan hacked out of a tree trunk by the youth club. At the 2003 Festival George Tremlett had delivered an incisive and inspired lecture in which he floated the theory that after his death Dylan's wealth had been hijacked by an old boys mafia from the City of Swansea.

New ground. If anything marked Laugharne as a force in literature in the new millennium then it was this amazing proposition. I discover the details from reading contemporary newspaper reports. George doesn't mention them at all.

Corran Books, named after the Coran, a minor tributary of the much larger Taf and source of Laugharne's original name, Abercoran, is most people's idea of how a second-hand bookshop should be – battered, holes in the roof, a name board which looks as if it hasn't been repainted since Georgian times, and a sprawl of assorted vols, unordered paperbacks and boxes containing twelve inch long players by Gary Glitter, the Band of the Welsh Guards and Leo Sayer. Last time I visited the basement contained what appeared to be the entire back stock of the

now defunct Five Arches Press of Tenby – runs of the *Anglo-Welsh Review* and *Dock Leaves*, slim vols by Roland Mathias, Alison Bielski and Robert Morgan. Today that's been reduced to several gross of the collected stories of Geraint Goodwin and two copies of the Writers of Wales (books slim enough to read in a phone box) on Sir Lewis Morris. The once tumbling and endlessly exciting back rooms where stock ebbed and flowed like the tides are now barred by a door labelled "Internet Stock Room – No Entry". George sits up front, writing on his pc. An out of town biker, tattoos, Midlands accent, comes in and buys an album of Elton John's *Greatest Hits*. £1.00. Over George's shoulder I glimpse on-screen the words he has just written: "and Dylan then …..". The industry rolls on.

Up the hill in the grounds of medieval St Martin's is Dylan's grave. His cross is in the new graveyard accessed by a bridge crossing a sunken, cobbled lane. White painted wood bearing his name and dates in Olde English script. Him one side, Caitlin the other. Overturned rose in a pot, small conifer. No pilgrimage offerings or poems or scrawled graffiti screams like those Jim Morrison gets in Père Lachaise. Rough cut grass. Buzz of dragonflies. RIP.

For a small town Laugharne does pretty well in terms of newsworthy controversy. Down the lane from the Boat House millionaire Eric Eynon has been battling both Carmarthen Council and the Four Seasons Holiday Camp over his plans for road widening. Things appear to be constantly coming to a head. Stand-offs, road blockages, restraint orders, poster campaigns. The *Carmarthen Journal* reported that its own reporter was ordered to stay away from a planning meeting of Laugharne Corporation by Portreeve[5] Sid Evans. The *Journal* has taken up the matter with the Charity Commission. Down here they really stride the corridors of power. Most recently rival teams of construction workers had faced each other off across hastily erected fences. No sign of who had won when I got there. The narrow lane was deserted. Dylan's Walk, as it's now known, runs from DT's well painted and re-roofed cliff-perched writing shed to the Boat House itself. Another version of this writing shed in exact replica sits in the Dylan Thomas Centre in Swansea. Both claim to be original. Neither look the same as the one shown in the 1970s Philip Madoc-fronted HTV video showing at the Boat House itself. Neither show any sign of wood rot or weather beating, or even the repair of such, amazing for 90 year-old sea-facing wooden buildings.

The Boat House is now a museum where you pay to go in. In the 1980s the native American poet Thomas Raine Crow managed to get himself a residency and stayed here for a month writing US impressions of Dylanesque Wales. The woman taking the ticket money knows nothing of this and Crow's book is not among the Dylanobilia for sale in the shop. The tea room is downstairs and there are museum cabinets up. Unter Dem Milchwald. Bajo El Bosque Lacteo. Porträt Des Künstslers Als Junger Dachs. Out at sea the late afternoon light comes in from Mars.

Down on the salt marshes TV actor Neil Morrissey has bought up the ancient farm of Hurst House and is turning it into a hotel with swimming pool, spa, cinema and high-end restaurant. He is also owner of two town centre taverns – the Mariners, upgraded for the youth market and, more controversially, Dylan's watering-hole, Browns Hotel[6]. The bar at Browns he has promised to leave intact but

elsewhere in the building he intends to establish a boutique hotel for the American literary market and to create a ballroom in the Hotel's grounds from the bungalow that currently stands there. Four hundred locals turned up at the auction at the Laugharne Millennium Hall which sold Browns in 2005. A good number of these interested parties appeared to be in action in the front bar on the Saturday night when I arrived.

The cabinet of Dylan drinking items – beer mats, sketches on the back of fag packets, pint mug, ashtray, photos of the man pissed or getting that way – had been replaced by a bandit but elsewhere everything looked as if it had been in place for decades. The locals were mostly seven sheets, all smoking, most of them singing at full volume to the recycled Beatles roaring from the juke. Hey Jude Juddijude Judy Jude. The guy  with the striped hair I'd seen earlier in the chip shop was performing into the end of a collapsed umbrella masquerading as a mike. The fatties who'd been in the Spar were dancing, or at least their version of that thing. Wave, slump and sprawl. Two pensioners, plastered, and with demolished double rums on their table were swaying their upheld arms from side to side in true Neil Diamond style. All that was needed to complete the picture were cigarette lighters flaming in their hands. I turned back from the bar to see that they'd found theirs and had lit them. Neil Morrissey's literary Americans will no doubt have the ball they'll be told to expect.

To the west, over Sir John's Hill, beyond the salt marshes where Hurst House pulls in the new rich and the Army exercises across unmarked lands and in places which do not appear on any maps, the ground flattens, drained by ditches, protected by bunds and sea walls. Land of the Flemings, little England beyond Wales, where the Welsh tongue thins to invisibility and the new Welsh Netherlands begin. Laugharne is the gatekeeper. How much does it cost to stay here, I ask the manager at Hurst House. £140 a night. That's reduced because we have the builders in. Do you have any vacancies? Nope, all full.

ST DAVID'S

The St David's peninsula is about as far west as you can go and still say you're in Wales. You could boat it to Grassholm with the guano and the gulls or land on the Bishops or the Clerks or the other brown

scratches of rock out there in the Irish Sea which, if we were Greek, we would by now have painted flags on. Or at low tide you could look for the drowned lands, of which Wales has so many, and hunt out fossilised tree stumps, the remnants of great forests that once grew out on the greater Wales which fills the vastness between here and America. You could, but you don't. In Wales we don't care so much about borders or marks on maps. The A487 which runs down here from Haverfordwest, seventeen miles and sixteen hills, turns right at Cross Square into Nun Street and then slides north east, back to Fishguard, that's border enough.

The path around the peninsula, 10 miles from the Pembrokeshire Coast Path's total of 180, is, in the scale of paths, about as good as it gets. Landscape, water. Pembrokeshire's inimitable mix of colour and light. The view of the world bending away from you out towards America. Infinity in that place where the sky meets the sea. The red ochre soil, the honey gorse, the thrift, the squill, the heather. Abandoned lime kilns. Places where you can semaphore Eire. Arthur[7] is here. His burial chamber low on the cliff side. Remains of industry where coal was once dragged from these soils, surface scratches, drift mines, hidden now. Overgrown but not yet lost.

In the eye of it all is St David's, the town, the city and at its edge the birthplace of the saint who gave the whole landmass his name. Dewi's Land. Dewi Sant. Saint David. Good boy of those ancient times. You walk through the streets and down the road to Caerfai, past a scattering of cottages and the stump of a tower which was once a windmill, to the birthplace, his birthplace, where the great man came into the world. At St Non's, chapel on pre-christian foundations, spring gushing from the rock at the very place where the patron saint of Wales was born. There are standing stones here. Fields which slope and slide. Remains of ancient buildings. A stone roughly inscribed with a circled cross. Non was David's mother and she gave birth in the midst of a great storm. Most of today's population know the name of her child but not who he was, where he came from nor what he did. What did he look like? Do we have an image? We do not. The spring, St Non's well, is bricked, arched, lipped, cluttered with catholic insignia and scattered with notes and beads and small crosses, the holy rain-washed relics of the supplications of pilgrims. Anoint yourself and make a holy wish. Drink. The water is pure. On the bushes are fragments of string. Weather washed cloth. In the water are coins. The christian mixing with the pagan, the impure, the desperate, the hard-up, the down on their luck. At holy wells, if you believe, then the world can change. The wells were there before the Christians came to these lands and, rather than close them down as homes of heresy, the early believers simply took them over. The Sisters of Mercy have a retreat across the field. Peace and spiritual passion by the Pembrokeshire sea.

From St David's Head you can see Ramsey, the flat stretch of beach that is Whitesands, the basalt outcrops of Carn Hen and Carn Llidi behind you. This is an old landscape full of glaciated slabs and erratic boulders. On the peninsula's tip is the Warrior's Dyke, Clawdd-y-Milwyr, man-made rock ramparts and ditches and iron age hut circles. There are celtic field systems on the lower slopes, scratches on a surface that seems as if it has been here, untouched, since the dawn of time.

The Cathedral at St David's sits in a hollow. You don't see it until you stumble on it, south of the preaching cross at the bottom of High Street. First look, from above, says this place is venerable, medieval, a repository of belief and history. It is unexpected, here at the end of the Welsh world. And set as it is on marshy ground and with springs below it washing away its foundations it is also unstable, jerrybuilt,

buttressed, with a floor sloped from true by at least 5 degrees. Walls lean outwards, window frames bend from square. You realise this slowly as the full-frontal magnificence and obvious hugeness release their immediate hold.

St David founded the place, made the site a place for meditation back in the sixth century. A succession of churches followed, at least four, before the Normans began their upgrade

programme in 1181. By the fifteenth century the great walls had begun to lean and fall and remedial work began. Struts and blocks and underpinnings. Inside are the tombs of Giraldus Cambrensis, traveller, Edmund Tudor, father of Henry VII, and Rhys ap Gruffydd, prince. There's a box behind a small wrought iron door which contains the mixed bones of St Justinian and St David, with St Teilo as well. Carbon dating in the twenty-first century put them as originating in the thirteenth. Fake relics. A mix of the skeletons of at least three people, one of whom was a woman. In Wales is nothing real? There are misericords on the undersides of tip up seats. Oak leaves and acorns. One or two of boat repairers. Monks overeating. Sir Gawain being ill at sea.

St David's itself, the town, is actually a city. The town hall on High Street has the words 'City Hall' carved above its entrance. Inside are tourist leaflets, the library, the City Council office and a shop selling jam, knitted hats and things previously owned. This is the smallest city in the world not to possess a traffic light. Nearest is in Haverfordwest or perhaps Ireland. Or maybe down there in flooded Atlantis, where no oil was ever found, in the Celtic Sea. St David's – population 1600 – incomers, non Welsh speakers, restaurateurs, craft workers, waitresses, candle makers, boutique managers, gallery owners, importers of fashionable shoes.

Up on Nun Street I'm trying to find traces of the poet, painter and wandering star Stan Rosenthal. Stan lived here during the nineties, painting himself into the lore of Pembrokeshire. Into the soil. Into the rocks and outcrops and shapes and colours of the land. Stan had come late to painting although if you asked he'd tell you that he'd always been involved. In the sixties he'd been a poet advertising in the local press for female assistants to help him create. He was a Buddhist meditator and led classes. He did fighting tai chi. He ran Zen Arts from Cardiff's Dickens Arcade, opposite the castle. He sold Bonsai and imported carvings and flower-child knick-knackery, scented candles, beads. Madam Romany who had the concession opposite turned a steady wage telling fortunes to snaking lines of the middle-aged. The queues blocked access to Stan's display windows, filled his doorway. He took down the Book of Changes and asked a question. Fight or sleep? Stay or run? Look to the future, the verses told him. He opened the following week as an I Ching consultant. Discern the future with Stan. £5 per consultation. You couldn't keep trade away.

Then Stan moved to Cilgerran. North Pembrokeshire. Castle, river. Zen Arts moved to St David's. Opened on High Street where Ma Sime's Surf Hut now is. Stan left Cilgerran, bought a three story stone house, up the road from the new shop. Sold it. Moved in over the store. Sold up and bought a cottage in Nun Street, the birthplace of former Archdruid James Nicholas. Bought a gallery a few doors down. Sold and moved to Solfa. Sold again and went to Mabws Fawr. Could never stay still. He was a Russian Jew whose grandparents had escaped from the Urals to London's East End to beat the pogroms. Like an emigrant crossing the American great plains, the idea of moving west was in his blood. Pembrokeshire with its abstract landscape and its clear light was a gift. He painted from a studio set up in the shop's corner and sold a rolling vision of the county he saw. Fields full of light. Hills bending into the sea line. Crags slashed by rain. Beached boats. The architectural rocks and slabs of Trefin in anticline. Felin Canol near Solva in a mound of purple. Cwm Gwaun in a sea foam of green. St David's Head in Mondrian blocks of colour. Carn Ingli as a darkening smear.

If anything it was 'The Red Flash' that made him. A painting of a field at the end of the St David's Peninsula where the light has turned at least three quarters of the canvas a solid, vibrant red. He put an illustrated advert in the Sunday papers and sold reproductions by the hundred. Framed, unframed, rolled, flat. Fame assured. He went on then to paint the rest of Pembrokeshire and sold it in a variety of reproductions made up in any size you liked. Tourists could take home native art depicting the very part of the county they had visited. The bay they'd walked across. The cliffs they had climbed. Stan's work was

on restaurant walls and in galleries and gift shops from one end of the
National Park to the other. You could buy a map showing the location
of everything he'd done. A mesh of squares and arrows. Stan
Rosenthal, Pembrokeshire in his blood.

And then he was gone. Moved to Hastings and then to Rye. Back
to Cowbridge and then Narberth. Now beached up at Battle, East
Sussex[8]. The St David's Gallery kept Rosenthal stock and for a time
his vision hung on but today, peering through their closed window,
most of this appears to have gone. The boutiques and gift shops and
restaurants have Margaret Jones, Beth Robinson, and John Knapp
Fisher on their walls. No traces of Stan. Instead there are new and
different takes on the bending, illuminating, magnetic landscape. The
man at the garden centre, where I bought a gunera in 1991 and which
now has leaves five foot across, remembers Stan moving around a lot.
Hadn't seen him for some time. Couldn't say where he'd gone.

At the hotel, full of noise and failed shower fittings, they have
paintings on the wall but not by Stan. In a car park at the town lim-
its is the National Park Information Centre. The woman behind the
counter hasn't heard of him. A few years back Stan launched his great
book, *Stan Rosenthal: Approaches to Art*[9] in this very place. A coffee
table masterpiece. Full of pictures of St David's and the landscape in
amazing light. No longer on sale.

I have a huge argument with the hotel owner about the size of my
bill. The night before he'd run a disco which had thrummed the floor-
boards until the early hours. From my bathroom I could hear the
punters below, every word, shouting about beer and women and
farming. I ask for a reduction but the owner won't give me one. He
says I'm trying it on. Discos aren't offensive, this is Pembrokeshire.
The whole thing feels like Fawlty Towers. Maybe he imagines I have
a house brick in my case. Or that I travel in spoons. Maybe he'll come
outside and beat my car with a tree. We compromise, eventually, and
I pay ten pounds less. Outside is the sun. Under its rays herds of
Wildebeest swarm down the coast.

SWANSEA

When I first arrived in Swansea it was a return to the industrial heart
of the nineteenth century. This was in 1958 and no one had yet
thought about clearing up the wreckage. No one could afford to.
Austerity, bomb sites, supply failures, shortages. Rock and roll had

only just begun to brighten the night skies. The place was bust, bug-gered and breaking apart, the parts I saw, steaming in on the Western Region, along the Neath and then the Tawe. Down the valley through Plasmarl, Landore, and Hafod. I was crossing a landscape I'd only ever experienced before in the novels of Edgar Rice Burroughs and H.G. Wells. A red, broken-brick fantasy of furnace, yard, smoke stack, and collapsing workers housing mixed with slop and slag on a cinder-black ground. Could this be hell? It could, but hell deserted. Hell with no one around. This was the lower Swansea Valley after the tinplate and copper and spelter had been abandoned. Swansea Vale, Villiers, Landore Sulphate, Middle Bank, Upper Bank, Llansamlet, Mannesman Tube Works, White Rock, Hafod Phosphate, Hafod Isha Nickel and Cobalt, Morfa. "The most extensive contiguous area of industrial dereliction to be found anywhere in the United Kingdom," contemporary report.

Spelter – another name for Indian Tin, Bismuth, Zinc. Used for galvanising metal. Does not readily deteriorate with time or atmos-pheric conditions. Doesn't stain. Twenty-third most common ele-ment in the earth's crust. Protects iron and steel from corrosion. A component of the alloys bronze and brass. Comes in ingots, slabs and plates. Can be readily repaired. Fire and heat and raining dust. You lived for just a short time if you were employed in its making. Arsenic and sulphur for air.

You went nowhere further when you got to Swansea High Street Station, and you still don't. The train from London to Carmarthen leaves the way it came. High Street is a dead end. Trains come in, stop, then reverse back out. Dust. Echo. Victorian cast iron. Platform tickets. Uniformed porters with trolleys. Guards with flags. None of that now.

Wind Street[10] takes the baton from High Street running south from the station to the water. This former banking and business district has today totally given way to pleasure. Piss up bladdered belch hammered shot-shooting sprawling on your long legs or in your shirt. Lloyd's Bar, Walkabout, Yates, SoBar, Varsity, BarCo, Adelphi, The Bank Statement. I take a look down Salubrious Passage once home of poetry readings and second hand-bookshops. Deserted. A hand-written sign on a store door says open afternoons only but the space beyond it is empty. Another bar soon, more space for vertical drinking.

At the lower end there's a subway which runs to Somerset Place, home of the Dylan Thomas Centre built into the refurbished Guildhall[11]. The Centre, known as Tŷ Llên (*House of Literature*), was opened in 1995 when for twelve months Swansea was created European City of Literature. A home for bards, novelists, and literary raconteurs. Tŷ Llên is clearly a hard name to pronounce. Hardly anyone calls it that now. Inside are the doors to Dylan Thomas' writing hut lifted from a skip at Laugharne. These are the originals. At Laugharne the refurbished hut on the cliff side has another set, also original (see p.76). These are twenty-first century equivalents to the bones of saints, fragments of the true cross, the chisel which Moses used. On e-bay recently someone was selling a pair of Dylan Thomas' trousers. Do not destroy, recycle. The subway is scrawled with DT quotations, posters replaying 'Fern Hill' for the hundredth time. "Oh as I was young and easy in the mercy of his means…." The poem rolls on wall and floor, printed, painted, carved in benches, on plaques and in stones right the way across the southern part of western Wales. Dylan in our hearts and in our souls. In our beer and our cafés. On our plates and our tea towels. Our shortbread and our jams. They visit here in their hundreds to touch the places where that short, stubby man once walked. Where he talked. Where he dreamed.

Swansea is built on a hill, a town on the escarpment of Mount Pleasant, like Edinburgh but without the grandeur. 6000 people in 1801. Sveinn Sae'r. Sweynesse. Sweinesei. Sweyn's Ey. Swanzey. Scandinavian. Germanic. Little to do with Swans. Nothing to do with the sea. No Romans. No Saints. "The Haunt of gull and plover"[13]. The industrial revolution made the place, the smelting, the mining, the tinplate works, the ferrous metals and the port through which the everything travelled. For a hundred and fifty years Swansea boomed. Then the Depression hit and hard. And during World War Two so did Hitler. Much of the industrial south, the docks, and the civic centre was flattened in a series of vast raids and rolling firestorms.

Swansea Bay is a great arc of sand running from the docks right round to the world's most eruditely named village, The Mumbles. A tram, one of the earliest of passenger rail links, once ran the whole length of this great curving. It's now gone. Ripped up. Replaced by bikeways, covered in tarmac, Mr Softee vans parked along it, kids with skateboards, cans and drugs. The tram ran along a sort of bund, with a wall on the seaward side. Perversely from the present road you can't see the water at all, a Swansea Bay of endless sky. Full of size and light.

Swansea became a city in 1969 when Charles, as part of his princely investiture, made it one. Swansea Jacks had long reckoned that the place should also be the Welsh capital, lost, fought hard to become the home of the National Assembly, didn't succeed, got instead the Maritime Museum hacked apart in Cardiff and rebuilt here as a high tech all singing and dancing make the computer displays work just by waving your arms family-friendly sop.

> The buildings of Swansea, the Swansea bricks, the Swansea gullies, the Swansea poets, the Swansea proletariat, the punters, the Swansea face, the Swansea voice, the Swansea hat and head, the Swansea style, the Swansea walk, the Swansea neck, the Swansea skin, the Swansea ribbon, the Swansea shawl, the Swansea brew, the Swansea tongue, the teeth, the lip, the Swansea nose, the Swansea eye, the Swansea money.

Swansea believes in itself, circles around itself, honours itself as a great city and the real psychological authority behind everything Wales does. There's an air of this in the streets and the bars and the places where Swansea boys doing Swansea things gather. In their suits and their shoes. It's slick but it isn't the West end. Swansea power. You can feel its sea blown grip weaken as you cross the Tawe going east or the Loughor to the west. Swansea, the town on a hill, stretched back behind you like an urban myth, And as you head away on the clogged M4 you wonder was the city there or did you imagine it. The lovely rubbery Dylan town, old, faded, but with new gleaming glass and concrete right along its front. Swansea where everyone is still talking and nobody hustling. Bars, cafés, new generation SA1 waterfront cool and yet still hundreds of brown-stained ancient pubs.

TREFDRAETH

The mujahadeen have yet to reach the far west. On these streets there are no signs of anything other than M&S tees and khaki chinos from Cotton Traders, mail order. In these far reaches of Wales where, if it were not for the earth's curvature, a look over the cliff edge would reveal south America, not even the restaurateurs have yet come in number. Tajmahal Tandoori in Fishguard, Golden Dragon in Cardigan, nothing in Newport. No mosques in Trefdraeth, St Mary's Church still holding the high ground, the old god still in the hills.

This is Welsh Wales, where the ancient tongue hovers just below the surface, where the unreality of tourism, like a patch of oil, slides above. Sometimes out here there's a palpable desperation for integration manifest by the goodly, well-meaning, liberal elite. Among those

who organise cello recitals in the Memorial Hall and sessions of storytelling at the chapel there is a fervent desire to welcome the seeker of asylum, to let them blend with this ancient society, to adopt the local ways, to fit in. But they do not come.

Trefdraeth, *tidrith* as the locals say it, town on the sand, called Newport in English, was dark when I reached it. Western Power had a man with a shovel in a ditch. The Golden Lion was lit by candles. An old woman emerging from her mortar roofed cottage complained in an English she rarely used, and with eyes wide with amazement, it's dark, it's all dark.... Newport of 1124 souls with no lights beyond those of flame, unchanged. And that's one of the great joys of this town, it rarely alters. No new roads are driven through its midst, no pipelines thrust beneath it, no building complexes sprung upon it, no water's edge enhanced by the glass and aluminium of apartment life, no new pontoons to accommodate the yachts of the rich and the rising from the rest of the world.

Trefdraeth might once have been a settlement on great sands which have now been lost beneath rising seas. The whole of Pembrokeshire is eroding, its coastal path is constantly redrawn to avoid landslips and places where unstable cliff edges have crumbled into the waves. Trefdraeth, they say, in the time before the Romans, was once a city of lights out beyond Traeth Mawr in the deep Irish Sea. I've encountered this myth time and again in my travels – a Wales that once was, a bigger, more glorious place, rich with giants and magic, of cities and power now vanished, drowned, fallen. The Romans never reached here but before them the ice did. During that age the glaciers were 3000 feet thick covering the Pembrokeshire soil with boulder clay and erratic stones. When those ice sheets melted their waters made the Gwaun Valley, the great Welsh backwoods, full of trappers, and hunters, lost folk who live from the soil and still speak with an insular tongue.

Newport sits at the mouth of the Nevern, tree stumps in the bay at low tide, cromlechs, standing stones, and a blanket of ancient memory, rolling back inland. Near the estuary is five thousand year old

Carreg Coetan Arthur, a nine foot diameter capstoned burial chamber now sitting in a twentieth century bungalow's backyard. Death and retirement almost hand in hand. Through here came the Stonehenge bluestones[13] taken from the Carn Meini and Carn Alw standing stone factories high in the Preselis above. Did they? Rolled in woven hay, strung with floatation chambers made from logs, loaded on rafts and sailed the roaring waves of the Bristol Chanel to land in north Devon and then on across the forest and high moorland to their two hundred and fifty mile distant Wiltshire ancient energy home. How did they do this? Flying saucers took them. Ancient levitation oiled their passage. Stone age magic made the very rocks float. Researchers have suggested canals, leather-hulled curraghs, hot air balloons, stones rolled by slave armies, on logs, carried by giants. Pushed by ice sheets. Bent through space time. The Millennium Commission funded attempt to repeat the trick in 2000 using 250 local Menter Preseli volunteers ended up with a three metric tonne bluestone slipped from its inadequate raft and lost in Pembroke Dock, still 200 miles from home. Undeterred and ever mindful of justification there's a new memorial stone to the project's failure up in the rain swept hills.

At the time of Christ the Mujahadeen were the Irish, landing here on their ways to St David's, spreading their Celtic religion among the farmers and fishermen who lived on these shores. With this early start Christianity has been strong in these western distances for longer than any other Welsh place. There are hand scratched crosses from the seventh century on the rocks in St Mary's churchyard, a grey place of standing slates and weather-worn grave engravings, not a soul present when I visited, not even a bird.

The castle, high on the slopes of Carn Ingli, was built by the Normans, knocked down by Llywelyn ap Gruffudd, rebuilt by the neo-Norman Lords of Cemais, decayed[14] again, fell down, stones stolen and used for local housing, church repairs, building of barns. Rebuilt in 1859 as a private residence, the ruined gatehouse and Hunters Tower turned into something habitable by R Kyrke Penson, architect. Extended thirty years later by David Jenkins, Llandeilo. Central heating installed. Dillwyn Miles, Herald Bard, antiquary and Pembrokeshire author lived there. Today a private mansion owned by the Baron of Cemais, Hyacinth Hawkesworth. To view the castle peer at it through hedge growth and trees from the other side of the road. Or go knock and ask. They may say no.

Newport twenty-first century suffers from being on the A487

Cardigan to Fishguard, no where else for this road to pass unless they dug a tunnel underneath. The Pembrokeshire County Car Run, two hundred classic cars pass through – Minis, Austin Sevens, three-wheeler racing cars, e-types, an aged Bentley, Hillman Imp, Lotus Elan, Ford Prefect – men dressed for the drive: caps, scarves, driving jackets, string-back gloves, silver cigarette lighters, Benson & Hedges. This was a recreation from the era when you went out on a Sunday for a drive, for the travelling, not to reach anywhere, never to get out of your vehicle unless it was for a pint at a country pub or for a cup of tea poured from a tartan coloured thermos into a bakelite cup. The idea of transport is big here. In the East Street antique shop amid the old tools and cracked vases there is a plethora of railway memorabilia – the station sign from Narberth, books on signalling on the London Midland, a fireman's handbook, a manual on how to shunt, pictures of long-gone steam giants on fire, a history of the Vale of Rheidol.

The town is dominated by the mountain above it. Carn Ingli, pre-historic volcano, mountain of angels named after the giant who built it. This is a Preseli mountain range outrider, at 1100 feet hardly a world beater, but with its jumble of dark igneous and its two-pointed jutting presence still a force to be reckoned with. The twin peaks are iron-age hill forted, ditched with entrances, a mess of built rampart, scree and fallen stone. Inside are at least twenty-five hut circles. Brynach[15] communed with angels here. The climb isn't easy. Drive out along King Road, park, bang straight up through the descending mists. A mistake, certainly. This frontal assault is across acres of rising rock rampart, scree below heather, surface fractured by ice action moving below your boot, no waymark, pull, balance, pull again. Sometimes maps lie, sometimes the routes they show do not exist, have moved, flowed sideways with the shifting topsoil. From the peak the mud-sweep of the Nevern estuary, the dark sands at Parrog[16], inland to the standing stone of Bedd Morus and Carn Cŵn where there is a well which cures warts are all swept by mist. My ears are wrapped in wind. Brian John who lives in the Gwaun Valley and wrote five books of historical Welshness set on Carn Ingli, self-published, and then sold them to Hollywood, runs inspirational guided walks up here, talking up his characters, naming the rocks and explaining how they fit into his fictional but ever so real history. He's absent today.

Signs of literature in this western black hole: Attila the Stockbroker plus support Make Poetry History at the Memorial Hall. Brian John literary stroll on Carn Ingli. Poster for WordzworkWales 4th annual festival of writing at Llandysul "Money from writing – is it possible?" The Welsh world is still asking that. Poem by John Tripp set on the coastal path beaches. Llyfrgell[17]. Books by John Donne in the Llys Meddyg guests' bookcase (glass fronted). Idea for a poem about Abu Hamza while sitting on bench outside the Golden Lion.

Newport's Barony still appoints the Town Mayor, manages the town's Court Leet, and appoints the fifty Burgers who sit on it. This anachronism which once had the ability to fine people for the crimes of theft and vagrancy now has no real power other than to consider developments on Barony land. The feel of this residual feudal power is hardly native, more that of gentry over hill farmer, of landowner over tenant. Incoming squire over native farmer. On the streets the local youth squawk at each other like escapees from *Little Britain*. The light has come back. At the Herbal Dispensary homeopathy has had a good day, the traditional butchers have sold a dozen rabbits, the bookshop[18] has shifted another two or three copies of the history of the Welsh stick chair, the Llew Aur[19] has sold more beer than it did when the lights were on. Free house, real ale, hand pumped. Two restaurants do fine dining and four pubs sell curry. No one has an illuminated sign. Not yet.

ABEREIDDI

There are times out here in the slanting rain in the far west when Abereiddi feels like absence. Abereiddi is empty, nothing here. When I first came, on a day of brilliant sun, it was a discovery like no other. The bare beach, a flat foreshore of slate waste, the Eiddi snaking through water pasture, no one else there but me, no habitation, cliffs holding back the intruding land. And on the western edge, among the overgrowth of gorse and grass, a line of roofless cottages, a wrecked lime kiln, a path rising to a slate brick house without roof and with one of its walls missing. I climbed it, the path, cut in a slow incline towards the headland. Took my breath away. At its end was the blue lagoon – a slate quarry at the edge of the sea with its outward face broken open to the waves. In the sun so unexpectedly and violently blue. A nylon rope running from a high mooring into the deep blue waters. A beach of wrecked slate, rusty blue. Quarry terraces still walkable. Engine house, dressing sheds, powderhouse, forge. Brick and broken rock. A place where men had once sweated. Took the slate down with great explosions and iron hammers. From 1838 to the end of the century. Fifty-eight slate workers. Five Railwaymen. One powderman. One owner. Gone. What they left softened now by encroaching green.

The discovery was sequential. The flatness first, then the emptiness. Then the row of slate workers' cottages half-hidden in the gorse. The path they stood along and the route it took you. The slow climb and the expectation of headland. Instead, the blue lagoon on the sea's very edge. The eyes widening. Why does this discovery impart joy?

What does it give? The past hanging on, the mark of men softened by time, out here at the end of Wales.

The Pembrokeshire slate industry was a pale shadow of its northern rival. Pembrokeshire slate as roofing is a poor material. It degrades so easily. Roof timbers rot below it, lichen grows above. When the men worked to slice it to slates the split was inevitably irregular and the surface shelled. Put this stuff on your house and the rain would soon come in. The solution they invented was to load the poor slate onto the roof timbers and then to torch it with a coating of mortar. Many older Pembrokeshire roofs look like this. A hard-bleached khaki colour, a sort of ancient plastic. There are one or two examples nestling at the side of the road which winds down to Abereiddi. But none on the sea front. Here the wind blows unhindered.

There's historical evidence that slate was cut from Abereiddi before the land was eventually leased to the big operators, Ward, Williams and Jones, in 1838. Their enterprise, Barry Island Farm Quarry, cut roof slate and building slab for the industrial revolution. Populations were expanding exponentially in Britain's cities. Bulk slate was cut and shipped out by boat from the beach. Earlier some stone had been cut and sent to Haverfordwest, some to Tenby, a little to Ireland. Abereiddi slate for gravestones had gone to Gower. In the mid-eighteenth century roofing slates had been sent to Margam House in Glamorgan. But it was small stuff. Ward, Williams & Jones' grand enterprise was designed to beat the world. Nonetheless it fell apart after three years. A London syndicate of Benjamin Hill, Robert Norman and John Bradley bought them out, bought up nearby Porthgain with its harbour and easy access and expanded everything. Steam engines powered the slate lifts, hand-pushed trams came up the slopes, a railway was built to carry their products over the headland. Barry Island Slate & Slab. Knock on the door and buy what you want for your Victorian fireplace, for your lintel, for your slate doorstep, for the new roof on the lean-to. Call in with your wagon, land on the beach in your one-masted ship. Get the horses to drag the stuff on.

No one lives here, now, in Abereiddi. There's nothing left. The cottages that once stood have let time wash them. Early Pembrokeshire homes were walled mud, with straw roofs and wattle and daub chimney. They were held together with rope bandages. They hardly had the strength to last a winter. The decades saw them out. Where examples remain their thatch has been covered with corrugated iron and their walls with stone and mortar. Same site, same shape, the fabric totally changed. These cottages moved when the land did, took the rain and let it soak below them. R.S. Thomas had one just like it, huge slate-slab stones ugly in the living room, up there in the distant north. Where he ended.

Down here he'd have had his poems cut into slate slabs and fixed, Bashö-like, on the routes to the lagoon.

Wales slate frozen, blue cracks, blue splinters.

Ginsberg would squat in front of his blue slate Buddha, slate beads in his slate hands

St Paul's vision in the desert would be of the slate Christ rising

Ernest Rutherford would split the slate atom in Welsh slate Manchester, the blue slate rain roofs gleaming

Faraday would make slate magnets pull in beams of blue slate light

Glyndŵr would fight the slate English, sinking their slate ships and breaking their shelled-slate castles

Captain Beefheart in his slate waste desert would make slate trout dance in the blue sunset.

The masks of Rebecca would glow in the soft slate light

Did they do all that here? There are no interpretation boards, no leaflet dispensers, no sign boarding. On the rain swept front a mobile hot dog has set up an awning and four Wal Mart plastic chairs and two white plastic tables. The stall offers tea and cans. In the slanting rain there are no takers. I go by round-shouldered in my waterproofs, overtrousers which are too long and slip down, catch my heels, red day-pack on my back with whistle and compass, map in case, hat and gaiters. I walk the trail, check the cottage row, climb to the lagoon, grey blue, and up above it, to the cliff walk via Barry Farm and another sea's edge, deserted quarry, to the harbour of Porthgain.

This might well be the best walk in Pembrokeshire, the coast path a line drawn in thick crayon right round the county's seaward edge.

The lagoon below me, wind pouring into my face. The world becomes slate grey then blue then green. On the trail up here the paths once taken by the Porthgain trams are empty of everything but their straightness. A single brick leaf of the quarry master's brick house, weathered to flaking dissolution, still stands. In the sea grass among the thrift and honey yellow gorse are stones which might have held rails, might have been moved there by nineteenth century hands, or might have been the latter day, work experience, twentieth century leisure repair.

Dr Who in his black and white days, the tapes the BBC have lost forever, came here in the early 1960s to fight the Daleks. Pembrokeshire is the planet Dido, is Vortis, is Vulcan. William Hartnell, the first and best ever Doctor, in his black and white cloak walks and worries among the black and white slate.

Then the rain goes and the sun once again makes the whole landscape bright. The sea blues. Painters arrive in their dozens to catch this magic. We are nearer something here than anywhere else in Wales. The need to record, to fix the experience becomes overwhelming. Graham Sutherland captured the curves of the lanes and the way the rocks lay, riddled with leaf and root. John Knapp-Fisher who catches the county's dark cottages has a small studio on the road side back up from Abereiddi at Croesgoch. Free to visit. Postcards. Long, dark illuminations. The spirit of how it is to live in a white painted stone house at the end of Wales. What keeps them? The light. David Bellamy lowers himself into a dangerous inflatable to float, full waterproofs, souwester and life jacket and seaboots, right up to the high cliffs, to catch them from a viewpoint that most will never experience. The light reflects off the sea. The light hits the slate grey rocks. Brendan Burns[20] makes art from the shape of the sand and the wreckage that's in it. Light lit smears and light lit blobs. The essence of how this life looks in Pembs. Touchable. Slate and sand at the ends of your hands. Sarah Young makes the landscape into advanced Rosenthals, recording the shape and the light of the landscape in clean, clear sunlit lines.

I cross the three miles of headland and see the beacons[21] of Porthgain before me. There's the best pub in the world here, The Sloop, black rib-eye and Brains, served in a ramble of rooms and old tables which spill out onto a slate harbourside terrace, local crab for sale, chips, sun. Sarah Young works behind the bar here but it's her day off.

Porthgain is busy. Gentrified now, like Solva. Didn't have time to lapse, moved from industry to leisure without a gap. The Shed Wine Bar and Bistro. The Harbour Lights Galley real art and cards. And a restaurant that gets into the Good Food Guide. Porthgain is dominated by the remains of great limestone hoppers and enormous crushers. These brick-made industrial relics tower over the small harbour, ghosts from the time Britain used Pembrokeshire rock for its roads and Abereiddi slate for its buildings. Slate waste was made into bricks at Ty Mawr, the large square works in the centre of the village. 50,000 a week. Tea, cake and postcards now. Men in soft shoes not boots. Women in quilted jackets. No shawls. Kids playing football. Nobody dying of lack of anything.

The rain has ceased. I take thirty steps back towards Abereiddi and get the sun behind me. Dazzle ships out in the bay. Blue slate below. The bustle of Porthgain fades. Blue slate silence once again.

PEMBROKE DOCK

The wagon trains did this, they went west. Tripp is in philosophical mood. Sober and vaguely unshaven. Grey hair in his ears. We're in my car heading for Pembroke Dock. We don't do this, travel together. Poets on a job. We rarely leave the city with its taxis and pavements and structures uncluttered by wind and sun. Readings cluster around the Marchioness of Bute in Frederick Street, the room upstairs at the Blue Anchor, near the terminus, across the wrought iron tables at the Conway, once in the grand Park Hotel with legendary results, and when it's big time, on the first floor at the Central Hotel. All of St

Mary Street visible rushing down to the Bute monument, the place where striking miners march, where CND rallies swirl, and where the writers suck up the nation before returning it done up with stars. The Great Welsh Novel. Poems to Change The World.

But this time we have ventured. Someone has invited us, offered £30 and a night's accommodation. Not far to travel, really. You been there, JT? Never. Me neither.

My car, metallic green, leather top, silver wheels, GT badge on back, bought for style has been cobbled from wrecks. Welded frame, clock turned back, boot from something that got smashed on the M1, engine lifted from a wreckers yard. Sold on as perfect. Leaked oil from the gear box and rusty water from the heater ever since. JT is still impressed. We rise along Stalling Down at speed chasing the sinking sun. JT is lighting up, smoke not dope. He had a poem where he called it maryjane and I told him he should update his slang. It dates you, makes you older than you are. No one calls dope maryjane today other than maybe trad jazzers and the regional press. Nineteen seventies. Got to keep ahead. So he changed it, called it dope, but as far as I knew never smoked it. JT stuck to beer and whiskey when he could get anyone to buy him some. Nothing yet today. We speed on.

Gwyn Thomas is our great man, JT is telling me. Our Henry Miller, a writer with an intellect and an imagination that fills all four corners. Knows the people, who they are, what they do, where they're going. Fills his books with them. Problem is he's too clandestine. He's the man who's writing the Great Welsh Novel and no one knows. What about Jack Jones? Crap. You don't mean that. No. Emyr Humphreys? Never heard of him. Yes, you have. Well, maybe. But what has he done? JT, looking out the window at the passing Vale of Glamorgan countryside, green fields, hawthorn, telegraph wires. Wants us to have a Jack Kerouac, a Laurie Lee, a John Wyndham, a Lawrence Durrell, someone bigger than the landscape. All we've got is craggy Raymond Williams and lovable Glyn Jones.

I don my sunglasses, a measure against both the booming sun and the imminence of barbarians. We talk instead about JT's rise as a TV presenter (anchorman on an arts programme called *Nails*, falling figures, now taken off) and his lapses in short fiction. Never many. Takes too much. It's the same process, he tells me, get the idea and let it go. Follow where it rambles. I've published John's collection of poems in praise of the greats of lit, *The Inheritance File*. This is his take on Rimbaud, Dylan, Lowell, Hart Crane, writers who had died difficult deaths. I've gone more than the full mile with this one – commissioned a JT silhouette from Martin Dutton and run it in rows on the cover like Warhol would, added orange flyleaves, illustrations, made both paper and cloth editions, had huge hopes. Mostly unachieved as history would tell. *The Inheritance File* went critically unremarked, as if it represented a blind side alley of JT's productivity, something that led nowhere, or was the end of something, or was sometimes fake or borrowed. I got a letter from a reader suggesting this. But in the seventies it was the best *second aeon* could do. John Clare, the drawing you've got of him, with flat cap on, looking like someone out of D.H. Lawrence. How does anyone know what Clare looked like? Well, there were portraits. Bet he didn't look like you show him. Clare staring at me from page fourteen looking more like A.E. Housman than the mutton-chopped seventeenth century mystic he actually was.

We've been booked by a local group who meet in the Library. Small beer. JT would have preferred it to be big beer and a do in a tavern but in the fledgling literary scene in the uncertain Wales of thirty years back you need to take what you can get. We are beyond Swansea, car still rolling, greenness everywhere. This is where Wales is, says JT. You mean that wasn't Wales back there where we came from? Well, it was, but not Wales like this is. He gestures with one hand at the fields out there through the windscreen. This was the first inkling I had that there might be more than one country inside the one that I came from. Not like Bargoed, is it? JT always claimed he came from Bargoed, although details are sparse.

Pembroke Dock can trace its origins far more precisely than many Welsh places. It was created, a new town out of nowhere, in 1814. That's when the naval dockyard was dug on a stretch of flat, creek riddled farmland. Britain had been fighting the French ever since they'd had their revolution and needed more facility to build warships. Wooden ships with sail and cannon – at the time the scourge of the world. The Pembrokeshire Paterchurch lands which stretched from Pennar Point to Cosheston offered protected coast, tidal inlets and flat land difficult for Britain's enemies to access. A pater tower, a defensive farmhouse, had existed here since medieval times. It was incorporated into the new defences. It's still there, the buildings around it burned down or demolished. Pembroke Dock wondering what to do with it next.

The Dock flourished. Between Napoleon and the First World War it built five royal yachts and two hundred and sixty three other vessels. But the time of the steel warship was coming and the Dock, miles from anywhere, had no ready steelworks nor method of transporting the metal in. Although early ironclads and submarines were built here, slow decline led, by 1926, to ship building collapse and mass unemployment. During the Second World War the RAF arrived and for a time Pembroke Dock became a base for Sunderland flying boats, the white whales that bounced along the top of Welsh seas before lumbering almost impossibly into the air. The Nazi bombing of the Pennar oil tanks launched a fire which destroyed a thousand homes and burned for eighteen days. The longest British conflagration since the fire of London.

By the time JT and I arrive, hair over our collars, wide lapels, aviator dark glasses, the Dock is in seemingly free fall. Everything closed. Doors barred. Windows gone. *Dock Leaves*[22], Raymond Garlick's revolutionary literary magazine has already transformed itself into the *Anglo-Welsh Review* and moved away and on. It's good to get out of the car. JT has removed one of my harmonicas from the glove compartment and been blowing on it in a desultory manner since Carmarthen. He sounds more like Larry Adler than Howlin' Wolf. Was that the blues, I ask him? Certainly not. That was Frank Sinatra.

The streets are straight, wide, built on a grid like most naval towns. We park and walk about to stretch our legs. Tripp sucking on a slowly smouldering fag, me chewing liquorish imps. Good for the voice. There's a store on High Street which sells things that no one could possibly want. Stacks of cloth shoe hangers, buckets with no handles, giant nut crackers, tins of Russian fish from 1946, bakelite devices for opening the milk, kilner jars minus rubber seals, and a tin tray showing the mop-top four Beatles circa 1964. I buy one. 40p. You've been done, says JT.

The reading at the Library starts at 6.30. I do a warm up with poems that these days I've largely abandoned and then JT launches into his act which moves between laughter and literature like a snake. The audience is tiny – women with carriers, a man wearing two pairs of glasses, a couple of youngsters in jeans and cheesecloth shirts. At the interval half leave including John and the bloke with two pairs of glasses who head for the Dolphin Hotel. I do the second half on my own, talk about JT's *Inheritance File* and read a poem or two from it. When it's all over I sell a single copy and am asked by the purchaser, a woman wearing a giant cardigan with wellington boots under a long skirt, if I'd sign it. I do. For a moment I'm tempted to use John's name. Who'd know the difference as time moves on?

The b&b round the corner from the Dolphin, reached after a huge amount of delay by JT finishing his beer and talking to all the regulars as if he'd been drinking there all his life, is part of the deal. The group secretary has booked us there in advance. There's the expected vagueness about who actually pays the bill. Our reading fee will follow, someone has told me. The secretary wasn't actually at the reading itself. Communication was made earlier via ball point letter on Basildon Bond to JT and a brief phone call to me. We are now living on beer-clouded hope.

But it's okay. They know we are coming. Turns out the whole town knew we were coming, although less than a dozen managed to get to the Library to hear us. The secretary had done the rounds putting up posters and handing our flyers. People feel content to know that literature is happening around them although they seldom take part. My bed sinks in the centre by at least a foot. The carpet is woven nylon riddled with cigarette burns. The ensemble is dominated by a double wardrobe big enough to house eight Japanese but, when I open it, is entirely empty. In the drawer below I find an ancient *Western Mail*, a Gideon Bible and an Italian pornographic magazine. I sleep like a Pembroke Dock warship, keel on the springs, guns ready for the morning.

JT is up before I am, double fried egg and bacon, read the *Daily Mirror* and got through two cigarettes. He wants to get out of this place. What's there to see, he demands. Let's get back. On the mantelpiece is a model of Big Ben made out of matchsticks by the landlady's husband. He's passed on. Left this memorial to his life and endeavours in this western extremity of English Wales.

Outside it has started to drizzle. The Irish Ferry will build a terminal here soon, they'll build a bridge across the Cleddau to Neyland and the Dock will recover briefly when the WDA opens call centres for ITV Digital here in the 1990s. But it won't last. In six years time in an eastern hanger of the Royal Dockyard that once housed Sunderlands, Marcon Fabrications will build the Millennium Falcon[23], flying saucer star of *The Empire Strikes Back*. There'll be other attempts. Objective One funding. Small factories making pipes and drills, aluminium replacement windows, parts for aerospace. Concern and consideration. High retired demographic, significant long-term unemployment. Writers still meeting[24]. No bookshop.

Was that Wales, then, I ask JT provocatively? Who knows, he says.

CARDIGAN

Early success would have been fatal. Cardigan lay beyond the Landsker, the wrong side of the Preselis, beyond Crymych and Lampeter, where the Gwili Railway did not run. A place where the sea itself was Welsh. How could anyone from Cardiff ever reach it? Aberteifi, where the river from the heart of Wales flows, a place of coracle fishermen and utter strangeness in stovepipe hats. The fast roads got to Swansea and then petered. Beyond the Pont Abraham services magically labelled *gorffwysfan*[25] there was nothing but impenetrable green.

Aberteifi, place of myths, my mother told me. Where they cover their chests in lard to ward off the cold and carry their babies in shawls. Where they keep their money under stones and there's mud in the streets. She was wrong. We came through here on a bus to Aberystwyth when I was eight and she looked slowly out of the window. Saw the castle and the shored-up castle mound. Great slabs of wood holding back rock. Someone sitting at the bottom smoking a pipe. Most of the myth was invented from that.

It could be that the problem of Wales is that we do not know ourselves. Think we do but don't or, more likely, simply can't be bothered to spend the time. It takes effort to drive here from the populous east. But, amazingly, nothing like as much as you'd think. Horse's Mouth visited here in the wham-bam eighties. Tôpher Mills, Ifor Thomas and I did our stuff at Theatre Mwldan, the town's arts regeneration, in a hollow on Bath House Road. It was winter and we came on the new roads they'd built north of Carmarthen, along the winding tree-covered highway that climbs through Cynwyl Elfed and Rhos then explodes through Newcastle Emlyn's tractors, full of light. The gig was fast and efficient and after collecting the brown envelope containing our miserable cheque we vanished back to sophistication through the night.

Cardigan is two places – the west Wales Welsh capital and far western Drop City, land of hippie and leather biker, a Welsh Glastonbury of beads and incense and hairies levitating up Pwllhai and into High Street. The market is housed inside the 1858 Guildhall, Ruskinian Gothic, made from stone quarried near Cilgerran. 1892 clock tower added on top. In the street is a captured Russian field gun from Balaclava. Upstairs there's a café with rainbow prints on most walls, a collection of war-time utility chairs, no two matching. All of them scuffed some part repainted. Yellows, bright blues. Peace prints.

Granola and sprouts, alfalfa,
lentils, black beans, garbanzos,
sunflower seeds. Was, last time
I went.

Cardigan's Norman castle
dates from 1093. Maybe. Built
by Roger de Montgomery. Or
it could date from 1110,
erected by Gilbert de Clare.
Then attacked and ruined by
generations of Welsh princes.
Taken in 1170 by Rhys ap
Gruffydd who changed
Norman wood walls to native
stone. He put on an early version of the eisteddfod in 1176. Check
Brut y Tywysogion, forerunner to the *Cyfansoddiadau*. There were
chairs for the winners but we no longer know who they were. When
Rhys died the castle was sold to King John. Llewellyn the Great
recaptured, wrecking the place in the process. At the end of the thirteenth century Edward I won it back. Cromwell took it during the
English civil war. More wreckage. John Bowen instigated repairs in
1805. In 1827 Castle Green House, a Georgian mansion, was built
on the inner bailey. Gardens were landscaped. The new and the
medieval meeting in glory. But not for long. Costs rose. Maintenance
faltered, slowly over the decades. Visitors were not encouraged. In
2003 the Castle plus mansion failed to make it to the top in the BBC's
Restoration series. The £3.4 million on offer went instead to a
Victorian swimming pool in Manchester. English industrial age
leisure beats Welsh national heritage. In 2004 CADW stepped in with
the money for a restoration report. Decline has stopped but the steel
buttresses still dominate Bridge Street and the Strand. And the Castle
is still out of bounds.

In 2007 I go past bound for Gwbert, estuary beach on the
Ceredigion coast, just round the headland from Mwnt where Rhodri
has his caravan. I'm early so I stroll the streets, dry hot dawn in a July
so far full of rain. The town's drop-out leanings are strong. On the
corner of Quay Street a chalk board tells me that Live 2Nite
Cottonmouth Do The Blues. I pass Gardd Gandalf which sells lime
green garden chairs and chrome ornaments. Before I get to Middle
Earth Books in Pwllhai, I turn into the 1763 former Shire Hall now a
cavernous multi-floored enterprise selling Harley-Davidson knick-

knackery, DVDs, war games and rack on rack of music. The blues are a Welsh weakness. In a bucket of CD doubles from Kokomo Arnold, Memphis Slim, Big Boy Crudup and Big Joe Turner I find John Lee Williamson and Bill Broonzy. Big Bill. These country singers were almost always physically enormous. As I'm paying I spot a used vinyl of Hendrix's *Electric Ladyland* stickered at £120. This is thirty years old, man, says the Willie Nelson look-alike shop assistant, pony and leather waistcoat. Interested? Shake my head. I've got one. Haven't played it since 1968. This town feels like I used to be.

We gather at Gwbert to celebrate the completion of phase one of the town's EU-funded regeneration project. In the early 1800s Cardigan was a port of some substance. Five shipyards built more than two hundred sailing ships. Thousands of Welsh people left here for the new world. The *Active* and the *Albion*[26] went to Canada. The *Triton* sailed to New York. Frank Lloyd Wright's family from Llandysul took that one. What was there to keep them in Ceredigion? Think of the fortunes they could make in Australia, Canada, America, Patagonia. Those were the new worlds. Wales was the old.

The several million pound regeneration project has dredged the snaking Teifi channel. It's done this from the sea right back to Cardigan's Prince Charles Quay, hard by the arches of Pont Aberteifi and the reclaimed warehouse that was once a sail loft and granary but is now the Cardigan Heritage Centre. The harbour wall has been fixed and ceases to crumble. There are three hundred new moorings, three new slipways, a new landing stage and a new visitor centre. There's a poem too. The former Welsh National Children's Poet, Ceri Wyn Jones' englyn is set in 942-point Arial on yellow boards and stuck to the sea wall. Making it a permanent carving will happen next. The *Tivyside Advertiser* calls him "Poet Bard Ceri Wyn Jones". That's two poets. And we only pay for one.

The instructions for the grand opening ceremony tell you to "park your car on Patch Beach (the tide will not come to the top of the beach that day) and board Ermol 6 for transit to Glanteifion pontoon,

Ceri Wyn Jones's poem reminds us that this quay was historically a point of both departure and return, and, as such, is a site of contradictory emotions. For those leaving or returning, and those bidding farewell or welcoming loved ones home, it is a place of beginnings and endings, of sunset and sunrise; it can be as bitter as brine or as comforting as...

Y Cei

Fel glaw hallt, fel awel glyd, fel hiraeth,
fel y wawr a'r machlud,
mae ffarwel a dychwelyd
yn yr afon hon ynghyd,

St Dogmaels". We do this in style. We are accompanied by a flotilla of yachts, row boats, RLNI inflatables, hangers-on, trumpet blowing musicians and a motor boat dressed up as a dragon. Jim Evans, project officer, face reddened by endless Cardigan sun, has on a t-shirt which bears the harbour wall englyn on its reverse. Dafydd Wigley is dressed in a red fleece suggesting a new political direction (for this is the time of the Plaid-Labour coalition). When we get to St Dogmaels there are jokes about passports and a 24-point double-spaced speech from a chain of office wearing local leader. There's another from Melfydd George, Mayor of Cardigan, delivered when we reach Prince Charles Quay. It's poundingly hot and he's dressed in red robes, ermine collar, gold chain, tricorn hat, serviette lace and sensible shoes. He speaks almost entirely in Welsh, looking like a Ceredigion version of Les Dawson. His lady mayoress is wearing trainers. For the concert we get Ryeland Teifi, Catrin Finch and Lowri Evans. By now there's a huge crowd of locals and a ice cream van hammering them out. No one is drunk. No one has been sick yet. It might be that so far no comestibles have been free. Apart from begrudging tea at the Gwbert marquee. This, after all, is the heart of Cardiganshire. In the Grosvenor Hotel (listed, late C18, refurbished with Objective One finance[27]) there's an exhibition and more speeches. The man from the Crown Estate talks about the importance of the Estate's urban, rural and marine sectors. He gives us the magic words to open the magic door. Dai Olch One Fawr. The sounds of a Welsh Janis Joplin come up the stairs from the bar below.

There's much more to do. The channel needs deepening further so ships of ocean-going weight can dock. This place has suffered two hundred years of people leaving it. Now it's time for some to return. Back at Patch Beach my car has not been inundated. There's a pensioner with his back against the sea wall eating a sandwich, someone flying a kite, and a few seabirds fighting over a dead crab. Slowness. Peace. Why we come.

SOUNDS OF THE SEA AT GWBERT

I'm in Paris, 1968, such a long way from the west Wales coast. I'm on Boulevard Saint-Michel. San Mich. Meesh, say it softly, meeshh, like the incoming sea. I'm with Robert Magasiner, regular pianist at Le Chat qui Pêche and on other nights at La Harpe, Bvd Saint-Germain, downstairs. They go for Leonard Cohen, these Parisiens, he says, they can't understand a word but they love the melancholy in his dreary voice. We've come from La Harpe where Morgans has done his bottle-neck slide Robert Johnson impersonation prefaced by J'habite le Pays de Galles et suis ici pour l'aventure, l'excitation et le monnaie. Got none. Someone bought him a beer. Morgans the unlikely musician. PhD at Cardiff University after study into why jelly sets. Morgans is still at the bar. We're in a record shop. I'm holding *The Songs of Leonard Cohen*, Suzanne, Marianne, Sisters of Mercy. Magasiner shakes his head. Buy these, he says. Get something real. He's holding two discs. *We Are The Sea* by the Tamba Four, Brazilian jazz samba, waves breaking on golden beaches. *Environment – la forêt /l'océan*. Thirty minutes of the forest at dawn on side one, thirty minutes of the sea at Cape Hattaras on the reverse. Le voyage suprême. Beyond boredom. Mesmeric. Like Warhol's *Empire*, eight hours five minutes, black and white single shot of the Empire State Building. The lights come on, the lights go off. Three reels, the last almost entirely in darkness. Watching it you pass from confrontation to ennui and then out the far side into some sort of black and white high-plain nirvana. The sounds of the sea are like that.

Long way from Gwbert in 2007. But the sea still sounds the same. Out there on this soft warm day in the estuary distance, flat and regular. Increasing by measurable degrees as it slowly approaches, then fading as it returns. There are recesses in our souls where this sound goes, you relax the mind to let them come. No longer hear the sea but the sound that is beyond it. Back of the mind rides off on the updraft. Pulls back with the undertow. All the time it's something but it's nothing. An old rhythm. A process that's been rolling at Gwbert and over the cliffs at Mwnt and round the edges of Cardigan Island for longer than history. Before the Irish, before Claudius, before the keltoi, the Celtai, the celts. Before anyone made much more than heads for arrows. Chipped at rock. Picked up sticks. Made pelts from bladderack. No one wrote anything then. But the sounds of the sea at Gwbert still came rolling on down.

Kerouac, novelist, French Canadian, born Lowell, Mass., never came to Wales. Nearest he got was in the minds of his followers. Ed Thomas, James Dean Bradfield, Lloyd Robson. Kerouac knew the sea and the sounds it made. He went to the cove at Big Sur in California to manage a breakdown and in among all the premonitions of madness that progressively engulfed him were the sounds of peace, the background noise the world made slowly ticking, the sounds of the sea. He caught them and rolled them out in a poem of roar and risk and long meditation, *Sea – Sounds of the Pacific Ocean at Big Sur*. Language bent into shapes that only the surfing sea could resemble: "the machinegun sea, rhythmic / balls of you pouring in / with smooth eglantinee / in yr pedigreed milkpup / tenor- / Tinder marsh aright rrooo - / arrac'h – arrache-- / Kamac'h – monarc'h-- / Kerarc'h Jevac'h- / Tamna ----- gavow --/ Va – voolva – Via-- / Mia— mine-- / sea".

My copy, a Four Square Book, paperback, 3/6d, *Jack Kerouac, The Story of the Crack-up of the King of the Beats*[28], I found in a box at the front of the porno book shop on Bridge Street in Cardiff. 1965. Wales mostly uncharted territory for me then. Took me forty years to get to Gwbert. To stand here by the big, cliff-backed beaches, looking south-west, listening for the surf out there in the far distance. Administrator, writer. No Kerouac, although I might once have liked to have been.

The poem stayed with me for most of my creative life. In 1987 I took it to Plymouth, *Beat Dreams*[29], read it on stage through a loudhailer, extemporised as I imagined Kerouac might have. Red wine and dope. Played it like an alto, post-bop through the southern night. Kerter davo kataketa pow. ke ke ke ke ke ke KEK. Kwakiuti Kik. Kara voom. Arms. Sway. God I've got to believe in you / or live in death! Every syllable windy. Kara kara VOOM. Alexis Lykiard in charge. Carolyn Cassady, wife of Neal Cassady[30], one time lover of Jack Kerouac, was in the audience. A direct connection to the man I was so in awe of. It felt like it does when you are about to ask someone out. Fear of failure. I overcame it. I blew louder. Sounds of the sea pouring through my ears. She said hello afterwards but didn't shake my hand.

You can get inside these sounds. Let them mix with whatever happens to be there in the top layer of your consciousness. Once you've set the storm in motion you let it go. Stop controlling it. Stop wanting to make it make sense. Let it flow beyond conventional meaning. Forget about meaning. Stick with the sea and its whooshing. Pour back out what comes to you. Third mind. Not you, not the Kerouac as he wrote it but something else. Beyond it, above it. Within. I'm standing on Gwbert beach with this faint sea back out there, letting it trickle into me like the 240 slowly recharging an old car battery.

Bryan Aspden had a poem back in 1984[31] where "The waves revise their tenses, their soft mutations: / 'Ll—', they say coming in; 'L—' going out.". The beach at Gwbert is not steep enough for this. Bryan was from Llandudno where the sea roars. Here it aspirates. Gillian

Clarke whose cottage is only a dozen miles away, in the heart of Ceredigion, makes her sea say 'll-ll-ll'[32] as it breaks on the shore. Welsh sea. What else could it really be. I scuff the bladderwrack. A man in a safety jacket marked Beach Marshal, front teeth missing, face browned like Muddy Waters, smiles and tells me again that the tide will take a long time today. It's down there, he says, gesturing. Like it might not be. Like the sea might go out from Gwbert and vanish. Blue gone silent. The meditation entered and never exited. It'll be here again later. He smiles some more. I walk the tide line. Sun on my back.

Things In The Western Sky

Buddha
Boundless
1024 milibars rising
Storm Cone
Skybolt
Cirrus
Saucer
West Minster migrant saint
Shed of air
The western skies are full of
vapour crimson (why) shards of ice
(delete shard) sheds of ice (substitute crisp)
crisp shatter
light full of translucent altocumulus
shape of bone hoard
(add hymn)
Jehovah
guide me
pull me on

sky full of rain

sky full of light

notes

1. Manifest Destiny – 1845 – the belief that the United States was destined to expand from the Atlantic to the Pacific.

2   Translates to English as: The surroundings are the bare dwellings of my youth, Foel Drigarn and the tall mountain, all behind me, all full of their own opinion.

3   Actually Laugharne is so small that almost all of it is back of the Castle.

4   Soon to be defeated in the 2007 Assembly election by Conservative Angela Burns.

5   Laugharne is one of the last places in Britain to retain a working medieval corporation. The Corporation is presided over by the Portreeve.

6   Neil Morrissey and his business partners have subsequently sold on Brown's Hotel for more than £1.5 million to finance the redevelopment of the Hurst Hotel, and expansion of the private members' club, Hurst House in Covent Garden, London.

7   Coetan Arthur. Neolithic cromlech. A large flat capstone supported by a single low vertical pillar. 3500 BC. In Wales Arthur is omnipresent.

8   Web site www.stanrosenthal.com Stan's a father again. A new daughter, Ibakha, was born in 2005. If past practice is anything to go by then by the time you read this Stan will almost certainly have moved again.

9   Stan Rosenthal & Shelagh Hourahane – *Stan Rosenthal: Approaches to Art.* Gomer 2002.

10 *Wind* as in the thing that turns rather than the thing that blows.

11 Built originally in 1825 by Thomas Bowen, incorporated into Thomas Taylor's Corinthian palazzo in 1848, made of Bath stone. In 1993 with money from Europe reconstructed by the Wigley Fox partnership. John Newman's *Buildings of Wales* says it is noble. Swansea Council is proud.

12 Sir John Lloyd.

13 The inner circle of bluestones at Stonehenge are proved to have come from Pembrokeshire's Preseli mountains. But how they travelled 240 miles in the stone age remains a mystery.

14 "Utter ruyne and decay and hath been so for a long tyme" (Rental of 1583)

15 Sixth Century Irish Saint who visited the Gwaun Valley to free the villages of the sound of howling and communed with angels on the peak of lonely Carn Ingli, showering a love of Christ on all who followed him.

16 The Parrog – as Penarth is to Cardiff so the Parrog is to Newport. A run of houses on the slate sea front, a place where before the estuary silted up ships took locally quarried slate to a wider world. *Parrog* could well mean a low-lying area near the sea shore. There's one at Goodwick and one called the *Perroge* at Swansea

17 Library.

18 For Sale as a going concern in September, 2006.

19 The Golden Lion.

20 In Morgan's garage in Roath Cardiff are rolled canvases by the early Burns. Great things like carpets. Like awnings. They are splashed with paint. We could slice these, like Turner did, and sell them, I suggest to Morgan. Better not he replies.

21 Two white painted beacons mark the entrance to Porthgain's small harbour.

22 *Dock Leaves* was edited and published in Pembroke Dock from 1949 to 1955.

23 Twenty-three tons, seventy foot diameter, couldn't fly. Floated a millimetre above the floor on a bed of compressed air installed to make it easier to move about. Travelled to the studios in Elstree in sections on the back of lorries.

24 At the time of writing a group gathers at the Community Centre in Albert Square, Monday mornings, although it's doubtful they were the ones who invited us down.

25 *Gorffwysfan* – resting place.

26 For America. The fast sailing brig called the *Albion* of Cardigan, Llewelyn Davies, Master,

intends sailing the beginning of next April, from Cardigan with passengers for Saint-John's (New Brunswick) and New York. January 1920. *and New York* crossed out. Text repeats in Welsh. Source: Emigration pictures Data Wales.

27 Most of Cardigan centre seems to have been similarly refurbished. The EU and WAG funded Townscape Heritage Initiative has paid for the fixing of everything from new first floor sash bay windows to the Delicatessen at no 56 Pendre to a complete makeover for the five story nineteenth century Edwards Warehouse. Check www.cardigan-heritage.co.uk/ for more information.

28 Jack Kerouac published *Big Sur* with Farrar, Straus in 1962. The ride from *On The Road* through *The Subterraneans, Dr Sax, Maggie Cassidy, Visions of Cody, Mexico City Blues* and *The Dharma Bums* was over.

29 *Beat Dreams & Plymouth Sounds*, 1987. Out of print.

30 Cody Pomeray or Dean Moriarty in the Kerouac novels.

31 Bryan Aspden (1933-1998) *News Of The Changes*, Seren Books, 1984

32 Gillian Clarke from 'Not', in *Welsh and Proud of it*, Pont, 2007. "her father passing the time with stories / as they drove to the sea, saying the words, / the 'gw' and 'w' of wind and water, / the 'll-ll-ll' of waves on the shore."

CENTRAL

Y HOLL FFORDD LAN I'R CANOLBARTH[1]

The idea was to go north, where the air would be different. Four of us in John's small Renault, heading to Newtown, the far north, three hours of trees and turning roads. If there was a Wales up there beyond our destination then we were unaware of it. Dave had heard of Anglesey but its exact location was a mystery. For Cardiffians, and that's who we largely were, Wales north of Brecon was mostly mountain, myth and forest. This was the early eighties, walking as a middle-class leisure pursuit had yet to arrive, the crags were untraversed and the land was still pretty empty. The A470, that twisting backbone of our country, was still a bag of minor roads. Towns did not have bypasses. Traffic stuttered.

The weekend was to be a residential creative hothouse in the company of a couple of English novelists of some worth – Ian McEwan and Alan Sillitoe – and best Irish short story writer Wales had yet produced, Harri Pritchard Jones. Wales had imported the idea from California. Put writers and students in the same place for a weekend of readings, talks and tutorings and somehow, by stealth, by desire, by osmosis, the ability to create convincingly with words would move across. The venue was Gregynog Hall, a Victorian great house six miles north of Newtown, Montgomeryshire. Or maybe it was Powys. The names of the Welsh counties change, borders shift and, rather like the great wheat fields of the American mid-West, new administrative empires are formed. Locals, however, cling to the older designations: Montgomery, Merioneth, Eifionydd. If they could manage Cornovii, or Deceangli, or even Ordovices[2], then they would.

Of the actual journey I can't remember too much other than a violent swaying as cars rocketed towards us missing by a breath, and a clinging to the window winder on my door and a hiding of my head in my chest and my arms. John drove as if he'd never done it before. Other road users were a mystery. Bends were delusional. Junctions a fantasy. We drove along green verges, we went through bushes, we stopped in ditches. The three hours the trip should have taken turned to four. To five. The hills became higher. The sun was in the sky. There were trees everywhere. The oldest of our group, Graham Jones, dramatist, musical hall poet, a man who had once had the British Council stage one of his plays in, of all places, Bosnia, had seen it all before. On a journey like this my son put his Renault into a stream and it never came back out. What model? Dolphin. Our Welsh road was rising through the cooling Welsh air.

Newtown, if we'd been able to stop there would have been discovered as a middling market town of around 12,000 inhabitants set on the side of the quiet yet often flooding upper reaches of the River Severn. Robert Owen, founder of the co-operative movement and social reformer came from here. So did Pryce Jones, founder of the world's first mail order business (drapery – special patterns by post) at the Royal Welsh Warehouse, a building still known locally as Pryce Jones. The man may have gone but his tradition lives on with what was once Kays Catalogue still operating from the glory of his former store. There's a railway (Shrewsbury to Swansea), Laura Ashley and a motte and bailey castle (motte still visible, bailey not) and an excess of charity shops, and places with boards across their fronts. Wales? Just about. But with John driving as if this were another planet we passed straight on.

Gregynog now belonged to the University of Wales who, when they were not using it themselves, rented it out to academic groups running courses. Scientists met here to discuss the acceleration of particles, cosmologists to look for god in the deep far reaches of the universes, historians to argue about Llywelyn, mathematicians to chase probability and try to pin down chance. As a great house it was largely fake, its extensive black and white faux-Elizabethan rendering was not ancient wood but early painted concrete. But the place had a history. There's a reference to it in a poem by Cynddelw Brydydd Mawr in 1150. By the fifteenth century the house had become the seat of the Blayney family. Charles I passed by in 1645 just before he was defeated at Rowton Moor. This was then a hall, a manorial seat, but in keeping with its position on the Welsh side of the Marches, and despite the extent of the grounds it sat in, small.

In the 1840s with ownership gone to the Hanburys of Pontypool the house was extensively rebuilt. So extensively, in fact, that it is hard to see much remaining that predates the renovations. Rooms were heightened, walls moved, more rooms, passages, stairways and whole storeys added, roofs rebuilt, backs and sides rendered. The marsh land in front was drained and sunk and planted to create the famous topiary-filled Gregynog sunken garden. The render was painted a striking white and black. A new seat of ancient power at the centre of 18,000 acres, visible through the tress. Concrete bridges were built on the estate, concrete cottages erected and a concrete school built for the nearby village of Tregynon. All this was under the control of the head of the Hanburys, the fourth Lord Sudeley, who ran out of steam and money in 1894 and put the lot up for sale. After a short period in the ownership of Durham mining entrepreneur Lord Joicey the estate was split and sold. The Hall and a mere 750 acres was purchased by Gwendoline and Margaret Davies, granddaughters of Davies the Ocean, opponent of Bute, builder of Barry Docks and owner of the Ocean Coal Company. You can see his statue[3] on the main road in Llandinam, eleven miles south of Gregynog. We saw it as we swayed our way past but by then we were too shaken to care.

The Davies sisters were the ones who established Gregynog's reputation as a great centre for the arts and crafts. They filled its walls with French Impressionist paintings, Rodin busts, the work of Richard Wilson, Whistler and Augustus John. You could do it in those days when great art was cheaper and many of the great artists collected still alive. They built a music room, started a choir and began the Gregynog Music Festival. Adrian Bolt, Vaughan Williams, Elgar and Gustav Holst all attended. The Warden, Glyn Tegai Hughes, tells the story about an a advertisement they placed in the local paper: "Gardner Required; Tenor preferred…". The thing they were most famous for, however, was the establishment of the Gregynog Press – one of the world's great private presses which, between 1923 and 1940, produced forty two books[4] – hand letterpress, special papers, fine bindings. Worth a fortune today. There's a complete set in the Gregynog Library. When the sisters died the house plus annual endowment passed to the University of Wales who turned it into a conference centre and, in 1976, revived the press[5].

We are to sleep in a great dormitory, four beds separated by acres of distance supposedly to ensure privacy. I put my bag on my ancient brass bedstead, shout across to Dave but he's been so addled by the manic journey that he's gone deaf and is lying down. Gregynog exudes pre-War elegance. Not yet interfered with by the need for televisions, computer networking, disabled access and ice machines. Food is served in a refectory half a mile away. It feels like that. We take introductory tea and cakes in the company of seventy-four cosmologists here to discuss red shift and the expanding universe. It's hard to tell writer from scientist. Maybe the writers smoke more. The scientists, other than the women, all have beards.

Glyn Tegai, Warden, erudite, urbane, author of critical works on the Welsh poet, Islwyn, on German romantic literature, and on the history of the great house we are visiting, tells me that, in addition to the ancient trees growing in the Great Wood that surrounds the house, Gregynog is now famous for its lichen. The 350 year old oaks support moss and varieties of lungwort unseen elsewhere. Naturalists are excited. There's a leaflet guide. Where to see them, what they are called. Glyn, one of the nicest of men, speaks in English with a sort of county accent which would not be out of place on an insurance salesman or a BBC newsreader on the Third Programme[6]. In Welsh he becomes unintelligible, to me anyway. At this time my command of *yr hen iaith* is tenuous to say the least[7]. On his recommendation we take a walk through the Dell and then the wood. Past the sculpture of a hand emerging from the ground, the most photographed piece of public art anywhere in Wales, past sessile oak with their green smears of epiphytic lichen, wild cherry, copper beech, blue atlas cedar, Japanese larch, Douglas fir, purple sycamore. Birdsong, silence, sky. Alan Sillitoe in his leather waistcoat, pipe smoking in the distance. Clusters of wannabes wandering the front of the building. Harri PJ carrying a bottle of red. Air. Elgar came here, did he? The place has the right amount of grace, and almost enough Englishness. But it's still Wales.

In the tiny bar down in the depths of the main hall basement I discover that course attendees are expected to sell and serve drinks themselves and end the evening with the till (minus five pound float thoughtfully provided) balanced. Saves on staff costs. Perhaps. Dave and I volunteer, neither of us ever having pulled a pint before but keen to try. Things do not go well. Beers will not stay in their glasses. Bottles will not open. We do not know any prices and cannot work the till. Actually there is no till, just a drawer, closed with a loose nail. After a period of writing it all down we give up and simply guess. We sample the wares to ensure quality. Forget what we are drinking and sell it to someone else. I fail to get the optics to work, take the bottles down and pour freehand. The crush in front of us increases. The writers all want serving simultaneously. We have no idea of precedence. The scientists, visible earlier, all seem to have left. Someone wants wine, I hand over a bottle and a corkscrew and suggest they open it themselves. McEwen asks for a lager. Tutor, famous. Serve him first. Forget to charge. Lose the ability to add up. Bottles get knocked over. Push onwards. Try our best. Somehow the evening ends, I'm back in my room. Spinning. I've handed on responsibility to another volunteer. Dave has vanished (later found sleeping under a bush). The room turns and sways. Much like the car journey up.

The big day in the great hall has McEwan, at the time hottest short story writer in the land, so hot he appears to have completely and single-handedly reinvented and repopularised the form, perversely reading from *The Cement Garden*, a novel. In the question session that follows I ask him for advice on managing rejection. Can't help you, he says, it has never happened to me. In Alan Sillitoe's dark country workshop my own fiction, laid on the public block, is decimated. Plotless, characters like stick insects, unmemorable title, opening line as appealing as candy floss. Dave remains silent. Too hungover to move or maybe just unwilling to join in. Yet writers need to be told how it is, when and where they are going wrong, why their pieces don't work. Told with truth. Too often all they get is misplaced praise from friends and family. The world's a hard place.

Fixes: too uncertain; too modern; no music; too long; doesn't go anywhere; beyond your experience; too guilty; full of fear; hasn't slept; not pure; like a chicken; too old; doesn't do anything; fanatical; exhausted; feathered; brings pain; Jesus; difficult; blue; fails to blossom; embalmed; unepic; disproportionate; drunk in bed; country; no confidence; Ezra; wrong information; grasp; kiss; lack. Harri explains it all with patience and smiles.

When the weekend is done I accept a lift south with Cliff James who talks of sheep farming and growing potatoes in a barrel. He drives at half John's speed but at least stays on the road. His first Gregynog also. A drunken retreat among the creative spirits in a pre-modern house made of inspiration and cement. My first truly post-modern experience, art where all forms repeat simultaneously and minority has equal value with majority, but that hasn't been invented yet.

LLANWRTYD WELLS – EDGE OF THE GREEN DESERT

Llanwrtyd is on the edge of that slab of population free Wales which Harri Webb once christened 'the green desert'. Depopulated, sheep full, and in the endless rain so green. Like many I'd always thought I'd been here before, passed through, Builth, Llandrindod, Llangammarch, the Victorian wells of Wales. But it's obvious, confronted by the huge statue of a kite near the bridge on the bending Afon Irfon, that I haven't.

The town is in the river valley between the military's forsaken Epynt and the walker's paradise that is the Cambrian massive. Llanwrtyd has the air of a place, like Blaenafon, in which post-industrial decline had once been slowed with a bit of repair and some tarting, and then allowed to slip again – road dirt washed into doorways, wood rot, paint flaked, boarded stores, kids in boombox Peugeots.

This is the smallest town in Britain, one bus, by arrangement, every evening, to Builth where there are shops. On the spring Saturday when we reached Llanwrtyd, the town's only newsagent finally closed down.

We are here to write up the Carlton House restaurant with rooms for the Which? *Good Food Guide*. I say we, I mean my partner, she's the food writer. I am from the school of pot noodle and the emptying of tins into small saucepans. I'm here for the scenery. The deal is that we book in anonymously and sample as much as we can of the menu, wines included. Neither of us can order the same dish and Sue gets to taste everything on my plate. Small price. The owners, of course, never suspect a thing with Sue making pencil notes throughout the eating and me taking digital photos of the wine list, the day's specials chalk board, and the menu. Carlton House[8] is a Victorian town dwelling, painted render, tall, battered a bit, but comfortable.

Before the arrival of the NHS with daily free doctor's surgeries with cure-all antibiotics and steroid rubs, sulphurous waters were regarded as the natural retreat for the scurvious, the sick and the maimed. Drinking them, bathing in them, allowing them to enter your every orifice managed the unfixable. These waters come from the earth's depths and have that gaseous nose of rotten eggs. They are the result of rains from the Late Pleistocene, trapped below for millennia, slowly reducing the rocks that hold them. They surface through a vast interconnect of fracture systems to seep, after all those years, into a contemporary Wales that once revered them but now has no time left.

At the Tourist Office the expected collection of home-made guide books and mapless leaflets for walkers has been supplemented by an interesting range of confectionary. I buy a Milk Chocolate Riding Outfit (horse, stirrup and riding hat) reduced from an obviously too expensive £4.25 to a quite reasonable £3.90. I was tempted by the Milk Chocolate Gardening Kit but the secateurs looked a little frail. The girl behind the counter (style and substance Visit Wales dark blazer, dragon on the pocket) says she's lived in Llanwrtyd all her life but only worked in the visitors centre for a year. She's not sure about the wells nor where they are. When pressed she offers Dol-y-Coed. Try in the park, but I don't think there's much to see.

Nor is there. Dol-y-Coed, where's there's been a manor house since 1535, was once a grand hotel. The spa baths dispensing mineral waters to imbibe and to dive in were housed at the back. Still there, but locked and wrecked. The bath house windows are all boarded and there's evidence among the smashed window frames and cracked render of arson. The magic sulphur runs in small streams to lose itself in the greater Irfon river. I drink a handful. No effect.

For a long time Llanwrtyd Wells was known as Pontrhydyfferau until, in 1732 Theophilus Evans, the Vicar of St David's church, discovered the health-giving properties of the stinking waters. Scurvy, heart disease, gout and rheumatism could all be kept at bay. The medicine show had arrived. And, as was the case right across this slice of mid-Wales, the tourist rush was begun. Llanwrtyd Wells, renamed to make things easier for lost Victorians, was swiftly developed. The railway steamed in. The wells at Dol-y-Coed were joined by those at Victoria. Hotels were built. Taverns opened.

On the wall next to the town's honesty bookshop is a plaque commemorating the fact that on this spot in 1895 one Talog Williams accompanied by the Rev D.M. Davies composed one of Wales' (and especially Llanelli's) unofficial national anthems, Sospan Fach[9]. The bookshop is a spill of the useless abandoned, shelves falling into heaps and volumes collapsing in on themselves like stars. *The Human Factor In Aircraft Accidents, Trade and Growth in the Philippines, The*

Soviet Impact on Commodity Markets, Lawn Care in Central Africa. Unaccountably, nine copies of Nigel Jenkins' tall book in the Writers of Wales series. *John Tripp,* 1989. A stamp inside tells me that this volume is AMHERFFAITH – imperfect. There's a water stain on page 119. And the endpapers are scuffed. I buy two copies.

Along the valley is the church of William Williams

Pantycelyn, he of *Arglwydd, arwain trwy'r anialwch* – Guide me, O thou Great Jehovah – sung to the tune even the godless know – Cwm Rhondda. There's a celtic cross here from 1500 years back and the graves of famous bards. Poetry is always near the surface in the greenness of Wales.

In the town the Peugeots roar. There's one on the square, opposite the Neuadd Hotel, suspension throbbing, baseball cap on backwards, fag and vacant eyes. Someone has painted flames along the sides of their new red Toyota Supra, huge spoiler, gleaming chrome. The Stonehouse Inn hosts a band called Slugman – 'loud, lively & lunatic'. Important – Please note – any person who causes trouble resulting in a ban, will automatically be banned from All Pubs in the Builth area. Free House. Homebrew. A white van is parked outside, covered with stickers. Good Rocking Tonight. Elvis No 1. Elvis The King.

Up Zion Street The Bell Bar doubles as a launderette (which in the world of weird combinations is beaten only by the launderette in Lindos which doubles as a bookshop) and half a chapel, church glass still in place, and inside twenty chairs lined up waiting for someone to use them. God is big here. Was once.

To survive, Llanwrtyd has become the twenty-first century home of the surreal and the outlandish. The Man v Horse sprint runs here. So does an annual Bog Snorkelling contest in which flipper-clad adventurers swim up four foot deep peat trenches cut into the bog of Waen Rhydd. There are food fantasies, beer festivals, red kite frolics, mountain bike races, a morris in the forest weekend and something called the Real Ale Bike Wobble which consists of getting legless and then cycling for thirty-five miles. How else do you survive when the waters have left you?

By contrast Carlton House is sophisticated calm. Alan and Mary Ann Gilchrist, who have cooked here since they came here in 1990 from Australia, offer just the right mix of old world charm and present day craic. For the *GFG* my job is to describe the ambience. Post-industrial Victoriana with touches of both Magritte and Mackintosh.

The first name of both those guys was Rene[10]. I order Chardonnay at £12 a bottle and admire the Gilchrist's Bryan Westwood[11] painting of a deserted slum. All shadows and sun. He's painted a child's slide abandoned in the middle of a Sydney street. The house windows lack glass. There are no people. Alan says it runs in the same territory as Hopper. It has similar public loneliness, the same dark and light and use of space.

I manage organic salmon followed by beef with black olives, saffron and parmesan mash and the best tasting spinach in the Welsh universe, wilted, according the menu, young, small and not left in the heat for long. It works. The menu is free from the usual restaurateur's jargon of goujons, fleurons, flambé and marinated medley. Although there is some jus and further along a chive velouté. I polish it all with a Goldackerel Beerenauslese. This is a massively expensive Austrian desert wine and one which is supposed to enrich me with taste trails of peaches and honey. The Felinfoels at the pub down the road earlier do not let these through. Instead the alcohol sings. High C. My fellow diners glow like angels. All fourteen of them. You can extend your arms out here and touch nothing. Warmth and space. Mary Ann emerges from her kitchen to regale the assembled with tales of Australian sauce making, the power of cheese, and life in this place where everyone seems to be from elsewhere. I pull again at the sweet Goldackerel. Smile. So much better than sulphur.

LLANELWEDD

There were once wells too at Builth but they are long gone. More spa water that smelled like gunpowder. Pools you bathed in and springs from which you drank. Made you better. Snake oil without the snakes. There was a castle too, a vast thirteenth century fortress, and that's gone as well. Its stones fallen and stolen, dragged off to make the walls of barns and houses. When the mighty are fallen that's what locals do. All that's left is an empty motte and some grass-filled ditches, reached along a small path behind the Lion Hotel. The greatness of the conquest reduced to earth and green.

Builth, of course, is on the way to somewhere. A dog leg veering east on the snake of the A470. Lorries still come up from Brecon along the treelined side of a Wye they never see to roar through Builth's outskirts. They turn right at the town's Victorian Assembly Rooms (now the Wyeside Arts Centre) and cross the river to head past Wales' worst Little Chef[12] before banging on north via Rhayadr or Llandrindod. Builth itself is a market town hammered by the Black Death in the fourteenth century, almost burned to the ground in a great fire during the seventeenth and then revived as one of the four Welsh centres for the taking of healing waters in the nineteenth. The railway arrived and so did hundreds of Victorians all determined to

beat their rheumatism, heart problems, gout, poor skin, loss of vitality, balding pates, impotence and failing eyes. The waters were the town's salvation – or at least like Llanwrtyd they gave it a few decent inns and the odd hotel.

The rail station today is out, way beyond the Llanelwedd Royal Welsh Showground, up the A470 on the way to Llandrindod. Builth Road it's called. It sounds as if it should be in the town centre, opposite the town hall, next to the Builth bus station, facing the Builth sex shop and Builth burger bar, clustered with Builth taxi ranks and Builth stalls selling polos and the Builth *Evening Post*. But instead it's a good three miles away, up the slope to the Llanelwedd Arms, the nearest place to stay, and the Little Chef, the nearest place to eat. The unlucky, thinking they can let the train take the strain, are obviously unaware that this is rural Wales.

Builth, three hours south from Caernarfon and yet, to some insular Cardiffians, still regarded as being in the north. A place that once sold sheep at the junction of three rivers, the Wye, the Irfon and the Chwefru. Llanfair ym Muallt – St Mary's in the Cantref of Builth. Muellt, Muallt, Bealt, Builth. Add Wells to illuminate the waters and in the thin tongue of the anglicised east you have arrived.

Today if Builth is still famous for anything then it is the great agricultural show held on meadows just across the bridge in the parish of Llanelwedd. The Royal Welsh Show, the biggest annual agricultural four-day event in Western Europe. 250,000 visitors in 2006. 100 acres, sun blazing for four days. If you have any association with land or tractors then for a short time Builth is the centre of the world.

The size of the show is enormously impressive – it takes at least a day to walk round its one thousand stalls, its three display rings and its countless pavilions, sheds, yards and pens. Seven thousand animals are brought here to compete. Best in breed, best turned out, best looking, best smile, best to eat. There are displays of just about everything of interest to rural people – from thatching to fencing, from red tail falconry to harness trotting, from bailing machines to tractors, from breeding ponies to chariots of fire. There are exhibitions of fence posts, coils of fence wire, huge brightly painted receptacles for slurry, yellow oil tanks, immense red septic tanks that need to be buried in twenty foot pits and then lines of machines that can dig that deep.

At the Native Breeds competition the stockmen often resemble their stock. A ponytailed white-coated giant leads a Welsh Black the size of a Mercedes delivery van. They stride together, in perfect time, the perfect match. Highland cattle with long hair and exemplary horns, Aberdeen Angus, Herefords, Devons, Dexters, Red Rubies, then iconic, docile, long-lived, hardy Longhorns. Cefn Gwlad[13]'s Dai Jones, white shirt and tie in all this heat, has himself filmed with the cattle passing behind him. The Welsh Blacks win. Rosettes, cups. A contract to supply Marks & Spencer.

Names for the competitors: Ridge Dean Artaban, Furzeland Appear, Millington Tangerine, Syfni ap Rhys, Villy, Archie Greenyards the First, Lowerhope Orange, Hallwood Nibbs, Gwenog Vindicator, Gower Armani, Newstart Vindicator, Pelletstown Valerie the Second, Celtic Noelle, Moretonhall Supersonic, Widewath White Mountain, Haughton SAS Joe Louis the First, Gorse Lollipop, Idlenot Henryetta, Moomin MacDuff, Challenge Showboy, Tommy's

Girl, Smarty Pants. The rappers have nothing on us.

In the sheep shed up beyond the massed craft displays of hand built greetings cards, dried flowers in frames and displays of cheese and paintings made from stuck on shells and bits of cloth are enormous crowds. Shearing here is a spectator sport. The women do two sheep each, the veterans five but the youngsters, at the height of their game, have to cut the coats off twenty. The animals, amazement in their dull eyes, pop from shuttered boxes. The contestants shear as if they were scraping away blistered paint. As each animal is finished it is kicked back down the hatch and the button pressed for another. The crowds roar on the edges of their seats. "Get in there, boy, shearing, exactly as it should be shorn." The women in this crowd have on cowboy boots,

PEIDIWCH A DRINGO
AR Y TARW

DO NOT CLIMB
ON THE BULL

the men are in vests. No tattoos, no body piercings, hardly any jewellery. This is a rural audience. Jeans, sweat, smiles. Nearer the heart of the country than any other.

In the pig pens the animals are bigger than I imagined they ever could be. Great porkers lying exhausted in the heat, all of them, not one among fifty standing. Children poke them with sticks, touch their backs. Nothing stirring. Temperatures are up in the thirties. Drink sellers are making more than they ever expected.

That evening, at the cattlesheds where the great winning Welsh Blacks lord it for the joy they've bestowed, the cattlemen and cattle-girls party. The meat supply contracts have been hard fought for and won. At the height a woman dances on a makeshift stage and full of beer or vodka, strips. Someone catches her discarded thong on a pitchfork and offers it back. The stripper shakes her head. To cool her she's sprayed with a firehose. The crowd roars, drinks some more. The day has been great. On the one following Show officials, who heard about all this second hand, are recorded as being disgusted. There's a note on the Builth Wells community website from a journalist offering cash in exchange for the stripper's identity. No answers are forthcoming.

The great Llanelwedd showgrounds, purchased in 1963 by an agricultural society exhausted from the push and expense of taking their ever expanding show from venue to venue, have stalls of the kinds you simply do not expect to find in the fields of mid-Wales. The National Library, yes, the Assembly free tea, smiling and empty, the Welsh Books Council, the National Museum, the *Western Mail*, CADW, Llandovery College, the Environment Agency, the Police,

the Fire Service, yes, even Shire Tractors, the Ploughing Society, Teifi Saddlery and the Association of Welsh Coal Producers. But maybe not Gypsy Betsy Lee "her powers are strong", Free Designer Fragrances six packs all of them fake twenty quid, Doggy duvets five pound, Teme Valley adjustable beds and reclining chairs, stairlifts, things to clean floors with, slice veg with, steam clothes with, and what looks like a travelling branch of Dixons selling toasters, food mixers, wide-screen TVs, hi-fis, fridges, built in ovens and dishwashers.

The show could not be more different from Wales' other great annual field event – the National Eisteddfod. The Royal Welsh has hard-topped paths, brick toilets, and car parks that are easy to drive to. At the Eisteddfod the ground is always uneven and the crowds more earnest. Stand still at the Eisteddfod and the chances are you'll meet everyone in the world you know. Do the same at the Royal Welsh and you'll also meet several hundred you don't. Where is the heart of Wales? Llanelwedd, or in the mud of a northern village or on wasteland outside somewhere urban in the south?

Walking back into Builth, over a temporary road bridge made from scaffolding, past the fat man selling collapsible chairs at double their normal price, the householders flogging iced water, the tired and aged evangelist with his placard "What Think Ye of Christ?", the Asians selling gold chains and sterling silver bracelets, across the slow and empty Wye, you feel part of a great mid-Wales holiday. The only people formally dressed are the judges and stewards in the competition rings, in ties and suits and black bowlers looking like Ulster Orangemen. Everyone else is in t-shirts, sandals and shorts.

At the edge of the town stands Gavin Fifield's bronze statue of Caerynwch Tywysog the Sixth, a local Welsh Black, now symbol of the town. There's a sign which asks you not to climb on it. There are a couple of local teenagers lounging here. A hot hatch revving in the car park. Its driver sports an earring. His companion has celtic interlacing tattooed around her upper arm. All is still right with the world.

EPYNT

We're stopped here to admire the view. High plain, buzzards above us, a green moorland undulation that asks to be walked across. No fences. Few hedges. Peat, the sky so vast for the lack of trees. We've been driving for six hours down from the north Wales coast. Wales is suddenly enormous. We're giving Borbála Szekeres a lift to the south. She's Hungarian, a one-time party member, used to be red for expediency, she says, but today is capitalist and free. We've attended a literary conference in now distant Llandudno. Coast town of the soft retired, a Victorian backwater of endless quiet. When everybody else went to bed Borbála went clubbing. Found two places open. Danced and drank. Said she did. People from the East are different. That's clear.

Now we are heading south by back roads, taking in the sights and the deviations. Went through Blaenau Festiniog where Borbála collected slate, through Trawsfynnydd where she put her hand in the radioactive water, past drowned valleys and over ridges, across abandoned railtracks and through the great green rocky gulfs that make Wales feel like the last wild place in the world.

The plan has been to make the country as big as we could. So far it has been huge. We've come past the Drovers Arms, the only building in an empty landscape, a place where cattlemen walking their stock to the markets at Brecon once stopped for beer and cheese, now an empty ghost. *The Drovers Arms - Ministry of Defence* reads the inn sign. Renovated in 1994. Still resolutely closed. We've pulled up next to an enormous and wind-shredded red flag which warns us not to leave the road. Firing is in progress, but there's not a soldier in sight.

Where are the tanks, asks Borbála? Your tanks, you have hundreds. She knows this. Out there on the horizon is nothing. A distant copse of evergreens, set square for soldiers to hide in. Across this Falklands-clone terrain the regiments yomp. Half-ton packs, arms cradling their SA80s. They fill with dust and won't fire. Too often, on these well-trodden routes, nervous trainee soldiers encounter anorak clad Welsh

THIS INN WAS ONCE A WELCOME RESTING PLACE ON THE OLD DROVERS' ROUTE ACROSS THE EPYNT.
IT WAS ACQUIRED BY THE WAR DEPARTMENT IN 1940 AS PART OF SENNYBRIDGE ARTILLERY RANGE, AND WAS RENOVATED IN 1994 BY THE DEFENCE LAND AGENT, BRECON, WITH ANDREW M. DAVIES AS BUILDER.

walkers, day packs, maps, sandwiches. Bad for the training, hard on the nerves. The Army is thinking of moving its operations north to Scotland. But today there's no one. Borbála knows her red flags and her soldiers and is not impressed with ours.

The Epynt range, this whole upland tract was once farmed by sturdy hillmen - sheep, occasional dairy. All moved on when the Army bought it. The land was locked away from the locals, from the Welsh, in fact from anyone not in uniform. The winds blew in khaki gusts.

But things have changed. The Army has come to realise that the public dislike secret lands, especially those that were once not. They've opened up routes for walkers, built a welcoming website, gone in for way marking, guide books and printed leaflets. They've even done a formal HSE risk assessment for those who are fearful of crossing alien Welsh uplands. Spent rounds – do not touch. Sun – can burn. Ankles – wear boots.

We head on south, winding through Upper Chapel, Lower Chapel, Brecon the back way and out onto the northern slopes of the southern Beacons. The light is clear and bright, the green glacial slopes crossed by the giant moving shadows of clouds. Borbála is convinced that Wales is bigger than the central Hungarian plains, as large as Texas, obviously, although she's never been there, and as full of sun as Portugal, she's read that in a book. The people of Wales are dispersed in cities she has yet to be driven through, the history of Wales lost in a desert of farm and rock and hilltop. We enter Merthyr, slowly, watching for the remains of the ironworks, showing her Cyfarthfa, twisting on to roll down the Valley of the Cynon where at least she'll be able to smell the coke works, still functioning, I think, amid the reclaimed world. But there's nothing. The air stays clear. Industry has vanished behind lines of trees and repointed walls.

Eventually we pull into Cardiff and head on for Penarth. The pier there will echo the one we left eight hours ago at Llandudno. Victorian indulgences hanging on as outlets for ice cream and facilities for fishermen with stools and rods. They haven't got these in

Hungary, no coast beyond the lakeside at Balaton. No blue grey horizon. No salt in your lungs.

When we eventually get there we find Penarth slumbering in the dusk. A few lights along the promenade, coming on slowly now that the sun has gone down. About as lively as Llandudno. That was Wales, I tell Borbála. Unroll it and it's as big as Austria. Of course, she says.

YSBYTY YSTWYTH

The past holds on in this country. Its artefacts stay in the landscape. Pre-war Shell petrol pumps, glass covers broken, dials illegible and colour drained, stand by unpainted wooden-slat garage doors. Ford Prefects moulder behind hedges. There's a caravan with pock-marked roof and curtains that will crumble if touched. At the margins of the fields are piles of cleared stone that have lain there for decades. Corrugated tin sheds, bent by lack of foundation, rust-red in the Ceredigion rain. In a forecourt on the B road down to Aberystwyth is a stack of horseshoes. Across the fields the old pathways are still trodden. The tracks the lead miners made still pass through deciduous woodlands of Sessile Oak, Downy Birch and Rowan.

This is the west again, all Wales is west. We follow the sun, the Buddha, the light of God, the rays of hope, the sky that bends away from us, pulling our eyes. I've got Lucinda Williams' *West* on the player, voice like a mesh filter, "I know you won't stay permanently, But come out west and see." The road drops into Ysbyty Ystwyth. Spital. Hospice. Place of old custom where the race memory is

strong. Corpse candles abound[14] and the images of the dead and the soon to die continue to appear as reflections in puddles of water along the road.

In the dip that is Ysbyty there's a churchyard. The great chapel of Maes Gwyn, erected in 1874 and capable of accommodating hundreds of non-conformist divines, has been demolished. The first chapel of Dafydd Morgan,

minister, carpenter, gravedigger, the man who managed the revival of 1859 converting more than 36,000 to the Lord, still stands. It is full of plastic chairs and dust. Above it the graveyard and, at the top of the hill, the parish church of St John's. Still there with its old god wearing his ancient robes. Clustered today with Italian marble headstones mixing with those of native rain-worn stone.

When Hendre Felin[15] and Frongoch[16] lead and zinc mines were working there were two pubs here. Star Inn, Whistle Inn. Plus bakery and general store. Two chapels. Population 711 in 1891. The rail link was down the road at Strata Florida. The new industry was roaring. But when that ended the men who worked it chose not to stay. Went east to the coalfields. North to the slate. South to the clay and tin of Cornwall. There are just 50 houses today with a school that teaches 25 pupils. The pubs are long gone, there's no baker, and the village shop has finally closed. The population in 2007 is 104. The council local plan says that the nearest shops are in Pontrhydfendigaid. I've been there. There's no Marks & Spencer's.

In the long past Ysbyty Ystwyth was on the pilgrim route from Strata Florida to St David's and the Knights Hospitalers of St John maintained a hospice here. A place for the sick pilgrim to rest. God managed health and God managed the way we crossed His land. Ysbyty means hospital. It's the reason the settlement began. But it's lost now. The buildings have fallen and their foundations have been turned to other use. Perhaps it was at the edge of the village graveyard. Or under Maes Gwyn. Or hiding in the birch woods of Nant y Berws. Its power now under dismal earth waiting to be found again. Travellers still pass by. In their cars. Pilgrims en route to the old salvation at the far end of Dewisland. Industrial historians searching the lead mine relics. Sometimes curious visitors who want to see this place with its ancient name. People like me.

ABERYSTWYTH

At the Ceredigion Museum on Terrace Road just down from Clive's Continental Menswear[17] we are launching Judy and Ted Buswick's *Slate of Hand*[18], a self-published history of slate art. The book is full of pictures of slate quarries and slate gravestones, of sculptured slate crosses and slate spirals, and slate engraved and daubed with the swirling shapes of modernism. The Ceredigion Museum of folk art, industry and local history, built into a refurbished Coliseum Cinema[19], is a rich mixture of holiday attraction and intellectual escape. Shop dummies dressed as Celts, penny-farthing bicycles, cases full of pot and rock, the interior of a bedroom from 1850, a rack of ploughs and sickles, cases full of still otters and frozen hawks. The launch takes place in the art gallery where we are surrounded by abstract drawings by Pip Woolf, made at the National Assembly's Debating Chamber. Art in response to argument. Lines that bend around and around. The book is coffee table size, a serious study of the way in which dark rock has been used to illuminate culture. Apart from us there are five or six retired and time-rich in the audience. A woman drinking orange juice from a silver hip flask. A silent white hair in fawn Marks & Spencer trousers. A couple of members of museum staff. "Slate art isn't like poetry," Ted tells me, "you don't come because you want to take part."

I'm in Aberystwyth again to try to get a new feel for it. I've been coming here professionally for decades – to the Library, the Books Council, the Books Centre, for meetings of the Academi at the Conrah in Chancery, for debates with writers and publishers in bars and cafés and rooms in hotels – but those have been purposeful arrivals and never rambling tours. When I first came here in the fifties, as a child of eleven, brought by my parents in a coach with scratchy seats and cream doors, I thought I'd landed on the moon. How could that be a beach, that colour? And that truncated pier[20], a battered hang-on from a 1920s film. And people holidayed here? They certainly did.

John Barnie, the poet and former editor of *Planet*, is taking me round. He's lived here since 1985 and tells me that his early experience of Aber mirrored mine. He also came here in the fifties but was hunting a scholarship at the university. Got on the wrong train and ended up at Barmouth in thunderous rain. Cheap brown suitcase soaked. Reached his Aber digs at ten at night, shoes like pulp. No welcome. Everyone there spoke Welsh, John at that time did not. Misery. Met up with another young man also trying his luck. A few warm sparks and then that man got the scholarship and John did not. Bugger. Who was he? Byron Rogers. Future author of speeches for Prince Charles and the tale of poet R.S. Thomas's search for identity in the far west.

John, an Abergavenny lad, went to university at Birmingham instead. He went on to become a medievalist at Copenhagen before returning to Wales in the eighties, disillusioned with the academic life. He got the job of assistant editor to Ned Thomas at *Planet*, the Welsh Internationalist, based at Ned's old house in Cambrian Place. The journal moved to new offices at the Aberystwyth Science Park in 1988 and shortly after John took command. Between 1990 and 2006 he edited ninety-nine issues of Wales' most widely-read cultural magazine. I ask him about politics. "I'm a committed anarcho-syndicalist. I believe in equal pay for all. No one at *Planet* earns more than anyone else. All jobs are equal. I'm a socialist, of course, as well as being a complete nationalist." He tells me this over latté at the Orangery (no jeans or trainers allowed), an upmarket wine bar built on the site of Aberystwyth's 1857 Town Hall on Market Street. John learned Welsh while still in Denmark. "What you speak changes what you are. How you think about the world. What you do." And is Aberystwyth a Welsh place? "If you exclude the students, pretty much."

As a writer John pushes boundaries, and is not afraid to innovate. Yet he's no exponent of difficulty. Instead he's one of the most consistently readable writers we have. He's also at the centre of the Anglo-Welsh blues scene, if there is such a thing, playing guitar and singing about down home Alabama, Abertawe, Comins Coch, Route

66 and the A470 in a variety of skiffle, r&b, and poetry bands. He's been at the sonic centre of the Salubrious Rhythm Company, Y Bechgyn Drwg, Madog's Moonshine and a variety of other combos. His latest venture is a straight blues outfit formed with the poet Richard Margraff Turley. The blues ain't nothing but. Here, at the mouth of the snaking Ystwyth. Lazy Lester, Robert Lockwood Jnr and David Honeyboy Edwards have all played the Arta Centre. The blues flowing in the cymric world.

Aberystwyth is no burgeoning city, redevelopment is minimal, its skyline is not full of cranes. The sense of alienation you get in places like Cardiff and even Swansea is absent here. Aber wanted to be the capital of Wales when that honour was up for grabs in 1955 and put up a good case – geographically central, Welsh speaking, full of institutions. But there was more money in Cardiff. Business wins. Same thing happened again almost fifty years later when the Assembly was created. That institution also followed the money. Aber now contents itself with the title of unofficial capital. Welsher than anywhere bar Caernarfon. More cultured than Pontcanna. A place you can hold. Alternative capital. Gay capital. Student capital on sea. New Brighton. The hippie Biarritz of Wales. In 1994 Aberystwyth elected former Incredible String Band member Rose Simpson as mayor. This town does not slumber quietly. Indigenous population is around 12,000 to which can be added more than 10,000 students in term time. Physically it is dominated by its institutions, rising in a tiered stack inland. Bronglais Hospital, the National Library, illuminated at night and looking like a Welsh version of the White House, and then the vast and brutalist Penglais Campus of the Arts Centre, Science Park and University.

Down at the harbour, halfway between the northern Constitution Hill and the southern Penparcau outcrop, on the top of which stands Pen Dinas, an iron age fort, we watch the fishing boats unload shellfish, lobsters and spider crabs. Basket after basket. They go into tanks and get driven to Spain. A half life left for a few more days. Better price there than here. John points out the

flats of John Harris, literary academic and Ralph Maud, Dylan Thomas scholar. Literature fills these streets. In his excellent guide *The Literary Pilgrim In Wales,* Meic Stephens lists around thirty greats who have association here. Everyone from Richard Hughes to the Marxist poet T.E. Nicholas. The house of Caradoc Evans is in Queens Square (plaque on the wall courtesy of the Rhys Davies Trust "Er Cof Am Caradoc Evans 1878-1945" – WKD sticker in the window above it). Gwyn Jones, translator of the *Mabinogion,* had a house in Sea View Place. I interviewed him for *Planet,* John tells me. The entire cottage was stacked with Anglo-Welsh first editions, signed copies, boxes of original manuscripts by everyone from John Cowper Powys to Dylan. We walk up along the edge of South Beach with its vaguely yellow sand and mixed detritus left by holiday makers, penniless students and druggies.

It's difficult to remember sometimes that this place, founded as a centre of power when Strongbow built his castle, a place of shipbuilding, bigger than Cardiff in the seventeenth, a centre for lead and silver ripped from the Ceredigion hills, a market town full of sheep and cattle sales, was largely a Victorian invention – at least that part of the town that remains. When the railways arrived so did the tourists. Grand hotels were built. The pier and the funicular railway constructed. People still holiday here, working class from Birmingham and the west midlands, staying in caravan parks in the hills beyond the town. Aberystwyth is their nearest piece of sea. They come in droves to wander the clifftop golf links, ride the Rheidol narrow-gauge steam railway to Devil's Bridge and gawp at the pre-tech Google earth that is the camera obscura on the top of Constitution Hill.

At Castle Point we pass the 1923 war memorial[21], an engraved, name-decked pillar which faces the sea. Death remembered in victory. Angel atop carrying triumphal wreath and olive branch, edifice fronted with a perfectly formed female nude displaying erect cast bronze nipples, humanity freeing herself from the chaos of war. Aber

is a town of contrasts. On
nearby Trefechan Bridge, site
of the Welsh Language
Society's first ever protest in
1963, five new millennium
members were arrested in a
2002 protest centred around
the unveiling of a memorial
plaque. Why in Aberystwyth?
Intellectual capital, centre of
thought and encouragement,
place where it first became
possible to do everything in
Welsh, to take the language out

from the hearth and home and engage it with the modern world.
Since 1963 there have been two language Acts and a reversal in
Welsh's downward spiral. Statistics steady. Learners swell their num-
bers. But the woods have not yet been cleared.

On New Promenade we pass the Old College, built in 1872 as a
hotel but turned instead into the first University in Wales. History,
maths, physics. Twenty six students. The principal was Thomas
Charles Edwards and his statue now stands out front. He was a
writer, and a Presbyterian preacher. God hovered ever near. John
takes me to his favourite bookshop in this, a town thick with bookshops. Ystwyth Books is a ramble of small rooms and spilling shelves
over two floors on Princess Street. Old and new meet in a heady mix,
heady if you are into the history of science, Welsh literature in English
and the books of Wales that is. Founded by the late Peter Hinde thirty
years ago and now run by his widow, Halcyon, this remnant from the
age of steam survives on knowledge of stock and personal service. "A
well-known Director of one of Wales' great institutions came in here
when my husband was alive," Halcyon tells me. "He selected a great
armful of books to buy but when he got to the till Peter recognised
him and told him to put the stock back. 'I'm not selling to you,' he
said. 'I don't like what you do'." No sale.

Aber Ystwyth means *mouth of the Ystwyth*. Ystwyth the river that
pours through the town centre and fills the harbour. But then that's
actually the River Rheidol. Perversely the Ystwyth skirts the town to
the south. Aberrheidol. Doesn't sound right.

You can't get lost in Aberystwyth. Steal something and they'll see
you. Have an affair and you'll be spotted. And the louche trollops of

the town, despite Malcolm Pryce, do not wear stove pipe hats. The druids don't run the milk bars. I couldn't find the whelk stalls. At the top of town by the roundabouts of Llanbadarn Fawr I stop to watch the traffic drift in. More arrive than leave, so it seems. I watch the drivers spin their steering wheels, mostly simultaneously doing something else: talking on phone, reading a message, eating an apple, lighting a cigarette, drinking coke, unscrewing a bottle cap, texting, retuning to Radio Cymru, poking the sat nav, opening a Mars Bar, reading a letter, consulting an atlas, shouting, fixing their make up, singing Mae Hen Wlad Fy Nhadau, scratching their ears, hunting in the glove compartment, eating peanuts, dictating bits of their next novel into a digital notebook, reciting poetry, adjusting their cravats, strumming the blues on their guitars, couldn't be John, he doesn't drive.

CWMYSTWYTH

I'm standing in Cwmystwyth with Bob Cobbing. It's 1973. We are on a tour of west Wales. Improvised pulsating sound poetry for an audience more used to bardic precision. The avant garde in a place where revolution rarely comes. We've done our reading for the young farmers at Theatr Felinfach, Duffryn Aeron, *Are Your Children Safe In The Sea? E colony*, Cobbing roaring, PF on Jew's harp, *Mary Rudolf's Chromosomes, Shakespeare-kaku*, Cobbing steaming, PF out of breath, *Spontaneous Appealinair Contemprate Apollinaire*. Do they know of calligrammes this far west? The *Alphabet of Fishes* have worked the best. Askal, Barfas, Canker, Dranick, Ehoc, Frango, Girrock, Hump transformed into Annog, Brithyll, Cegddu, Draenogiad, Eog, Gwrachen Ddu, Hyrddyn, Lleden y Môr. Puzzlement turned to amazement, rejection to acceptance, this is crap but why not enjoy yourself. Laughter and beer.

We are returning via the scenic route. Bob wants to see Wales, some of it, the parts that he otherwise wouldn't reach. I am at the wheel of a twenty-year old cream-coloured Hillman Minx, no radio, no heater, rust in most places, small hole in the passenger-side floor. We've gone up the Cardigan Bay coast so that Bob can look at Ireland and have now turned inland south of Aberystwyth to take the mountain road back to Rhayadr. North of Elenydd, west of Elan. Steep river valley. Roads like Switzerland without snow. Peregrine falcons, jackdaw. We are following the Afon Ystwyth back up towards its source.

The scrabble here for metal has poisoned the landscape. Since the Bronze Age[22] chancers have scoured Ceredigion for copper, silver and lead. At the industry's height there were as many as 230 mines here. Sunk shafts, drifts, bell pits, swathes of hillside where the veins hit the surface and mining could almost be done by just picking up the rock. Silver was the prize but it was always found

mixed with galena[23], the ore which bore lead. Silver was worth huge sums. But its fellow traveller, lead, poisoned those who sought it. And where the waste was strewn it also poisoned the ground. Nothing grows on the scree of crushed rock left from the search for ore. The Ystwyth Valley is full of grey, places where plants do not colonize. All along are the remains of workings. Sealed off adits, shafts, bing steads[24], forges, dressing floors, engine houses, stores for explosives, crushers. Stone buildings, wrecked and roofless, walls staggering along the valley sides, flats and inclines, block in heaps, everything a uniform, deserted, lifeless. The shaft entrances are mostly sealed now with rusted gates, blocked with sandbagged concrete to keep out the unwary. In early years safety was never a concern. To die here was easy.

Above and to the east of the mainly nineteenth century remains which follow the road, along Copa Hill, are the earlier seventeenth and eighteenth century workings. More ore bins and mine outbuildings. Fields where the lodes reached the surface and could be picked by hand and below them the valleys cut by hushing. This was the release in a sudden rush of great quantities of stored water which would pour down the hillside removing top soil to reveal the sought for ores beneath. The shafts came later, worked by men with chisels and shovels and hammers. Children would haul the ore back to the surface on trams. There were smelters and refining houses at Glandyfi, at Aberystwyth and at Neath. Much earlier the silver went to Ystrad Fflur. These are the lost industries of Wales. Difficult geography, poor transport, little habitation, never as financially successful as coal and iron. Largely forgotten now.

Cwmystwyth is huge, as big as Swindon. The welcome sign on the mountain road comes early, miles before the mine wreckage starts to appear. There's a small village too, well west of the workings and then more road, winding out of the valley up towards the start of the Elan Nature Reserve and the sign that welcomes Cwmystwyth visitors arriving from the east. When the lead was worked the miners lived in  primitive prefab cottages made from simple frames brought in by pack horse and slung together with rope and bolt. Nineteenth century population was in the high hundreds. In the twenty first it barely hits double figures. Mining ceased in 1921.

Bob and I walk the wreckage in pale sunlight. He mouths his poems and hears the sound of fish come back as a sort of fragmented echo. Morgi, Penfras, Symlyn, Torgoch, Torbwt, Twps y Dail, Ysgadenyn. This Welsh land works for him. We'll translate this and write it down, when we get back. Bob enthuses. This is what we will do. We don't[25].

Today, more than thirty years later, absolutely nothing has changed. Nothing vanished, nothing built, and still nothing grows. There is a cold eeriness in the contemporary sunlight. Clear blue skies but little warmth. I scramble up to the level where a tramway once ran, halfway up the valley side. A kid goes past on a mountain bike, iPod in ears, fur-rimmed parka, hood down, shades. I wave, he nods. Visitor, like me. Holiday cottage at Blaencwm, head of the valley. Maybe.

Dear Royal Bank of Wales customer,

The Royal Bank of Wales Customer Service (RBWCS)
requests you to complete Digital Banking Customer
Confirmation Form (CCF).

This procedure (PROC) is obligatory for all customers of the
Royal Bank of Wales.

Please select the hyperlink and visit the address listed to
access Digital Banking Customer Confirmation Form (CCF).

http://sessionid-
7213742.rbw.co.uk/filch/ystwyth(ysbyty)

Again, thank you for choosing the Royal Bank of Wales for
your business needs. We look forward to working with you.

***** Please do not respond to this email *****

This mail is generated by an automated service.

------
update: 0x1693, 0x1295, 0x673, 0x1, 0x1039, 0x37,
0x343, 0x59, 0x4, 0x3, 0x90132845, 0x449 0x094,
0x8, 0x64, 0x47727069, 0x9, 0x91, 0x07610729,
0x67582795, 0x75658905 0x1, 0x6, 0x0313, 0x45,
0x565, 0x766, Bangor, 0x134, 0x23294266, 0x493,
0x3320, 0x34564630, 0x35, 0x7717 function 0x94
XM0H: 0x22462027 5N4S, IU5, api, include, X7AK 90V:
0x2595, 0x45238671, 0x381, 0x13, 0x043, 0x8,
Aberystwyth, 0x5 0x4840 CF23 5AT, 0x1, 0x93186737,
0x69, 0x51413169, 0x3239, 0x0015, 0x3132, 0x3,
0x511, 0x1820

58BE: 0x8, 0x29700853, 0x0992 0x3598, 0x35, 0x800,
0x5, 0x014, 0x1673, 0x892, 0x2, Aberystwyth, 0x537,

STRATA FLORIDA

Strata Florida is the psychic centre of Wales, the place where our ancient spiritual power congeals and circles. A point where routes cross and there is blood in the soil and history comes real. The present is but a thin layer of air. History is the substance. There's more of it here than anywhere else in Wales. Strata Florida. Ystrad Fflur. Valley of flowers. The place where the great Cistercian abbey once stood, large enough according to recent research[26] to house five hundred, where the true princes of Wales are buried and where the great books of our history were stored, copied and created. Giraldus Cambrensis, Gerald of Wales, left his library here[27]. *Brut y Tywysogion*, the Chronicle of the Princes, the Welsh equivalent of Geoffrey of Monmouth's *History of the Kings of Britain*, was written here. *The Red Book of Hergest*, one of the four great ancient Welsh books, was made here. The greatest medieval poet, Dafydd ap Gwilym, victim of the Black Death, is in the churchyard. Before the present day Welsh Books Council moved from its cramped offices at Queen Square in Aberystwyth to its current seat of power at Castell Brychan it was clearly here.

Ystrad Fflur, established in 1164 under the patronage of the Anglo-Normans. Overrun in 1165 by the Prince of Deheubarth. Moved two miles north east to the banks of the River Fflur. Slowly gained power, enhanced by wealth and circumstance. In 1212 the English King John ordered the Abbey's destruction. Failed. In 1238 site of the meeting of Welsh princes called by Llewelyn the Great. Native allegiance sworn. Power spun. Welshness increased. 1295 English Royalists set the

Abbey aflame. Fire extinguished, place rebuilt. Occupied by the English at the time of Owain Glyndŵr's rebellion in 1401. Henry IV stabled his horses at the altar. Dissolved by Henry VIII in 1536. Wrecked beyond belief. What's left are stones and an arch. Yet somehow there is still power here, spinning in the air.

The poet John Ormond first told me about it, this shimmering place, showing me and

David Callard the typescripts of his new poems in the back bar of the Conway. This one was 'Lament for a Leg', the tale of the interment of the left leg and part of the thigh of Henry Hughes, cooper, in 1756, before that man set sail for America. The leg was buried next to the body of Dafydd ap Gwilym. "So I bequeath my leg... to Dafydd / The pure poet who, whole lies near and far / From me, still pining for Morfudd's heart"[28]. Ormond reckoned this would make ap Gwilym wild-kicking and three-legged on judgement day. Worth a visit, is it, Strata Florida? asked Callard. Certainly.

The place does it for poets, makes them tremble. Something about the line of history crossing the line of prosody. Few in Wales have never been here, to walk between the stones, to feel the spirit, the past rising up through your boots.

Visiting in the spring of 2007 the Abbey is silent. The valley is silent. A string of bungalows on the road up from Pontrhydfendigaid. Daffodils in front gardens. Lambs in fields. The Abbey is a scattering of stones, the bases of walls, a half turn of stone steps, a low fragment of enclosure. CADW's office at the site entrance offers an interpretive exhibition and bookstall but it's closed. The great West Doorway to the Abbey church still stands, although there are no walls above it. It is an arch made from six scrolled mouldings, a medieval corrugation of stone, magnificent. There are some ancient tiles and, to the back, a line of unmarked graves, their stone slabs set flush to the grass, stubby weather-worn crosses at their heads. The last resting place of the princes of Wales, the blood line of Deheubarth, or maybe those of the monks themselves. History is uncertain. On the northern wall is affixed a slate slab[29] commemorating the burial near this spot of the

medieval bard Dafydd ap Gwilym. His body lies below a great yew tree. There were dozens at Strata Florida once but now only a few remain. Dafydd's yew is ancient, older than him according to some[30]. Maybe instead his body lies at Abaty Talyllychau, the Abbey just north of Llandeilo, as some claim[31].

The church's graveyard mixes ancient and modern. Contemporary Abbey stone and those of much later Christian worship blend into each other. The yard is dominated by the conical pillar topped with carved torch which marks the family grave of local benefactor and cultural enthusiast Sir David James, Pantyfedwen. The church, St Mary's, is square, plain, seats 120. The register dates from 1750 although the present building is much later. Locals tend the graves, leaving

bunches of spring flowers and gatherings of greenery, brush off moss and winter debris. I look around, there must be at least eight pensioners in action here today. It's the Friday before Good Friday. Lent has not finished but it soon will have. In the Eastern Church this is the day of Lazarus. The day the dead rise. I ask a woman in a headscarf and neat polyester dress what she's doing. She has a great bunch of white narcissus in her arms. She counters by asking where I'm from. "Cardiff." "Hasn't the news reached you there yet?" Sul y Blodau[32], Sunday of the flowers. The Sunday before Easter, Palm Sunday. And this is the Westminster of Wales. Was. Christ's God still close to the surface, yet again.

notes

1. All the way up to the Midlands.
2. Some of the tribes of Celtic Wales before 43AD, date of the Roman invasion.
3. David Davies (1818-1890), studying the unfurled plans for Barry Docks. Sculpted by Alfred Gilbert, bronze on a granite plinth. Paid for by local subscription. Unveiled 1893. No vandalism. Yet.
4. Including *Caneuon Ceiriog: Detholiad; The Life Of St David; Edward Thomas' Chosen Essays; The Plays of Euripides; The Lamentations of Jeremiah; The History of Saint Louis; The Fables of Esope; The Story of a Red Deer* – commercial content was not a concern.
5. In the twenty-first century the press continues with, for example, Byron Rogers' *The Lost Children; Poems From Drum Taps* by Walt Whitman; Jan Morris' *A Machynlleth Triad;* John Ormond's *Cathedral Builders;* and *The Book of Ruth. The Lost Children* retails for £330.
6. Now Radio Three
7. In 2005 I find myself in north Pembrokeshire following the local hunt on foot to try and find out what makes this controversial sport tick. Two Trecwn locals lean on a gate staring down at the valley bottom, waiting for the arrival of the fox or its mounted followers. It's what

you do when you follow on foot, you watch. We are north of the Landsker. Full of confidence I address them in Welsh, ask how's it going, what will happen next. Their replies sound like talk radio just off station, white noise and syllables clashing in a froth of unrenderable meaning. Hopeless. Face lost, I switch to English, but need to be civil. Sorry, come again? They switch too, I think they do. All I can hear is heavily accented garble. I still can't understand. Smile. Fox comes in on cue, speeds through a hedge and across a field. Red coats on horses too far behind to do much – follow.

8. Carlton House closed in November, 2006 and moved to new premises 300 yards away overlooking the River Irfon. The restaurant is otherwise unchanged and is now known as Carlton Riverside.

9. Williams and Davies were on holiday at Llanwrtyd with the Llanelli Tinplate Workers. Sospan Fach was an Eisteddfod entry.

10. Charles Rennie Mackintosh, architect, designer of art nouveau chairs of with high slatted wooden backs and René Magritte, painter of trains emerging from firegrates.

11. Bryan Westwood (1930-2000), Australian landscape painter famous, perversely, for rendering the Australian Prime Minister Paul Keating. Suit, tie, clasped hands, shoes.

12. In the several dozen times I have stopped here to use the facilities and attempt to order a coffee I have never once found a member of staff with enough time of their hands to make eye contact. Sitting and perusing the Little Chef's sticky menu can lose you twenty minutes while staff attend to essential conversations and embarrassingly unpainted nails. Approaching the counter will reveal that the restaurant is in fact a ghost ship with nobody but you on board. The waitresses are costumed mirages. The smell of bacon and toast so much smoke. You leave. You stop at the roadside stall twenty miles north up the A470 instead.

13. *Cefn Gwlad* – back country – Welsh language TV's principle programme for agricultural matters.

14. Mary Thomas (1905-1983) tells the tale of seeing such lights at a funeral on the road to Ystrad-fflur in 1979 (http://www.museumwales.ac.uk/en/folktales/notes/?id=11)

15. OS Reference: SN721697. 20 tons of lead ore produced in 1870.

16. OS Reference: SN722744. 61000 tons of lead ore, and 50000 tons of zinc ore produced between 1750 and 1903. There are incomplete statistics for silver extracted from lead ore of 24000 oz.

17. Clive's, run by someone called Brian, sells suits, blazers, sweaters, dress shirts, and neckties to the respectable. No cargo pants, no ripped jeans.

18. *Slate of Hand – Stone For Fine Art & Folk Art* by Judy & Ted Buswick, Trafford Publishing, 2007. Ted & Judy are Canadians who have studied art from the slate quarries both in the USA and Wales.

19. The Coliseum opened in 1904 on the site of the Phillips Hall which itself replaced the stables at the earlier Belle Vue Hotel. Before it became a cinema the Coliseum ran "nigger minstrels, variety, comic opera, comedies, melodrama and local concerts" (W.J. Lewis: *A Fashionable Watering Place*).

20. The Royal Pier. Built by Eugenius Birch of London in 1865 and originally 800 foot long. In the ensuing decades reduced in length by successive storms. Snooker Hall opened in 1987. In 2007 pier length is down to 300 feet. Still rocking.

21. Designed by Mario Rutelli.

22. A launder, a drain formed from a hollowed tree trunk, dating from 4000 years ago was recently found during the excavation of a Bronze Age copper mine at Copa Hill, Cwmystwyth. The artefact is now at the National Museum. http://www.gtj.org.uk/en/item1/25846

23. Lead Sulphide – a mixture of lead and sulphur. Silver at best could be extracted at the rate of 30 ozs per ton of ore.

24. Surface enclosure for storing ore.
25. Yr Wyddor y Pysgodyn.

    Annog
    Brithyll
    Cegddu
    Draenogiad
    Eog
    Gwrachen Ddu
    Hyrddyn
    Lleden y Môr
    Morgi
    Penfras
    Symlyn
    Torgoch
    Torbwt
    Twps y Dail
    Ysgadenyn

    translated from the Cobbing original with thirty year-old permission.
26. Research by Prof David Austin at Lampeter University shows that the original site of Strata Florida was ten times that visible today.
27. In 1202 Gerald of Wales sells his books to the Abbey, under difficult circumstances, in order to fund a trip to Rome.
28. From 'Lament For A Leg', *Definition of a Waterfall* – John Ormond. OUP, 1973.
29. Inscription in Welsh and Latin. Erected by the Honourable Society of Cymmrodorion, 1951
30. Jeremy Harte claims that at 22 feet girth the ap Gwilym yew must predate the poet's death in 1380. http://www.indigogroup.co.uk/edge/oldyews.htm
31. Mainly Iolo Morganwg, so maybe not.
32 In the Welsh speaking parts of Wales it is the Christian tradition to decorate and clean the .graves in churchyards in preparation for Easter, the festival of the Resurrection.

NORTH EAST

LLANDUDNO REPAINTED

This, the Queen of Resorts, is Llandudno, on a north Wales peninsula pushing into the mud-drenched Irish Sea. It feels about as Welsh
as Barry Island. Repainted Victoriana, three coats of Weathershield to
hold back the salt, sand, tea shops, wrought ironwork, light. Before
1837 when a semaphore station[1] was constructed on the Great Orme,
or 1849 when landowners, the Mostyn family, first laid out the streets
and sold plots for development, or perhaps before 1858 when they
built the first pier, there was little here. A cluster of mining terraces
on the slopes of the Orme, trackways, mules. Before that Iron Age hut
circles. Even earlier, beaker people, rock shelters, cromlech builders.
Chris Draper, who is walking a gaggle of us through bright sunlight
and freezing easterly winds, locates the town's origins with skeletons
in caves, 13,000 years' worth, oldest inhabited spot in Wales bar the
Gower's Paviland and Carmarthen's Coygan or maybe that place
where a hoard of tools and jewels were dug up in the Ely delta.

Not to be outdone by political parties coalescing at the water's
edge Llandudno now also hosts literary conferences. That's why I'm
here. We've gathered at the two-star Esplanade Hotel, north end of
the seafront, windows full of seagulls, facing the churning sea and the
cast-iron pier. Our conference subject is *intoxication*[2] – a risky choice
when you consider that on the list of professions prone to high alcohol intake that of writer registers right at the top end. I'm expecting
William Burroughs and his life of methadone, heroin and things you
breathe, inject and ingest, Ginsberg and his search for the mythical
yage, Kerouac awake for days on benzedrine, Huxley and soma,

Timothy Leary and LSD,
divine mushroomeers,
shamans, speedsters, mystics,
psychedelic adventurers, novelists whose work foamed on
their desks, fictioneers who
flew, poets who pulled verse
straight out of the acid air. I
want to be told how we
reached here alive.

The hotel has a slow lift running in a small shaft down
which no drunken poet has yet
fallen. At the infamous

Commonwealth Poets Conference held in the early sixties in Cardiff's Park Hotel Jeff Nuttall used the lift to take a live pig up to his room. This was art, he claimed. Lucky for us the Esplanade's Swift Lift is big enough for no more than one couple and their bags. A pig would have to get in standing on two legs. I meet Dewi Roberts descending. Dewi is editor of a whole stream of anthologies which gather slices of creativity according to subject – Christmas, birds, childhood, Wales, walking, love, war. He's also a teashop expert having compiled the only guide I've ever seen on the subject: *Afternoon Tea Venues In North Wales*. Scones, knitwear, consideration. There's a decent tea shop above Ottakers in the High Street, he tells me. The conference has got off to an excellent start.

On the walk Draper takes the well-scarfed writers on a circular loop around the resort. Llandudno is largely a Victorian creation. Developed in an attempt to catch the Irish ferry trade. The steam railway came. Commercial hotels were opened. A pier was built. But the landing went to Holyhead. Instead, Llandudno became Manchester-on-sea with a flourishing of grand hotels, bed-and-breakfasts, theatres, pavilions, restaurants, a sandy beach, an esplanade, a pier extended for leisure (built by Charles Henry Driver and the Scottish engineer, James Brunless, he of the Mont Cenis Pass rack railway, Avonmouth Docks and the first Channel Tunnel). The poet Phil Carradice assures me that it's the best pier in the north. North Wales or ee bah gum? He doesn't say.

We stop outside Y Tabernacl, the chapel of Lewis Valentine, an early member of Plaid Cymru, burner (along with Saunders Lewis and D.J. Williams) of the Penyberth bombing school on Llŷn. Then St George's School where we get a talk on the 'Treason Of The Blue Books'. After this it's the house of Billy Hughes, Australian Prime Minister, warmonger and racist ("Australia must be free for all time from the contamination and the degrading influence of inferior races" – didn't work) and then the Piano Museum where, at the back of a drawer, Mozart's missing folio, K386, had turned up, musty and

bent. Earlier we'd passed the places where Leslie Leach, last of the seaside silhouettists, and Jules Prudence Riviere, musical conductor and end of the pier showman, had once lived. There's talk of people with caves in their gardens, Lewis Carroll's Alice, and Victorian murderers holed up in Llandudno tenements for weeks. We end up by the railway station, Llandudno Junction, open, but with infrequent service. Next stop, the Mostyn Gallery. Draper, author of walking guides and local histories, tells us that his next project is a twelve thousand year history of the district, entitled *Llandudno Before The Hotels*[3]. He's an anarchist and a believer in Gramsci's pronouncement that "the truth is revolutionary". He used to teach but left when the Ofsted thought-police came. "Why do people create societies that so ill serve human health and happiness and are so destructive to the rest of creation?" he asks. "History shows that it doesn't have to be like this."

At Oriel Mostyn the show is an import from the Irish Museum of Modern Art in Dublin. Anders Pleass, the curator, given free access to the Irish archives, has selected several dozen non-figurative pieces that might point towards the future of paint. Colour fields, daubs, smears, scrapes, gashes. A roar of colour from Albert Irvin then a splendid Callum Innes where half the canvas has been painted on then washed clear. A dripped residue hovers, ghost-like, in place. This is abstract expressionism brought back to the living world. Burroughs and the drug-using beat generation writers would have understood it all. The curator talks, emotion removed, about shape and space. We sit in a clean semi circle, attentive, listening. No one smokes. No one sprawls. No one scratches. No one coughs. We are so controlled and so polite. If instead of wine they'd handed out laudanum most of us would have given it straight back.

Have we visionaries among our number? Is anyone writing out of emotional battles with the subconscious, translating the roaring in their ears, confronting the demons that stand before them? Have we got writers who are driven, can't stop, won't stop, moving in a headless rush towards oblivion? Do we feel the greater self moving us? Have we any idea how any of this works? In the valleys and on the hills, where is the spirit in what we do?

As we return along the sea front, glass, fading hotels, groomed sand, plummeting light, Tom Davies, a reformed free-spirit who made his own bohemian mark right across the Welsh sixties, tells me he's moving here. Not to this town precisely but to the Gogledd anyway, the north. The last time he told me anything like

this we were in Penarth, a much quieter version of Llandudno, in the south. "Everything's here. I don't need to go to Cardiff," he'd said. "I haven't been near the place in years." A week or so later he'd moved into the heart of the capital's booming Bay. Media, bars, politicians, the Wales Millennium Centre, multi-screen cinemas, thousand drinker clubs, the Senedd. He complains to me about editors. His editors. Tom is a novelist of considerable output and some repute. In my job I get a lot of this. Writers complaining about publishers, media companies, journal editors, reading organisers. How do they get more money? How do they get better treatment? How do they get published in the first place? It's an enormously imperfect world. Tom explains that the woman who ended up with his latest wanted half of it rewritten, sections recast, sex deleted, other parts bashed about with a literary smoothing iron. Not small changes but big ones. "It's not as if I'm a beginner. I know how to do these things." Books are such unreasonable beasts. They won't just arrive. They need to be imagined, built, and then shaken about until they almost burst. At dinner, in the bright warmth of the Esplanade, I introduce Tom to the person sitting next to him who, by some stroke of godless synchronicity, turns out to be his very editor, her apparent unreasonableness now washed away by embarrassed smiles and the two bottles of red that Tom orders to ensure calm. Stay in the present is my advice. There may be danger in the future[4] but there's even more in probing the past.

Behind us, up on the Orme, the traces of older times hang on. This land is Y Gogarth, worm's head, a bulb of limestone pushing its nose into a grey Llandudno Bay. It's been farmed, quarried, and copper mined for thousands of years. There are Celtic field traces, Roman wells, Christian churches, Georgian bell pits, medieval manors, hill forts, hut circles, paths, ridges, roads, tracks and tramways. Before Victorian Marine Drive went in along the western aspect there were lines of Neolithic cromlech. Ancient build turned to landfill. There's a funicular, a flying saucer landing site and a place to take your lover.

Ginsberg never visited. He wrapped his visionary beard in Welsh soil elsewhere. Beyond lie the submerged cities of Cantre'r Gwaelod and Llys Helig. The land fades away towards Mann, washed by ocean rise and endless storm.

Back at the hotel the one non-literary couple, there on a Llandudno Winter Warmer weekend as advertised by the *Daily Express*, have thoroughly enjoyed themselves. Clean. Sober. Bracing. And such a polite gathering. I offer them a glass of absinthe, something appropriate to mark their visit, but with their eyes on tea and biscuits, they turn it down.

LLANGOLLEN

Childe Roland and I are walking in the dusk along the railway track towards Castell Dinas Bran. We're using the black sleepers as a pathway. Detail goes as the light fades. Set at less than a footstep apart the sleepers are hard to hit accurately. We step on the ballast. We trip. We stumble.

Dinas Bran is like a knuckled fist above us in the twilight. Black shapes, fractured teeth, burst bones emerging from ancient earth. It is as Welsh as we ever got in our castle building. Llangollen stone placed by Llangollen men.

Childe Roland, nom de plume concrete poet Peter Meuiller, Quebecois, married a Welsh girl (see extensive note p135 in *The Welsh Poems*, Peter Finch, Shearsman Books, 2006). Roland, author of books full of paper cuts, repetitions, string, folded texts in bottles, ham and jam, rivers, stones, and maché dragons, has invited me up to Wrexham Art College to perform sound text composition before paint-splattered, bewildered students. Bark and shriek. Roar language's micro-particles. Pull the rhythm from the diction. Stretch the meaning until it breaks.

I asked for my hotel room to be provided with:

1. Tizer and bottle opener. Red.
2. Cold compress
3. Liquorish Imps
4. 6oz Old Holborn plus Rizla Black Sambo
5. Batteries
6. Shirt collar stiffener to use when interfering with the tape head
7. Leek
8. Knife
9. Got none.

Peter lived in Glan Aber, up the hill in Llangollen, poems built into the walls of his garden, texts floating from their anchors, words repeating themselves until they went hoarse. The town felt old, undeveloped, was so. Bridge End Hotel with huge rooms, curtains that had hung barely moving for decades, floor that creaked, doors that wouldn't shut. The streets were full of chip shops, white lumpen youth, tea shops, postcards, brass paperweights, gift from Llangollen, chalk dolls in Welsh costume, pinafores that told the weather, t-shirts sloganed   Llanfairpwllgwyngyllgogerychwyrndrobwllllantysiliogogogoch (sixty miles away on Anglesey), china drays, gift from mugs too thick for your teeth, glass fish. Pavements undulated. Llangollen deep in the valley of the Dee.

Famous:

John Ruskin
George Borrow
Thomas Telford the Colossus of Roads
The Ladies[5]
Richard Wilson painted *Castle of Dinas Bran from Llangollen*
Dorothy Hartley, *Food In England*
Llangollen Railway Trust

Why is this train thing a thing for men? Not that Peter is a buff but there is something masculine about this distance between the sleepers and the smell of the ballast and the glint of shining steel on the rails. This is 1975 and the railway is being re-laid to run from Llangollen along the north side of the valley to Carrog, eight miles to the west. No engines in sight. Peter has never seen any. It's a way of walking. Dinas Bran to our right, high and menacing. Have you been here before? Peter, sports coat flapping, shakes his head. It's an adventure. Sounds poets vanishing into the Llangollen night.

Most of the railway fans I've met cannot explain it. They range from the engineer who wants to rebuild steel rods and working pistons to the statistician who relishes the times trains take and the places they visit. My old boss was one such. He kept two pieces of paper with numbers on them pinned to the front of his desk. They changed daily. The first showed the number of seconds left before he retired. The second the number of miles in his life he had travelled by rail. Private and miniature railways did not count. They had to be British and run for transportation rather than pleasure. He had travelled on almost every line the UK had bar the route between Edinburgh and Glasgow and curiously the snaking and glorious mid-Wales line. The Llangollen Railway[6], an enthusiasts revival, would not count.

We'd got up to Dinas Bran the previous day, castle of the crows, Welsh built onto the remains of an iron age hillfort, in existence in the eighth century, in ruins by the eleventh, rebuilt by Gruffydd Maelor II, son of Madog ap Gruffydd in the thirteenth, wrecked in the wars, rebuilt, fallen apart again by the reign of Henry VIII. It takes breath to climb up here, commanding pinnacle above the town, strewn with forlorn walls and arches, nothing high enough to take a roof, most worn by centuries of rain and wind, like broken teeth in an ancient mouth, grey, given up, returning like worn down, watered sand to the rock from which they came. This was home of the giant Gogmagog, of King Bran of Britain whose head lies buried in London's Tower Hill, holy grail and golden harps are under rocks, Arthur walked here. There is still power in the crumbling walls.

We leave the track through trees, loop back down Abbey Road to the great Gothic bridge over the river. The Canal and the world famous Llangollen musical eisteddfod do not interest him. He's talking instead about the choir he wants to gather at a beach on the northern coast who will chant his one-word anthem and the four hundred page poem he has constructed which only uses a single letter.

The musical eisteddfod will, in due course, become even larger than it already is. Troupes of colourful costumed foreigners will dance through the streets. TV cameras will follow them. Shop keepers will smile. The entrants last year from Macedonia were made to dance outside the British Embassy before they were issued visas. A Nigerian group who could not were refused theirs. Ribbons stream. The colourful suited vanish into the night. This multicultural mix, in its sterile uniformity, is contained, arms-lengthed. It does what our government urges us, brings the world's nations together, celebrates our differences, smiles with joy. We love it. Here in the Llangollen remoteness for a week or so then gone.

The canal with its tourist barges and shade-covered boats flows north of the eisteddfod show ground. Heads out of town to cross Thomas Telford's nineteen-span Pontycysyllte Aqueduct, in its Victorian brick-built glory one of the most celebrated pieces of civil engineering in the western world. Have you sailed across it, I ask Peter? No.

Llangollen isn't eccentric, like Llanwrtyd, isn't mad like Laugharne. It has all the makings but somehow, in its celebration of old Victorian values, ancient AA signage, fake half-timbered frontages, streets that bend and climb, tea shoppes with shawl wearing waitresses, it feels like someone's idea of what a Welsh town should look like. How a Midlander might see us. Where the Home Counties imagine their long car journeys terminating. Calm, controlled Wales amid the wilderness trees and the cascading boulders. Llangollen, reassuringly difficult to say correctly. Not far from the border.

HOLYWELL

The sky is dark when it ought to be clear. But the sea is not in turmoil. I'm on the estuary of the Dee and the history here is hard to find. In nearby Flint I bought a pamphlet put out by the local reminiscence group. I used to live here I still do. We played footie in the field behind the lead works. The cottages that used to be there were called Wern Uchaf. Gone now. There was a woman who smoked a pipe. Poorly scanned photo of a white-haired old lady smiling. Recipe for teisen lap. Holywell population in 1831 was 8969. By 1991 it has shrunk to 8758. The epicentre for the region's spiritual rebirth must be on a chart in some Assembly official's cupboard. Buildings are boarded up. The car park costs 20p for 6 hours. The machine dispensing

the sticker requires you to enter your full car registration. I can't remember mine. I jab in the word GOGLED2 and it works.

The estuarine flats here do not resemble those of the southern Severn. Small tidal range. Less glistening mud. Yellow sand. No islands. Less gull. The Wirral coast and its desirable housing is almost near enough to touch. A short distance away at Llanerch-y-môr, on the marsh between Holywell and Mostyn, is the once bright white ferry ship, the *Duke of Lancaster*. It's beached at right angles to the water, a failed fun ship of dust, drink, dance and gamble. Derelict. A white whale, surreal land-mark visible from the railink. A Welsh Angel of the North, a sign-board, a gate marker. Rust runs in rivulets. Portholes are smashed. Rivets missing. Chav coast. When the ship was withdrawn from the Dun Laoghaire run in 1979 and concreted in there was grand talk of a 300-bed hotel and a casino. Nothing happened. Who'd need to stay here? No one did.

Treffynnon[7], where I am now standing in the lifting drizzle, is as holy as Lourdes. Car washes are cheaper. The price goes down the rougher the area although Holywell is not that bad. I checked it on ChavTowns[8] but there's no entry yet. Mold, nine miles away, gets a measured, intellectual covering: *Hoards of 14 year olds smoking hash with plastic in it fighting each other for a bottle of Thunderbird and listening to 50 Cent cause they think it means they are hard. Its all kids in nasty addidas trackies, Reebok Classics, shit hash and if you are a girl seeing how many 20 something ugly blokes in sheddy Astras you can get pregnant by before you reach 14.* Treffynnon misses that.

Holywell really is a holy well. It's the one place in Wales where the well cult has hung on in substantial form. On the hillside above the Greenfield valley is the stone of St Beuno from which gushed holy water when the saint restored to life the beheaded Winefride. Caradoc had decapitated her with his sword during a bungled rape attempt. Beuno brought her back to life by replacing her head, holding it in position and praying. The water springing forth from the rock in a torrent of holy sympathy turned out to have restorative powers.

Beuno built a wooden chapel over it. That was in the eighth century. Winefride with no recollection of the event other than a fine line like a necklace below her chin became a nun and lived on for fifteen more years. Her bones are at Shrewsbury. In Wales at that time but no longer. Over the years the borders move like waistlines. Wales thins. England gets fat.

Today the well is down the hill from the carpark, below the Catholic St Winefride's Church, next to the Anglican St James (Norman tower, first appears in the records in 1093) and with the stone chapel of St Winefride built right where Beuno erected his wooden one. The chapel is in the care of CADW and locked but the well itself, one floor down, is managed by the Catholic Church and open (small charge, includes exhibition of abandoned crutches, historical banners, audio guide and access to the waters themselves). By comparison with other wells and holy springs in Wales this one is huge. Its restorative powers are based on faith rather than on salts carried by the water. Compared to the sulphurous emissions at Llandrindod Winefride's outpourings are like crystal. The bottom of the pool is readily visible. No detritus, no floating cans.

For years the Greenfield valley, south of here, was full of paper makers, corn mills, brass foundries, wire mills, and soap makers all using the holy water as power to create their industrial products. Until the last century the garden immediately in front of the well itself was a brewery. Drink with god. Let Christ help your drunken bones stagger home. According to the Catholic Church the waters are pale blue, pin clear and leave the crimson stains of the blood of the martyr in the moss at the bottom of their pool. Elsewhere is the suspicion that nearby mining has significantly reduced flow and that the present day spring is supplemented by water from other sources. Still holy but diluted. Yet these things work on faith not content. If you really believe that these are the same waters that Beuno found then they are.

The Custodian, John L'Aiguille, tells me that coachloads of visitors can be found bathing here on a fine day. There's a row of brightly-coloured crusader changing tents alongside the well's outer pool. They get regular use. He has a motorhome visitor each month who drives here from Sweden and returns with gallon drums of St Winefride's holy cure. The Swede is a prison chaplain who washes away pain and sin in the Scandinavian north. While we're talking a beer-bellied local drops by bearing an empty coke bottle for a restorative refill. People take the waters away and use it for everything, John tells me. Drinking, teeth, cleaning your knees. There's no charge.

The structure over the inner well dates from around 1500 and was built by the mother of Henry VII, and one of the wealthiest women in north Wales. It is this royal connection that saved the building during her grandson, Henry VIII's cultural revolution. The religious world elsewhere was rendered flat but the well's elaborate fan vaulting and carved roof bosses somehow survived. It all looks pretty wrecked today, open at the front to the elements, damp and moss grown, covered with a combination of worn engravings depicting scenes from St Winefride's life and historical graffiti rendered in perfect serif font from the saved and the cured down the years. R Norris 1770. Hirsh Wilshook Shacklicksohn. 1827. T M Carew Esq. Meath West. Cured here 1831. The well makes no distinction between faiths or indeed between those who believe in something and those who believe in nothing at all. Proximity works. Stand near and by osmosis cures can happen. Water taken away continues to function. The touching of paper made with these waters a hundred years back can still make a difference. Faith like radiation. True believers, of course, know that nothing happens simply. St Winefride satisfies all petitions but maybe not all on the first asking. Sometimes it takes two or three or even four attempts. Come back to the well, pray while kneeling damply on the stone of St Beuno, bathe again.

In the gift shop are plastic bottles in which to carry off the waters, holy soaps and prayers on plastic coated cards, crucifixes, illuminated crosses, plaster models of the virgin. Some Bibles. A mimeographed history. No literary works. There aren't many. There's something about pure belief that keeps them at bay. Gerard Manley Hopkins began but did not finish a verse play about the waters. "This Dry Dene, now no longer dry nor dumb, but moist and musical / With the uproll and the downcarol of day and night delivering…" Dense, even by Hopkins' own standards and complexly alexandrine[9]. The sort of verse that should engage and lift but rarely does. In Hopkins' drama Caradoc was to die from a blow by the finger of God but the text never got that far. How Caradoc, rapist, murderer, pagan warlord and lost Prince of Wales actually did die is not known. No mention on the audio guide, nothing on the panels on the interpretation centre's walls.

Back at the Dee's edge, heading south, towards Flint and Connah's Quay, post-industrial Wales increases. The thing that brought most of the population here from the hill farms, from Ireland, from the English midlands, mostly no longer exists. What's left are shabby dormitories waiting for reinvestment. Pubs with tables outside for the smokers. Closed garages. Spar. Farms. The politicians are full of European-funded hope but so far that's mostly all it is. I've rubbed St Beuno's bounty into the eczema on my right leg. Nothing has happened yet. Check here to find out if it does[10].

NORTHERN BORDER

For a long time I've thought that borders were absolute. One thing ends and another begins. No period of transition. Boundaries firm and fixed. Immutable, impermeable, they stay where they've been put. I was brought up believing this. Our house finished at the back lane. Peter Hughes's chicken shed started on the other side. Nothing crossed between. It was like this when I went to bed and it was all still in the same place when I got up in the morning. In the atlas the lines between lands were clear. Rows of dots that traversed plain and mountain. Switzerland here. Austria there. Bosnia Herzegovina becoming Montenegro. The ink went from green to blue, no shades between. Simple, clear. But the world turned out never to be really like that. I had my suspicions when my grandfather opened an ancient atlas that he kept in his roll-top desk. He showed me a map of Europe with countries on it that I did not recognize: Romania like a collapsed balloon, Poland pulled in like a plate, Austria Hungary huge like a hungry beast. This was not the world I knew.

In Cambria's far north Wales turns slowly into England and both of them somehow become water. There's a border that has snaked up the map from the Wye on the Severn Estuary, following Offa's Dyke when it wants to and then plunging waywardly off on its own. For a distance it tracks the River Dee, a current-borne demarcation of floating dots rolling slowly into the greater waters of the industrial estuary and then the wilder swells of the grey Irish Sea. North of Wrexham Offa's great wall of Wales has been industrialised flat. The official walkers path diverts to Prestatyn. Here the border becomes

truly political. It slices Saltney
and the Ferry Lane Industrial
Estate from Chester, makes
them Welsh. Leaves the city in
English Cheshire. It then
shoots like an arrow to cross
the bogland green of the
Anglo-Welsh Dee delta. Out
here where few live for the
floundering of foundations and
the overpowering roar of steel
works, paper plants, rolling
mills and power stations the
border shimmers.

Trying to get to it is something else.

Why I should want to do this is questionable but there is something
that fascinates me about the places where the sand turns to water or
the city runs out to become farm or forest. These border places are
where ambiguity is king and the rules bend like sticks in water. Once
in the Alps I found a town where France, German Switzerland and
Italian Italy had come to an accommodation, where all currencies
prevailed and any language would do. On the surface the place may
well have been a shopping mall of overloaded drink trolleys and men
staggering under the weight of a thousand cigarettes but underneath
it was a place of political freedom where everyone seemed, just for
that moment, equal. But in this place, at the watery edge of Wales and
England, there is no conurbation where such an arrangement could
be brokered, and no road either.

This is Deeside where industry still rules. I've driven on the A548
through Connah's Quay and past the four giant white towers of E.on
UK's 1420 megawatt gas turbine power station generating enough
electricity to run half of Wales. Here like science fiction iron maidens
with their arms outstretched and their bell skirts swirling a massed
army of pylons march towards the border. When Auden and Spender
were writing in the 1930s these skeletal structures in the landscape
were seen as harbingers of a brilliant future. The pylons "like whips
of anger" pointed where we should go. Make things, build things, flat-
ten the landscape, burn it clean[11]. And in some places that is just what
we did. Look around.

The road crosses the Dee estuary on a new bridge[12] held by cables
attached to a giant A-frame which rises, blue green and huge, a pylon

to beat all pylons, glinting in the smoggy sunlight. The road skirts the northern reaches of the steel works at Shotton, belch and might, sweat and roar. Up here, beyond the road, lost in damp greenness, lies the border.

Boundaries often surround themselves with de-militarised neutral zones, with buffers, with marches. Areas that although belonging politically to one entity or another actually blend the two. Regulations change. Reality shifts. In these regions things are allowed that would not be elsewhere. Voices meld. Tricks are considered. Lights flash. Rules bend like spoons. But in these north Welsh marches there is little to hang anything onto, bar fields and low hedges and the blend of grass to reed to mud bank and foreshore and tide and sea.

The border itself ends at a military rifle range. Access restricted. Off the roundabout at Zone Three, Shotton, is a locked barrier, a narrow hard-topped path protected by chain link and in the near distance numbered ranges. Red flag flying. On the map the words 'Danger Area'. Places the population are not allowed to traverse. World's end, world's change, permit only.

The place where the line actually hits the water used to be marked by the now abandoned Sealand Rifle Range Halt, a railway station on the old London and North Eastern Railway which ran between Chester, Wrexham and Seacombe. The halt was demolished in 1954 and the ground cleared. Today rifleers arrive by military truck. Or maybe don't now that RAF Sealand, the airbase once stranded on the edge of the Deeside Industrial Park, has closed. To the north, about the distance away a rock would go if you threw it, is the remains of an iron age hill fort, eroded almost to nothing. Burton Point. On the

sea's edge a century back, now facing salt marsh. Beyond is the Bagillt sandbank and increasing water.

In Wales we may seek to be neutral, to be unmilitary, to be bombless – no aircraft carriers, no airbases, no missile silos. A gun free country. A place of peace. But we've not made it yet. Here, where the country finishes, the residues of the military are all around me. Back there in real Wales are the castles of Flint and Ewloe and Hawarden. Beyond me men with giant guns once guarded Liverpool. But right here, on the roadside, nothing more than passing trucks and on the Shotton approach road a burger van doing a decent trade. Peaceable enough.

Llanarmon

Beyond Chirk   Church Street traffic-calmed
Castle medieval magnificent
fortress of the Welsh marches   2ml W of village
(missed this) I enter the
Ceiriog valley of lost souls green
silence   road rising through Pontfadog
Llwynmawr, Glyn Ceiriog,
Pandy, Tregeiriog
thinning like a cholesterol artery
scattered with wet tar and
loose gravel   edges populated by
pheasant juvenile grey squirrel badger
roadkill   grass
no other vehicles no orange
signal   John Ceiriog Hughes
Cymric Robbie Burns once watched
this mud track from his Penybryn farmhouse
made new folk tunes from
old Welsh airs   not today
silence like an air bag.
Reach Llanarmon Dyffryn Ceiriog. Valley head
beyond a green rise of silent Welshness.
At the West Arms ask a man with a pint of
Felinfoel if this place can be real.
Nah mate the real stuff that's further.
look out at the skyline
real Wales ah yes forever further
in the twenty-first never get there

FLINT

The best thing about Flint is the way back out – the rail track, a way to depart for London or Cardiff or anywhere. Take the new red-streak futuristic Pendolino tilting express. Catch the Arriva two-car, direct to the Welsh capital with no changes in four hours. Faster than a car, no more standing for hours at lovely Crewe, arrive full of canned lager from the trolley service, ready to rock. They've had trains at Flint for more than one hundred and fifty years but service went to the dogs during Thatcher's eighties. When the London main line using Virgin began to stop here again in 2004 the local council put on a firework display. Rockets and burning stars. Welcome to Flint. Don't get off here, get on. They tell me this in the library. Such a small town and now so easy to leave.

Flint is not the county town of Flintshire and nor is that county anything like what it was. Flint and Flint, a place they named twice. Before 1974 the county was in two parts, separated by a stretch of Denbighshire. Flint Detached, that part of the old county, lying on the western fringes of the north Shropshire plain, has now found its way into the Borough of Wrexham. Flintshire, the rump that remains, lies along the Dee Estuary and with the Clwydian Hills rising to its west, is now one of the most deprived areas of Wales. Industria deserta. Once full of smoke and toil now idle with high rise and lager. Flint, no Next no Gap no French Connection no Marks & Spencer. Bustling with the unemployed and the unemployable. This is a town with a population large enough to staff six mills, three packing plants, an iron foundry, a paint maker, a pickling bottler, a mail order ware-house, a marshalling yard, a dried food processor, a tin plate platery, six call centres, a casino and a string of night clubs. But there are none of these things. No longer.

The place is old. A bastide[13] in the debatable lands[14]. A town built on the north Wales sandstone coast by Edward I as part of his plan to subdue the unruly Welsh and extend iron fist English rule across the whole of the north. Bastides were planned new towns built in open country. They had straight streets laid out in a grid pattern. There are dozens in south-western France and a smaller number in Wales. They have castles and broad high streets. Caernarfon, Conwy, Flint. At Flint the castle stands at the head of the new town like a dot on a fat letter i. On Speed's plan of 1630 there's no A548 to Chester nor rail-way to Holyhead but a double-walled grid of streets and trees like a suburban housing estate. The goalposts drawn in the top left corner are the gallows. The gaol has yet to be built. The castle with its four corner towers and large rolling outer bailey looks like something from cartoon television. The vanished shire hall has a maypoll standing next to it along with an early version of the ASBO, the stocks. Deviate from society's norm and you'd not get fined or banned but clamped in public view to have clods of mud and worse hurled in your face.

But simply being ancient offers no guarantee of civilised demeanour. These present-day streets are not full of black and white half timber, antique stores, potteries, bistro restaurants, tea rooms and shops selling antiquarian books. In fact during my visit I could find none of these things. At the edge of town arriving from Flint Mountain is the Pain Relief Centre, on the way back out two seconds later is the Palace Social Club & Bingo, Harun's Kebab-Burger & Pizza House, the Ship Hotel (To Let) and then the large and rambling Injury Claims Advice Centre. On Church Street Lloyds Pharmacy, Iceland, Sayers Café So Fresh We're Famous, Pound Shop (closed), Digital Hearing Aids, town toilets with a large bilingual sign at the entrance: These Facilities Are Regularly Checked By Uniform Police Officers. Pushchairs. Prams. Women in white track suits. Men in bomber jackets smoking. Men with tattoos leaning against walls. They are all called Jade, Kelly, Gaz or Daz. They stand around eating sausage rolls from Sayers or talking on their mobiles. An air of undiluted hardness abounds. Older folk keep their heads down. Flint is a small town with two tower blocks dominating its landscape. City lofts may be a much sought after fashion in the urban centres of the south. Here there's no option. "Ellesmere Port and Flint are the ONLY places in the UK that we can look down on, and regularly do." (comment on the Chavtowns web site). Although Ellesmere doesn't have an 1840s octagonal-towered town hall with a panelled ceiling bearing the shields of the fifteen tribes of north Wales. The historical effect is diluted somewhat by the building being strung about with Save Our Hospital banners and the establishment of a drop-in centre on the ground floor.

There's a writers circle which meets on a Thursday morning but no literateurs yet have used Flint as background for their great Welsh novel. The poems, too, are yet to arrive. Unlike the Poles who, as they are in nearby Wrexham, are already here mending fuses and installing central heating systems. Projekt Otwarte Drzwi. Meets daily at the RiverDee Community Church in Castle Street. Papurau Polski on sale in the newsagents. Sausage in the food stores. Flags in windows. Dom Polski. Picking up the work we can't do or won't consider. Or both.

The real castle, as opposed to Speed's drawing or the versions seen illustrating tourist brochures, has an atmosphere of absolute command. It's separated from the town by the rail link and sits against a green and deserted foreshore in splendid dominance. At high tide the waters once reached the outer walls. The place feels real. Battered about, holes in walls, stretches of masonry collapsed but still amazingly strong. The sort of place you think of when you hear the word castle. Marred by the stash of empty lager cans in the dungeon and the hoodie-graffiti across CADW's interpretation signboarding. To the south east once stood the town gaol. It was demolished in the 1960s. Today the site houses Fflint Football Club, ground and bunker club house. Low, brick, no windows, welcoming in the way a bomb shelter is welcoming. Looks solid enough to survive a direct nuclear attack.

Before the Victorian era Flint had a holiday trade – sea waters were taken here, visitors in head to toe bathing costumes would walk the shore-line sands and bathe in the pure Dee estuary. Hard to imagine today with a silting river, vanished sand and the overpowering presence upstream of the giant four-towered Connah's Quay power station, smoking on the skyline. They built boats at Flint, there was a dock. Still is a dock, back of the small industrial estate on the edge of Flint Marsh. Mud addled, overgrown, water enough to land a coracle. Gun shots sounding out through the marsh bushes when I was there. Locals slaughtering animals, maybe, or shattering targets shaped like the outlines of bulky men.

The wings of the Airbus A300 are made in nearby Broughton. They travel on low loader to reach the sea near here before being united with their engines and the body of the plane in Toulouse[14] in France. Whoever thought up this method of aircraft construction certainly knew their economics. The giant wings leave by sea up the Dee estuary. They may well have gone from Flint itself if access had been provided and history had been listened to. Centuries of sea trade return to north Wales port. Flint in charge of its own destiny once again. But Mostyn, a few miles up the coast, put up a better case, had the infrastructure, built what it needed, bought in the cranes and the special jigs and dredged the mud. The wings by-pass Flint on the A55. In Flint dock are a few car wheels, the mud-encrusted frame of hifi display unit and the remains of wooden jetties in their last phase of recognisable existence before total collapse.

Flint has an air of a northern, 1980s Newport – a place lost now the industry has left it, never consciously Welsh, 64 per cent on the street smoking. A gateway to Wales bypassed, a place in transition.

Five miles up the road, hidden on falling land in dense woods, two fields back from a minor road and marked by its guardians so inadequately you'd think they were keen on keeping people out, is Ewloe. Llewelyn ap Gruffudd, Prince of Gwynedd's arms hand-painted onto the wall at its entrance. A Welsh castle, remains of, at the top of a north-facing slope, above two deep ravines where the streams, the Wepre and the New Inn, meet. Built at the time of Henry III as a native stronghold the place lasted in Welsh hands for a little less than a generation.

The castle does not feel nor look anything like the battleship at Flint. This is an armed stealth bomber, not shaped like anything the English do, walls folding across the contours, the tower melding naturally onto the rock on which it stands. This is Machynlleth as opposed to Cardiff, Meic Stevens and not Bob Dylan, Waldo Williams and not T.S. Eliot. It feels like you could live in it, if the roof was restored and the stairs which spiral up the Welsh Tower to end heart-stoppingly in mid air, were fixed. To stay you'd need to like rain and have little need of taverns. On your way to the road you'd get muddy. You could write the novel the area needs. If you wanted to.

WREXHAM

Wrexham, so good they named it twice. Wrexham Abbot, owned by the abbeys, and Wrexham Regis with its allegiance to the Crown. The boundary between these ancient townships can still be traced. It spirals in from the River Clywedog in Erddig Park to follow the railway into to Wrexham Central. It then rolls along the middle of Abbot Street, High Street, Yorke Street, and then Tuttle Street before turning back on itself, through the Coed y Glyn estate, to the meet the Clywedog once more. As disparate conurbations representing god and king, Abbot and Regis have faced each other for so long now that the differences between them have evaporated Protestants and Catholics in Northern Ireland undistinguished by surname; Palestinians and Jews without yarmulke and kufi; Cardiff and Swansea minus Burberry and Cyril the Swan.

Wrexham, population 42,576, is now the largest town in Wales. In the clamour for status it lost out to Newport, three times larger, in the last round of city creation in 2002. Before that, in 1998, it had offered itself and the splendour of the north-east as home for the new

National Assembly. Lost out there as well. Wrexham today is an independent-minded con-urbation of Welsh dimension. No visible cultural overload. There's an art centre and a lit-tle theatre, one too many branches of Poundstretcher and its clones maybe, but a total lack of pretension. The B-level students from the local Technical, Art and Tertiary Colleges fill the centre with goths, emos and skaters. There

are small town boom-box boy racers and a bus station unpolluted by porno merchants. You can walk here.

Over the years I've visited this place many times. And mostly I found it dismal, too small for sophistication, too big to be beautiful, and with smoke from the nineteenth century still in the air. But today, in the new millennium, with early sunshine filling the pedestrianised streets, I find a clean town, of easy proportion, with a scattering of fine Victorian and Georgian buildings still extant among the branches of Wallis, Next and Burton.

Wrexham Central with its hourly diesels to Liverpool could be in the running for the shortest station in Wales award. The stubby plat-form is in Regis but the track in Abbot. Where it used to run to in the grand days is now a shopping mall, kids wearing ear buds, women with shopping trolleys, men with boxes and plastic bags: JD, Holland and Barrett, HMV, car park, plantings, indistinguishable from retail parks the world over. Even the brewery that made the town famous for its lager has been demolished to make way for the Central Retail Park. All that remains is the original office and tun house from 1882. Empty when I visit, with the graffiti THIS SHOULD BE A PUB encouragingly scrawled outside.

But not all of Wrexham is like this. The central streets are narrow and beautifully car free. They have irregular rooflines, Georgian porchways, Victorian arcades and a timber-framed pub, in Hope Street, right in the centre. The Horse & Jockey is still thatched, and still serving local beers. Wrexham could be a town of inns. The vast and vertical drinkeries have yet to arrive. User-scale pubs dot the townscape. The Walnut Tree, Seven Stars, The Old Vaults, The One

To Five, The Elihu Yale.

Elihu Yale, famous Wrexham son, is worth tracking. How do you get to be called that? "Elihu" is Biblical. He was descendant of Abraham and antagonist of Job. "Yale" is an Anglicisation of Iâl. Elihu Yale's family came from Plas y Iâl in Denbighshire. He made his money in India and then spent some of it founding the great American university named after him in New Haven, Connecticut. He is buried in the yard at St Giles Church. The 500-foot church tower, one of the seven wonders of Wales, is replicated at half size in America. Yale's grave is marked with a monument of his own devising. "Much good, and some ill, he did; so hope's all even", runs the inscription in an eighteenth century serifed font.

Inside I am accosted by an ancient in a knitted cap who could have walked here straight from Dibley. Are you an engineer? God, do I look like one? Over the arch of the east wall is the famous early sixteenth century Doom Painting[16] put there to show the ignorant just what would happen when the trumpet of judgment sounded. Cartoon figures emerge from their coffins to rise towards God, fear in their sunken eyes, decay evident in their bloodless limbs. On the north side is a white marble memorial showing a woman also rising from her coffin[17]. Death might elsewhere be dark and still but here in St Giles they offer luminous hope. That's Mary Myddelton. The money her family made was used to make cannons. Famous for it. War and God, marching side by side.

Wrexham is not multi-ethnic to any significant degree. Few enrobed with djellaba, hijab, or burka. Nothing like Swansea or Cardiff although the arrival of refugee Iraqi Kurds at the tough Caia

Park Estate[18], dispersed there by over-zealous New Labour, did spark days of rioting in 2003. Hot summer nights and alcohol, claimed the media. In reality more to do with the pains of an impoverished and rarely represented white underclass. The Kurds moved on, some of them. But today Wrexham is the Polish capital in exile. Political parties print their election leaflets in Polish. There are Polish newspapers, day centres, shops and clubs. On the streets in 2007 you can hear as much Polish as Welsh, both mixing with an English whose accent owes more to Cheshire than Denbigh or Meirionydd.

The Town Museum was built to celebrate the Borough Council rather than ancient Abbot or Regis. Here, amid the displays of mayoral regalia, assemblages of embossed red Wrexham brick, and enlarged and grainy photographs showing how the world used to be before colour was invented, is Brymbo Man. A beaker burial discovered in 1958 by Ron Pritchard, pipe trench digger, outside 79 Cheshire View, Brymbo. Work stopped as the three and a half thousand year old bones, the cracked pottery beaker and the skull itself were recovered from the ditch. He's there now, in his museum case, lying on a bed of sand. In 1998 when he travelled back here from his period of somber analysis at the National Museum of Wales in Cardiff he did the trip in a hearse. Manchester University's Dr Caroline Wilkinson has made a face reconstruction. How he must have looked. Head in a glass case, lit by low light. I wanted him to resemble Grahame Davies but he looks more like Frank Hennessey, rosy Irish cheeks, 70s rock band hair, the frown you'd expect on a man with no body. That's unreconstructed, as yet.

At the library I hunt out the café made famous by Aled Lewis Evans in his Welsh novel[19] of old ladies, cream cakes and the mystic young who frequent such places Wales over. There's a 70 year-old reading the contents of his wallet, a pair of students encumbered by bags and files, a child eating an egg sandwich and two pairs of female pensioners eating scones. Attire by mail order. Primary colour – blue. On the window in white Times 30-point is an unattributed text – "He

is selling his flat to go to Brazil. There he learns Portuguese by reading *Folha de S. Paulo* in the café for hours and hours. He reads the newspaper with his dictionary in his hands. He meets his future wife. Six months later they come to the UK to meet his parents." I ask a middle-aged couple in blue anoraks if they know what it means. They don't. Art, says the woman. They nod their heads.

Near here, according to an exhibition in the Art Centre foyer (70 votes already cast, huge local interest), Landmark Wales will build a sculpture to mark the gateway to Wrexham. In contention are a blue and white tower, twin hands one in red the other in white, a castle that might be made from gravestones, a wreck of ornamental cast metal and a box of letterforms masquerading as dragon bones. My money is on the letters, which mix *Wales* with *Cymru*. A concrete poem for the age of the soundbite. Literature for the illiterate. Words for those who usually never bother. A Welsh marker for one of the northern beginnings of Wales. The chosen site is the A483 and A5 junction in nearby Chirk. Watch it as you drive past.

I've walked in a great Abbot circle, mostly the older town. In 1857 when there were only 646 registered voters the whites took on the reds and the reds won. The whites were the Liberals and the reds the Tories. Corruption was easy and rife. You only had a few hundred pockets to line. Today almost everyone can vote but most don't bother. John Marek, now defeated independent Wrexham Assembly Member, has his HQ in a poster-plastered end-of-terrace near the football ground. His urgings to keep him in power mix with those of Safeway Scaffold and the men there to fix his roof. At the ground itself, The Racecourse, just beyond The Turf pub, is a plaque celebrating the Wales v Ireland game held here in 1906 – the first filmed example of a football match. Men in black and white tops, long shorts and tall socks chasing a speck of a ball. Film by Mitchell and Keynon. The game was a 4-all draw although the plaque doesn't mention this. You can watch that game today on YouTube[20]. The plaque is surrounded by engraved bricks bearing messages from supporters.

MANDE WILSON LET THE GOOD TIMES ROLL. FANS FOR LIFE KEV, KARL & MEL SALISBURY BRUCE ROBERTS & CO SUPPORT WREXHAM FC. There are hundreds of them. Grahame Davies has recorded most in a poem. I'd considered turning the text I found in Abbot Street into a clip from Wrexham actuality – t-shirt slogans, half visible tattoos, street signboards, shop names, text on passing

vehicles, copy lifted from litter, warning notices, letter-forms created by the chance meeting of upright and diagonal, graffiti. I remembered this plan on the clacking Arriva two-car diesel that took me back from no-smoking Wales through bits of still smoking England, woman with fag on Shrewsbury station, man desperate for one at Gobowen, three kids with roll-ups at Oswestry, empty platform at Abergavenny, light rain as we enter Newport, southern hassle and an accent that opens drawers.

Wrexham, I'll make up your poem – Whatever You Wear This Christmas (sign on April bus) · Stryt yr Abad · FEARANDLOATHINGINWREXHAM at the Old Swan · This lectern may not be moved under any circumstances · This Stone Replaces One Presented To Yale University, U.S.A., 1918 · D J Hatty (Raverbaby) · It's Absolutely Bonkers at the Memorial Hall · Go In Peace And Sin No More.

notes

1. The semaphore station was a pre-telegraph invention to signal to the great port of Liverpool that a ship was sailing in. Stations began on Holyhead and ran right across the north Wales coast. Messages took five minutes to travel the distance although it is recorded that in one spectacular demonstration of 1830 word got through in 23 seconds.
2. *Intoxication*, the annual bi-lingual conference of Academi (Yr Academi Gymreig), the Welsh National Literature Promotion Agency and Society of Writers.
3. *Llandudno Before The Hotels* – Christopher Draper (Llygad Gwalch Cyf. 2008).
4. Tom Davies, "after being messed around relentlessly by publishers in his 25 years as a professional writer" has now taken matters in hand and set up his own publishing company, *The Berwyn Mountain Press,* which published his *The Tyranny of Ghosts* (based on an affair he once had with a famous ageing Shakespearean actress) in the autumn of 2006.
5. The Ladies of Llangollen were two Anglo-Irish aristocratic lesbians who eloped from Ireland in 1778 to set up home at Pen-y-Maes in Llangollen. Lady Eleanor Butler and the Honourable Sarah Ponsonby renamed their cottage Plas Newydd, developed it within and without, and lived a celebrated life there for fifty years. The house became a focus for intellectual visitors – William Wordsworth, Edmund Burke, Caroline Lamb, Josiah Wedgwood, Sir Walter Scott and the Duke of Wellington all came. Lord Byron wrote of their love. Plas Newydd is today a museum. The nearby Ladies of Llangollen Wedding Service offers ceremonies at £480 less than the national average.
6. GWR Prairie Tank 5199, Kitson Industrial Tank 5459, GWR Pannier Tanks 6430 and 7754, GWR 7822 Foxcote Manor, LMS Jinty 47298, Saddle Tank Jessie & Diesels. Others on the way.
7. Welsh name for Holywell.
8. http://chavtowns.co.uk
9. Commenting on the rhythm G.M.Hopkins wrote "It is in an alexandrine verse, which I sometimes expand to 7 or 8 feet, very hard to manage but very effective when well used… as the feeling rises the rhythm becomes freer and more sprung" – *Gerard Manley Hopkins*, The Penguin Poets, selected by W H Gardner, 1853.

10. No, at the time of publication. I do this everywhere. Take the cures. They never work.

11. Despite the reality Connah's Quay power station have gone to great lengths to up their conservation game. There are wildlife corridors across the plant, a designated SSSI, reserves to welcome pintail, shelduck, oystercatcher, redshank, teal, curlew, dunlin, lapwing, a lease to the Deeside Naturalist Society, visible vapour plume reduced hybrid cooling towers and less actual noise than you'd imagine. If you get the power station behind you then the views up the estuary are unrivalled. Yet the ground beneath continues to tremble. Little can be done about that.

12. Tweeds Construction. River Dee Estuary Bridge. 3.7K dual two lane road. 115 meter tower.

13. Bastide – French – *bâtir* – *the build.*

14. The Debatable lands, ancient Tegeingl, the Middle Country between aggressive England and recalcitrant Wales.

15. The wings go by ship from Mostyn to the port of Bordeaux where they are transhipped by barge on the River Garonne to Toulouse for assembly.

16. Vast early sixteenth century wall painting of the day of judgement, re-discovered after being painted over in 1867.

17. Memorial by Louis François Roubiliac of Mary Myddelton (1688-1747) of Croesnewydd Hall, Wrexham.

18. Population 11,000 with a high incidence of single white males. The Kurds were given hard-to-let flats in some of the estate's toughest corners.

19. Y Caffi, Gwasg Pantycelyn, 2002. The author claims the book to be not explicitly based on the café at Wrexham although his useful groundplan on page 10 seems to be an exact replica.

20. http://www.youtube.com/watch?v=qFtb7Sl0KAA

NORTH WEST

LLANYSTUMDWY

The Professor is in a red dressing gown and has his arms folded in a you can't do this moan. It's 2.30 am in the heart of the great house. The Professor is sleeping in the big room above the communal kitchen or rather he is not. The kitchen is full of poets and fictioneers eating toast and sorting how the writing world works. They are full of wine, most of them. Arguing, laughing, honing in on the way the muse arrives and where it heads after that. The Professor, who retired hours back, asks for consideration, demands it. Cap the noise. This is no way for the world to turn. He is offered a can of Heineken and a slice of wholemeal with marmite smears. He turns them down. Outside, under the hunter's moon, poets can be heard disagreeing about ancient meters. Essential for poetry. No they're not. This is Tŷ Newydd, set on rising land above the Eifionydd village of Llanystumdwy. Pop. 1796. Llŷn peninsula down the road.

Tŷ Newydd is a residential writers centre, a place where writer students come to spend time in the company of those with reputations, to learn the art of writing by inspiration, by example, by practise, by osmosis. Based on the model established by the Arvon Foundation at Totleigh Barton in Devon and at Lumb Bank at Hebden Bridge in West Yorkshire, Tŷ Newydd is one of literary Wales' great successes. You come here ragged and wild to have your muse trained. You live and work for a week with a small number of fellows, sixteen or less, and in the company of two top flight tutors, established poets, published novelists, broadcast dramatists. These are writers who know how to care and inspire, how to teach and how to listen. Walking gods

of the wider literary world. You cook together, eat together, talk together, create together. No radio, no television, no football, no clubs. One pub in the village. One small shop. Silence, sea and mountain around you. Attendees become transformed. Become inspired. Leave entranced. Face a different future. If this were a church then god would be on fire and the very rocks replete with miracle.

There's been a farm house on this spot for as long as history can remember. Sixteenth century records show a habitation on rising ground in the hands of Rowland Owen. A ragged place built on the site of much earlier shacks and lean-tos and places with turf and thatch and stones found on the ground for roofs. The site commands unequalled views across the Dwyfor and Dwyfach estuary and the sea of Ireland beyond. Llywelyn ap Iorwerth's castle at Criccieth is to the south, Bardsey and its five thousand saints in the fog and distance to the west. For all its life Tŷ Newydd has been added to, rebuilt and changed. First farm house then gentleman's residence, then working manor, an elegant retreat from the wet and muddy world. Slatestone roof, slab-coped and kneelered gable parapets. Flush-pointed lime-washed walls. Tall end chimneys. Tudor-arched openings. Irregular quoins and voussoirs. Heavily-moulded plaster cornice. Cellar below the Georgian parlour. Georgian range. 1500s vertical post-and-muntin oak partition screen. Built from local rubble on pronounced boulder foundations. Grass, rock. The grounds fill with sun. Owners have looked for decades for the well but it's not yet been found. Full of stones, lost below centuries of outbuilding knock-about, garden walling and land being dug and filled. Unused, unholy water seeping into the river below.

Rowland Owen, Humphrey Owen, Lowry Owen, Robert Ellis, Thomas Williams, Canon William Williams, Robert Williams, tenant names lost, John Goodman, the Broom Hall estate of the Joneses, David Lloyd George, Maiden, Farmiloe, W. Thomas Baker Ltd., Taliesin Trust. Farmland sold on after DLlG. Rain slanting in though the trees.

Lloyd George was born in Manchester but spent all his formative years in Llanystumdwy. He lived from 1864 to 1880 with his uncle Lloyd at Highgate, a tiny stone-made terraced cottage south of the river. This uncle was Richard Lloyd, bootmaker and unpaid minister at Pen y Maes chapel. Preacher, breather of fire and honourable dissent. Here Lloyd George acquired his life-time dislike of the land-owning aristocracy. His initials are carved by penknife on a stone in the parapet of the eighteenth century Afon Dwyfor bridge. DLlG MP. Elis, Tŷ Newydd groundsman, tells me that everyone did that.

In the village centre there's a museum for LG, exhibition, book-stall, lecture theatre, artefacts, car park, picnic tables, children's play area, peace, tranquillity, half a block from Highgate. Llanystumdwy is actually so small that nothing is more than half a block from anything else. Nothing built in blocks, come to that. Divided by the clean sliding Afon Dwyfor the village nestles in a cupped and rocky hand: church, Ranch restaurant, a couple of hundred stone houses, council-built white wall rendered outriders, Ty Canton, Capel Moria, Tafarn y Plu – the Feathers Inn (new management, flags of Wales and Glyndŵr flying large outside), Ysgol Lleol, Gwynedd T-Shirt Centre, largest car park in north Wales, recycle bins in its northern corner.

Lloyd George bought Tŷ Newydd c. 1938, briefly farmed, then died there in 1945. There's a black and white film of the mourners and the crowds and his horse drawn coffin leaving the house for the final time. I watch this at the Museum where the regulation Philip Madoc-fronted great man documentary is shown in the darkened lecture theatre. In the theatre with me are two Americans in shorts and a middle-aged couple from the English Midlands, both carrying day packs and badge infested walking sticks. The film plays, no one speaks. When we re-emerge among the Museum's million Lloyd George artefacts one of the Americans tells the Museum attendant that he thought Mr Lloyd looked a lot like Abraham Lincoln. Wasn't Lincoln Welsh? No, he came from Norfolk. Ah yes.

In the Museum amid the dozens of jugs and mugs bearing the great man's likeness, the talking head that plays his speeches, his library, his pens, and his many awards is the nameplate from the London Midland and Scottish steam locomotive that once bore his name, removed after his fall from power in 1922, and lost behind panelling at Kings Cross for decades. An era past. In its stead the Festiniog Railway running out of nearby Porthmadoc now has a double-ended Fairlie narrow gauge steam loco named David Lloyd George. Built in 1992, history like Hornby. Travel for fun and smoke and going nowhere. Men with cameras on Porthmadoc station. Kids with ice creams. None of this at Llanystumdwy. Outside, through the grounds and the great gates and over the road on the Dwyfor riverside is the Lloyd George Memorial. Designed by Clough, LG is actually under it. This is a grave below trees by the falling water.

Plaque by William Lloyd George. Memorial verse by his nephew, W.R.P.:

> Y maen garw, a maen ei goron, - yw bedd
> Gŵr i'w bobl fu'n wron;
> Dyfrliw hardd yw Dwyfor lon,
> Anwesa's bedd yn gyson[1]

Hard to get hold of, that fact that his bones are actually here, in the shade, among the leaves.

The area is thick with worthies. More for its size of population than most places. Jan Morris, author of the great *Pax Britannica*, up the hill at Trefan. Her son Twm Morys, bardd mwyaf yr ardal, in a cottage in the trees, Wil Sam, Clough Williams Ellis[2], architect of Portmeirion, lived down the road at Plas Brondanw, Penrhyndeudraeth. Traces of Clough embellish the entire district. He built Capel Moriah, put on the distinctive rounded ends, the roof decoration. He built Tŷ Newydd Cottage, the estate bailiff's residence, with its curved porch and trademark corners. He built the great curved first floor library window at Tŷ Newydd itself for Lloyd George to better view the land and the sea. Clough the unmissable.

In 1975 I'd signed up for local accommodation at the Dwyfor National Eisteddfod and to my amazement found myself staying at Plas Brondanw with Clough as my guide and the man who made tea for me in the morning. He talked endlessly of his wife Amabel's science fiction as he strode me though the great house's rebuilt wings and book-strewn halls. I was a writer too so I was bound to have an interest. She was out of this world, he joked. *Out of this World* was the series title for a whole run of sf anthologies she'd edited. How was I to know that? I thought he was just enthusing. Should I visit the Maes, he asked. Aren't I too old? He'd have been 91 then. Do it, I told him. In his bright yellow socks and plus-fours he did. Took me around Portmeirion, his great Italianate and complete fake

village first. Made me more tea. Talked about the great and ancient architects, the things they did in Rome and Greece, the way stones weathered and leaned, the way the landscape held them. Back at Tŷ Newydd his weathered stones are still there. In 2006 the architect Frances Voelker finished yet another set of alterations – this time a complete refurbishment, repointing, repainting, improved services, tutor accommodation upgraded, the main drive metal surfaced, and a glass conservatory housing three-floor disabled lift and sun-filled space for poem creation fixed to the side. The new extension is both audaciously modern like the pyramid in front of the Louvre and somehow totally invisible. Clough's round-ended library still juts its stuff and bends the sound of those speaking inside it. The house's hands through five hundred years of history are as full now as they ever were.

As a writers centre Tŷ Newydd's history goes back at least twenty years to when Sally Baker was running a language centre here in the 1980s. Her parents had retired to Llanystumdwy and bought the great house as a way of ensuring their daughter's future. Sally, meeting (and subsequently marrying) Elis Gwyn Jones at a pub quiz in Criccieth, ran music afternoons, chances to learn Spanish, bees and badger weeks and chances to try your hand at that emerging art and interest – creative writing.

Down at the Arts Council in Cardiff Gillian Clarke and Meic Stephens were looking into ways of establishing an Arvon-style writers operation in Wales. Tŷ Newydd fitted perfectly. Right history, decent size, perfect location and with two able and willing wardens already on site. After a fair bit of negotiation, wall painting, door fixing, money machination and mangled promises the Tŷ Newydd Writers Centre opened in April of 1990. It began with a week-long poetry course tutored by Gillian Clarke and Robert Minhinnick. Catherine Fisher was guest reader.

Today, 2006, with the centre just reopened the same course has been re-run. Gillian greater, Robert wiser and Catherine famous. A brand new set of students set on their ways to literary glory.

Sally's single-minded enthusiasm brings the students in but it is Elis, window-fixer, lawn-mower, and all round bricoleur who holds the place together. Bearded Elis, fisherman, raconteur, man of the Glyndŵr hills, family residency of Llanystumdwy for at least four generations, trap maker, wood turner, regular at Y Plu, never knowingly written a

poem, owns twenty-one sheds, scattered across the country from here to where he launches his fishing boat at Criccieth. At Cae Llo Brith[3], Sally's house up beyond Tŷ Newydd, Elis feeds us grilled plaice, self-caught five miles out with home-grown greens and potatoes. The real world here seems much easier to touch.

Fish caught from Elis' boat: Macrall, Cimwch, Cath Fôr, Lleden, Lleden Goch, Cranc Heglog, Ci Môr, Draenogyn, Mingrwn, Morlas, Gwrach, Môr Nodwydd, Gwyniad, Chwyrnwr, Tyrbotsan Cranc.

When Ifor Thomas and I taught a Tŷ Newydd course on poetry in performance we got Elis to cut the grass using a deafening petrol strimmer right under the Clough library windows. Inside the assembled acolytes were learning to deal with interruption. What would you do at your reading if this kind of thing happened, bawled Ifor. Ask them to stop, suggested the class front runner. Try it, commanded Ifor. Elis, ear protectors cutting all ambient sound, roared on oblivious. The noise went round the library in circles. Give up, suggested a harridan at the back. That's what we did. Went outside for a fag, went to the communal kitchen for tea. How do you mix poetry and lawn mowers? You don't.

Contents of Elis' sheds: six bicycles, a broken Spanish guitar, a selection of anchors, rope, copy of *Pilgrims Progress*, model railway, three outboard engines, skull of a seal, mitre saw, band saw, circular saw, scroll saw, jig saw, hand saw, briefcase that once belonged to the Dean of Durham, nets, arc welder, two chainsaws, lawn mower, rope, chair, wardrobe, vice, penknives, antique pedal car, compressor. lobster pots for repair, soldering irons, splicing handbook, assegai, barometer, anvil, chest of photographs, fire extinguisher, lifejacket, paint, beeswax, road sign, rope, .22 air rifle, stainless steel fixings, rope, rat trap, mouse trap, mole trap, wasp trap, oil, net, net, net, net, net, net, rope

In the coming year David Constantine, Jim Perrin, Pascale Petit, Maurice Riordan, Carol Ann Duffy, Menna Elfyn, Stephen Knight, Nigel Jenkins, Jackie Wills, Stewart Brown, Jack Mapanje, Patricia Dunker, Janet Thomas, Michael Longley, John Williams, Graham Hartill, and Mererid Hopwood, Bethan Gwanas, Manon Rhys, Ifor ap Glyn, Eigra Lewis Roberts, and Fiona Sampson will teach at Tŷ Newydd. Poetry, prose, drama. Travelling here over long roads by exhausted car or on the train from Birmingham via most of the wilderness of north Wales to the long platform at Criccieth. Somehow you don't expect that, real trains running so far from metropolitan anything. The spirit is great here. There's a poem by Gillian in the glass of the new front door and books by Tony Curtis on the new library shelves. There are a couple of Elis' sheds outside, beyond the redecorated back porch. Left alone in the latest rebuild. One of them looks as if it has been here since before Lloyd George. You never know when you need things, says Elis. Sheds like libraries, part of the culture.

CRICCIETH AT NIGHT

Hotels this far off the trade routes are rare. You'd miss the Bron Eifion if it wasn't for the white-washed rocks marking the drive entrance and the AA sign, in its pre-war font, hanging there from another age. Hywel Teifi Edwards, historian and world-standard raconteur told me once that the Bron Eifion was part of the home counties. Pearls, suits, voices that bark. This is the great house that John Greaves built in 1885. The slate master of Llechwedd, quarry owner at Ffestiniog, Lord-Lieutenant of Caernarfon. A stone house of size and weight, ivy-clad, balustraded, galleried and gardened, surrounded by trees.

In the great entrance hall, beyond reception with its polite notice informing guests that the hotel will be locked at midnight[4] there's a land of dark wood and great armchairs. Here a grand piano plays. Beethoven. The keys rise and fall of their own accord. Piano roll. The violin part, synchronisation failed, seeps from a speaker high on the wall. In the bowels of the long conservatory restaurant a lone diner sups asparagus soup. Amid the great and ancient furniture, over-stuffed settees, round arm-chairs made of tropical hardwoods and upholstered with the same kind of stiff, itchy cloth that once covered the seats on 1950s GWR steam trains, there's a notice. Framed on the mantelpiece. "We ask guests to refrain from re-arranging any of the furniture in this room". As if you could. The pieces are as heavy as rhinos. There is no mention of what would happen if you did move anything but none of the people I am with are capable.

Will you be dining with us, sir? Maitre'd in dinner suit, overlarge bow tie, accent somewhere east of Cracow. Maybe not.

Criccieth at night is like the cowboy west. Solid citizens gone home to their houses, doors bolted, visitors in small gangs roaming the streets in search of sustenance, locals, beer in hands, holed-up in the saloon. The town relies on gentle tourism. A row of old-world guesthouses lines the seafront. They are shadowed by the remains of Llywelyn's twin-towered and magnificent Welsh-build castle. It's up there on the promontory dominating all. Along the High Street are antique shops selling silver spoons. A florist. A baker. A failed surf shop. Chemist, library. Bank now a café. The George IV Hotel with its sizeable dining room is rebranded as a bistro. There are five customers clanking their cutlery in its olive brown interior.

The deal with dining in any town that is not your own is to walk the circuit of restaurants, appraising each for range as shown on their menu and on style and substance as observed within. These circuits can be miles in circumference. They usually involve a minimum of twenty calls at restaurants, cafes, bistros, bars, pubs, dining rooms, eating counters, burger stalls, and take-aways with eat-in tables for the lonely or the scared. It's pretty much a given that in any of these perambulations hunger will drive you to buying packets of crisps from shops you pass. You will also inevitably end up returning to the precise place where you started. There is never gold at the end of the gastronomic rainbow. And in Criccieth's case, after we get round the Poachers Restaurant, Tir a Môr, the Prince of Wales, and the Blue China Cafe (all rejected for being closed, for overuse of Formica, for having a poor menu or simply for being too full) and back to Granville's where we began, we discover that they can no longer accommodate us. Full. Their griddles going at full strength. The six-guns and the sharp-shooters, all three generations of them, in from northern England have got there first.

Siop Chips with a car park big enough for tourist coaches and full of light when we passed an hour ago beckons. A bag of pysgodyn & sglodion while walking along the dusk-filled sea front suddenly seems the obvious thing to have. It's 8.05 on a clear Saturday night. But when we reach it the door of Siop Chips is locked. There's someone in the back with a mop shaking their head. Siop Chips is closed.

In the end we retreat to the basement Bistro of the Bryn Hir Arms. "The Restaurant is downstairs through the bar" reads the sign. Down steps and round turns, along a corridor, past beer barrels, broken chairs, cigarette machines and Saturday night screaming from the lads smoking to the end of the world in the beer garden, another turn and another door and there it is. Five tables, nineteen sixty-six nylon carpet, no windows, and a feeling that the walls will shortly press in and squeeze us flat. I order a butterfly of chicken grilled bacon cheese with hickory sauce rather than the Bryn Hir Buster Beef Stew served in an 8" Yorkshire pudding. It was a hard call. Gill asks for mushy peas. The waitress says she'll check with chef, chef says sorry mushy peas are done. None in the pan, none in the freezer. Chef is seen looping in across the room, full-speed, in his chef's trousers, shaved head, long thin arms and chef's tattoos, bearing giant bags of frozen chips. The waitress takes my order. From beyond the ranch-style swing doors guarding the kitchen we hear a familiar ping. The waitress returns with my food on an overflowing plate. Ten seconds have passed. Chef is seen legging at high speed across the bistro bearing this time bags of frozen rice. The fat woman at the table in the back has spilled Bryn Hir Beef Balti (hot) down her front. Sue has Welsh lamb tagine (med). Ifor has cod plus peas that do not mush. Might be haddock. Hard to say.

Three minutes in, at that point where the cheese, chicken and bacon have all started to acquire the same texture and similar taste, something like Wrigley's once the spearmint has gone, there is a noise like road rage from out beyond the swinging ranch doors in the microwave-packed kitchen. You f★★%$★ what? I'm not f★★&@★ so f&★★ you F&★★er and f&★*% your job. There are crashes as implements are hurled. Then the sound of crockery breaking. You can F★★★&★ stuff it. Ranch doors slam outwards just as the waitress is entering bearing a great stack of plates and bowls. The effect is pleasingly spectacular. Plates shoot up into the air as if they were part of a roman candle. All, without exception, shatter dramatically as they land. Cutlery mixes with used gravy. Crockery shards spray like art. Chef, face red and still swearing at full volume bursts through the middle of this cabaret and streaks across the bistro and up the exit stairs. He is pursued by two members of the casually-dressed management who, in raised Liverpool voices, are saying things like come on now, please be reasonable, there are only a few extra orders after all, and we'll pay you. But no dice. Chefs the world over have learned from TV that prima donna mentalities are essential to their trade. They are expected to storm and swear. Diners would feel cheated if they did not. Our man is gone. The waitress explains that he had been asked to cook a few extra steaks for very late arriving diners. It's 8.45 pm. They should be ashamed of themselves. Members of the management, back down the stairs now and smoothing flat their hair, have re-entered the kitchen. Sleeves roll up. I hear a familiar ping.

Back at Bron Eifion, in the dark depths of the conservatory restaurant, I can see the lone diner wiping his lips on his pure linen napkin. The bar is empty. The tuneless Beethoven still tinkles but with the volume cut. Over Bron Eifion the sky is a brilliant wash of milky brightness. Stars like stars should be. It is 9.15.

The Teashops of Wales

particularly
prominent
bilingual
crowded
cooked
substantial
cream
navvies
tea towel
mats
homeopathic
best
hat
dreadful
nutritious
warm
beffro
post card
bara
large
melin
legacy
celtic cape
high

larch (ll)
glaze
graze
gaze
bap
peint
beint
pheint
locally
preserved
walking
oak
scone
pantry
accolades
sampling
flattering
cheese
cream
fish
stairs
carpet
hamper
hiker
blazing log
4 slices
of toast
4 tablespoons
of brown ale
minimum flat teabag lidl dust cheap white water no longer hot
enough insert yourself your spoon string un strung hope and press

BARMOUTH

I've by-passed Dolgellau, Cader Idris south of me, run the fast gully
with its over-bridges and not gone north winding with the A470
through Coed y Brenin to the long straight that flies to Trawsfynydd.
Instead I've followed my nose and turned east at Llanelltyd to drift
along the side of the Afon Mawddach as it opens and spreads and fills
with sand and salt in its great rush to the sea. At the estuary's lip is

Barmouth – the anglicised Abermawddach – slate-roofed home of north Wales ship building, fisheries and enormous skies. This is Merioneth, bastion of the language, Welsh home for the renegade and the rebel, retreat for prince and warlord. If Wales had a Taliban then they'd fester here. This road will take me on to Harlech, across the toll bridge to Penrhyndeudraeth, and on via the Cob to Porthmadog. The Wales of ancestral power.

Yet the coast here has been unaccountably eroded by immigration. This is now holidayland. Wales' own Sunny Beach. A conurbation of caravan park, converted cottage, inflatable beachbed, pork scratchings and beer that runs from Borth right up to Pwllheli. Butlins. Gay Friendly weddings. Field after field of mobile homes. Burger bars. Golden sands without end. At its centre is Barmouth. A hard-top seafront of men in vests, earrings, tattoos, all of then scowling. Grey roofed shops blossom with clumps of bright beach gear – clusters of red buckets and yellow spades, lilos decorated with fish, orange windbreaks, racks of hopeful sunstop, stacks of Welsh hats, lines of shorts and cheap tees. Sausage and pies, chips. Families with push chairs, swarms with ice creams and mid-calf shorts and bright white trainers and pink flip-flops.

Why are they here? Why haven't they taken a cheap flight somewhere on an airline that slices up flight costs like Burroughs did novels. Fly you places where it doesn't rain. Cactus, beer, heat. Nothing the same ever again. Is Wales still so desirable? Barmouth has four web sites, all run by local enthusiasts. They are full of tales of harbour fundays, yacht races, flamenco dancing, fireworks, billiards, three-legged pub crawls, beer gardens, islands full of shells. The fun never stops in Cardigan Bay. Barmouth pop 2500. Triples in a good summer. They bring cars, cheap 4x4s that rattle, coaches, there's even rail. Across the estuary is the toy Fairbourne – trains downsized from horse-drawn passenger trams to become replica steam mainliners where the drivers tower over their coal-filled tenders like Celtic giants. Full-size Arriva rolls in across the viaduct of Pont Abermaw, the great 900-yard Welsh Forth Bridge equivalent which carries the Cambrian Coast line from Shrewsbury to Pwllheli. Diesel diesel. You can get here with a suitcase and undamaged arms.

My own connection with Barmouth is slight. In 1971 Dave Cunliffe at BB Bks in Blackburn published a small collection *The Edge of Tomorrow*, A5 cyclostyle, stapled, 30 pages of poetry, half mine and half by Jeanne Rushton (Barmouth). In those days you always put where you came from in brackets after your name, like a badge. She described herself as "Sun in Aries, Moon in Cancer, mother, Taro reader, living in the Mawddach Estuary". Cunliffe, along with his partner Tina Morris, named their press after their postcode. It was an outgrowth of their sixties co-operative small mag *Poetmeat*. Poetry would change the world, came out of you like breath, was the heart of how we would soon all be, flowed like milk along our bomb threatened streets. That was the theory. Those were special times.

Rushton's earthmother verse was full of emerald and aconite and the potency of light. Thick with silver boats, jewels in the lotus, seaweed and jasmine and solitary ones who "keep their watch through the lonely mansions of the night". There's a badly scanned snap of her on the book's front piece looking like Buffy St Marie - long dark curls, strings of beads, embroidered cheesecloth shirt. That was thirty six years back when we were the people our parents were warning us against, when the world was about to become a wondrous place. Never did. Jeanne vanished. Never saw another poem of hers anywhere, never met her, never saw her mentioned, collected, anthologised or on the programme of any literary festival. Wiped. There were no launches for the book, no parties. *The Edge of Tomorrow* sank.

My contributions were all bird-filled paeans to life, full of love and lush rhyme. Looking back on them I wonder now how I ever came to write such vacant drizzle. None of them made it to the end of the decade. The book went out to the critics. No one replied.

In the dust-filled loft of my house in Cardiff, where the lack of felt below the slates has made the whole dark cavern of strut and rafter the blackest of spaces, I am shifting boxes. They balance precariously over the three inches of dark fibreglass insulation. Slip here and you are through the ceiling. Central heating man did once, leg and mighty shower of black mortar like a bomb in the hall. I go through the boxes of small mags by torch. *Iconolatre, Global Tapestry, Hapt, Earthship, Gong, Stereo Headphones, Curtains, Cosmos, Ludds Mill, Sad Traffic, Good Elf, Crab Grass, The Curiously Strong, Fountain of Light, The*

Waxing Moon. Blackbag them. Their four decade afterlife near the stars in Roath now over. This has happened before. I've left boxes of poetry in the bedroom of a flat in Llandaf North and great stacks of little mags in a garage in Whitchurch. This is what becomes of them. Their purpose. The poems flicker, for a moment maybe, as someone other than their creator reads them, if indeed they ever do. Then their pages are shut and they fade as the years roll, to vanish as time eats them becoming dust addled landfill or recycled pulp.

In the era these things came from there were poets around who thought they might change things, writers who actually went out and engaged with the world. Innovators, they altered the way it was done. They rocked across landscapes, climbed mountains, tracked the energy lines that flowed like psychedelic rivers between standing stone and standing stone. Eric Mottram, Chris Torrance, Paul Evans, Lee Harwood, John James. All Welsh elected to be Welsh, Welsh while they were here and, it should be said, always ignored by the Welsh establishment, clearly never Welsh enough.

There were literary magazines run from Bangor and from Caernarfon. In Pwllheli and a whole raft in Aberystwyth. *Ubu, Madoc, Mabon, Decal, Dawn, Dragon, Ram.* But never one from Abermawddach. But they are not needed now. The web has dissolved geography, made everything so inexpensive, made it all so easy that anyone without skill and without effort can do it, turned the literary world into an all-pervasive soup.

In Barmouth there are no mosques. Christianity, now the age of morals is over, hangs on, if it does at all, by a dismal thread. Welshness is a thin drift from Ireland and a roll from England. Adoptive. Smiled

at or ignored. The locals, those left, are appeasers, their culture kept boxed and silent, lost among the take away curries and the bright red plastic spades. What else can you do? Here Wales, long time centre of opposition, of the other point of view, has itself become the underdog, swamped by alien-accented arrivals from a post-industrial wider world. Does it matter? Can't go back now, can't do anything about it, lost the way, missed the chance. We'll have to manage, we'll get by, we've done it before, have we not, so many times.

I don't stop, I head on, out past mile after mile of caravan park clustered like so much industrial detritus along the sea line, heading north.

THE WATKIN PATH

Most mountain work is up. This is no exception. You have to get nearer to the big sky, to the ceiling, to the void. Pull yourself, one foot then another foot, climb. There are a host of mountain books on this subject – climbers lost in meditation and pain, pulling muscle, flagellating flesh, as they inch upwards to find their souls, their gods, themselves. The plan today is to get to the top to say I've done it. How is it possible to live in a country and never have come near its highest spot? Yr Wyddfa at 3560 feet. Snowdon, sunburst in the Welsh psyche. Snowdon the great northern starfish with its six ridges radiating. Snowdon the ancient burial place of the giant Rhita Fawr with his cloak of hair made from the beards of the kings he'd killed. Snowdon made of gritstone, mudstone, volcanic ash, slate. Snowdon with its subterranean lake full of dragons. Snowdon scatter ground for Arthur's bones.

The car is at Pen-y-Pass, locked against marauders who may visit the boot and steal our tooth brushes. The pull is up the Miners Track, winding to the lake, Llyn Glaslyn, a path built in the nineteenth century for the workers at the now abandoned Britannia Copper Mines. It's rough and eroded, rock strewn but with admirable views of the peaks and the crags. In the guidebook there's talk of an Edwardian madman from the Pen y Gwryd Hotel who drove his car all the way up here to the big lake at the top. The route is heavy with booted tourists, blue and red anoraks, walking poles, sticks, packs, compasses, maps in bags, kids, hats. No chance of solitude. God to be communed with among the banter and blather of the leisured class.

The lake is glacial, created by the terminal moraines left here by the melting glaciers of the last ice age. The waters are replete with mystery. Excalibur was thrown in here. The robed hand of the Lady of the Lake rose up from below the surface to catch it and to take it back down. The legend repeats at glacial corries right across Wales.

Beyond the waters the climb starts to feel real, it pulls the backs of your legs, it hauls and pushes, it goes, where does it go, it goes up. The heaving crowd around me hardly falters. We rise up the zig zag, stop to take the view, actually to draw breath, watch the skies, look out through the thinning air. I've got kids around me eating crisps, some-one stopped by the marker stone at Bwlch Glas to light a roll-up, a bloke with his mouth round a sausage roll, where did he get it from, why is he eating it here. The up and down mountain traffic merges, climbers with OS Explorers and cameras, whole families in matching hats, lone ancients in knee socks, hauling on up.

I'd like to be alone, I need to be on my own, can't do it, this heav-ing crowd like Saturday Queen Street, the mass mind like a cloud damping out all reason, no space left to think. Then there's a steam whistle, a great echoing, bouncing off the rock walls in a shattering scream. And bloody smoke up there on the ridge, hell's teeth, the train. I'd forgotten the Mountain Railway, the hour or so easy trip up the rack and pinion, sit in the coach with your newspaper. Alight at the top without a puff. There's something wholly irreverent about this, like chewing gum at interviews or wearing t-shirts to church. It's in your face, no effort, got here by helicopter, the pain and strain of the personal slog and sacrifice drained completely of value. The sum-mit comes into sight, surrounded by a great bubbling crowd. Women in white high heels carrying city-size handbags. A man in resort shorts and flip flops. A middle-aged couple dressed for dinner, creases in the right places, shine on their shoes, don't have any leisure clothes, for what do I need those. Here I am, top of the Welsh world, and I have to fight the massed punters for a toe hold. Heaven will be like this. You imagine you'll rush in aboard a golden chariot, you're wrong. It'll be queues and checkpoints. Shoving. Bad day at Terminal Five. Motorway Services when the football coaches have pulled in. Someone else comes by streaming coffee from a giant paper cup. Has to be a concession in the café. I can't bear to enter this concrete fortress. Folk emerging with clutches of postcards, ice creams, bags of sweets, t-shirts sloganed I GOT TO THE TOP OF SNOWDON. On the back it ought to say I COULDN'T BE ARSED I CAUGHT THE TRAIN.

Sue says we should return on the Watkin Path, be different, why not. Neither of us have looked at any maps, well I haven't. I just need to go. The track slides away southwards, a blob of paint to show where it is, to mark it as different from the rest of the sprawling scree. We plunge on down.

I always imagined that the path was named after a Snowdon mountaineer, a walker, a Wainwright of Eryri, someone who had pio-neered trails and trackways, a rescuer of goats and stranded children, a saver of souls lost in the mist. But this turns out not to be the case. Sir Edward Watkin, 1819-1901, Victorian railway magnate of the Great Central, Liberal Unionist for Stockport and later Hythe in Kent, a man given to flamboyant gestures, had the trail surveyed and then built for him. Watkin had started a Channel Tunnel which had faltered for lack of finance and then failed in an attempt to outdo France with a tower much taller than Eiffel's on the site now occupied by Wembley Stadium. Watkin's folly, which Gustave Eiffel had been offered the commission to design but had refused on the grounds that such a tower in London wouldn't do much good for France, had reached only 155 feet before the foundations were discovered to be too unstable for it to climb any higher. Sir Edward retired to Cwm y Llan at Snowdon's foot and had workmen construct a path up to the old South Snowdon Slate Quarry and then on through Cwm Tregalan up via the precipitous scree to the mountain's peak. The track was opened in 1892. Watkin got William Gladstone, then 83 and still British Prime Minister, to perform the opening ceremony. Just south of the quarry a giant rock was carpeted and temporarily roofed. The great man spoke to an enthusiastic crowd of over two thousand. Rock's still there, you can't miss it on your way down.

I climb south, down a slope that is suddenly far steeper than I'd expected and which then falls away almost vertically. It seems to be made entirely of loose boulder and sliding rock. Below the world opens in a great plunging vista. My legs strain. Vertigo, my old friend, my sweat, my panic, rises behind my eyes. I can't do this. Flexibility vanishes. I freeze and shudder. Climbers pass me, going up, breathless, smiling. I have fear of falling or dissolving or dying, of my pack and my arms loosed from me. The whole world spins. The climbers blur. Someone ascends with a two year old strapped to his back. Gurgling, laughing. Impossible. I have to go back up, look over my shoulder, cold rocks looming, can't manage that either. Maybe if I take off my glasses and let the world blur. Try this. Worse. Sue urges me to descend following her footsteps. Do it, so slowly. Death just behind my mouth. Hands shaking. The path sinks and falls. Goes on down for thousands of feet, like a ladder without rungs, nowhere to stop, no rest. This vertigo has to be conquered. I strain on down, feet sliding on the loose surface. Takes eternity. But I get there, inch on inch.

Eventually after what seems like a whole day of this but which in reality can't have been more than twenty minutes the ground begins to level, just slightly, enough for my rubber legs to shake onto, my hands to steady, and my breath to come back into me. The valley sides come up. In the distance is the Quarry and then Gladstone Rock. We move on, pain in every bone, but the clouds above me no longer swimming and swirling.

I've seen this landscape before, of course. These rocks played the part of the Khyber Pass in the film *Carry On Up The Khyber*. Sid James as Sir Sidney Ruff-Diamond came up here with the Third Foot and Mouth to take on Kenneth Williams, the Khasi of Kalabar, in 1968. Wales and India have always been close.

Beyond the Quarry the land opens up, greens, empties. No one here, no habitation, no one for miles. No anoraks. No candyfloss. No dragons. Wales again. "When at my feet the ground appeared to brighten, And with a step or two seemed brighter still"[5] We are, of course, nowhere near the car. This is the wrong side of the mountain and, when we get to the road after more hours of sun-filled downward walking, at least twelve miles from Pen-y-Pass. But does any of this matter? Watkin has been conquered. We hitch.

That was Snowdon. Centre of the Welsh heartstop wilderness. At a store in Betws-y-Coed I buy a picture of the mountain covered with snow, looking like Everest, brooding skywards. Show that about when I get home.

HOLY ISLAND

The name itself is enough. How many of these are there in the world? Islands where saints dwelt or were martyred or took off for heaven in streams of golden light? This one is on the far reaches of Wales where, given the land of the ancients' mountained remoteness, the geomancy of druidic power should still dominate. But in this western outpost of fading Britishness spiritual magic no longer exists. Instead there are six axle-prime movers, tankers, trailers, pantechnicons, white sprinter vans, overloaded European rigs with their silver pipework venting oil exhaust to the heavens, three-layer vehicle transporters, containers of fish and rags from Bilbao, Carpathia, Bratislava, Budapest. Engineered car parts from Cluj-Napoca. Immigrants from Plovdiv and Varna. The weight of twenty-first century logistics en route to the land of the celtic tiger. I'm here because I need to be. Almost everyone else is transient. Nothing to hold them. Bleakness. Rain.

I've set off from Cardiff in the deep south at 4.00 am. Miss the tractors. I've come up through the cotton fields of Merthyr and crossed the Rhayadr badlands in the morning dark, slick and swift.

Dawn rose in the mountains, Meic Stevens on the player, Solva ballads, so far from here as to be alien. Kyffin Williams, the late painter the well-to-do of Wales loved to love, came off the road near here once, so I've been told, car in a ditch, wasn't hurt, but couldn't get the vehicle back out. Iago Prytherch, weeding mangles in a nearby field, offered his shoulder. There was much pushing and wheel spin before Kyffin got back onto tarmac. He was so pleased he opened the boot and took out one of his sketch pads, charcoal landscape, Kyffinesque shepherds leaning on staffs, clouds. Tore it out and gave it to Iago by way of thanks. Worth hundreds, even back then. Iago looked at it briefly, nodded, offered mumbled thanks, folded the thing in two and in two again, then pushed it roughly into his overall back pocket. He touched his cap as Kyffin, as much in awe of the roots of northern Welshness as R.S. had been, drove slowly on.

The mountains give way to the coast and the A5 to the European-funded express way, the A55, dual carriage which crosses Robert Stephenson's tubular Britannia Bridge, leaving the fastness of volcanic Wales for the unexpected flatness of Ynys Môn, Mam Cymru, Ynys Dywyll, Anglesey, Welsher than Gwynedd if there was a contest. But there's not. The A55 is empty while I'm on it, speeding through early light. Meic Stevens becomes Lucinda Williams, country steel and chiming guitar, sliding to the west. We move on. Through Valley, lose the Four Mile Bridge, take the new one missing Telford's Stanley Embankment, onto another island, the Holy one, Ynys Gybi, Ireland beyond Anglesey. It's like that.

In the car, stopped alongside Holyhead harbour, waiting for the world to open I wonder what I've missed? Like most who come here I've driven straight across Anglesey without stopping, seen nothing, none of the pagan stones, Roman camps, cliffs and coves, missed the beauty, the tranquillity, got here to this battered place full of scuff and squalor. Fisherman walks past, rods and bait boxes, carry stool, catch net, boxed sandwiches, *Daily Mirror*, roll up.

There's something which links this place with Milford Haven, its southern equivalent, wide cambered streets, light, lack of grandeur, places that service the traveller, pound shops, beat up, sink, small pubs, traffic, places boarded, gutters full of leaves and moss.

Holyhead is the ferry port for Ireland. A border point where one world ends and another begins. Troops go through here. Men with dirt on their faces. Families with baggage. Cars and caravans. Now there's no oil or gas in the grey Celtic Sea, the Irish would like to build a bridge, been done already over a wider stretch of wilder ocean by the Japanese, six lanes, tall enough for tankers to pass under, lit like a city at Christmas time. The twenty-first century peril will not be the wars with Islam but our obsession with movement – endless, eternal – further, faster, Dublin to Constantinople in the time it has taken me to cross Wales.

I've come here, all this way, to read my poems. Poets do this. In the twentieth and twenty-first centuries. Increasingly. Small, clear, attentive audiences of aficionados, other writers, wannabes, coming to hear you tell them what you do, how you did it, so they can marvel and then bend your ideas into theirs. I've been involved in the system for more years than I care to admit to and still wonder at its confusion, its audacity, its place in the cultural firmament, its achievement as high art, its utter boredom for anyone not deeply or closely connected, its brilliance, its fulfilment of desire and description, its magic. And it can be magic be assured.

At Ucheldre, the arts centre converted out of a convent chapel once belonging to a French Roman Catholic order of nuns and still feeling that spirit in its floors and ceilings and doors, my small audience cluster at the centre of a great and hopeful swathe of chairs. Ucheldre, the conversion project, began in 1989 when Holyhead topped the tables as the most depressed place in Britain. Art was seen as a vehicle of salvation, just as Christ once was, and just as Christ once took over the sites of the pagans and made them his so the arts take Christ and turn him to a different glory. Green, local stone, sculpture park, exhibition hall, performance space.

I am the only one on the bill. No warm up act. I surreptitiously take a drink. The trick is to have enough to lubricate but never so much that control goes. Vodka. Clean and clear. Jeff Nuttall explained that it was possible to drink fourteen whiskeys and still go on. You took a deep breath and flung yourself into it. Could anyone ever tell, I asked? Always, he replied.

Fiona Owen introduces me as a writer who has carved new spaces and spent his life pushing at boundaries and I begin. How are these things different from actors coming on and reciting what they've learned? Why would anyone want to hear a poet speak his poems? Poems hang in the air like irresolvable difficulty, lumps in your back as you take to your chair, things that won't slide easily, won't massage the stress from your brow. The late Ray Handy travelled around Wales regurgitating the leaps and laughs of our poetic culture – R.S., Harri Webb, Dylan – stuff that underlined an older vision of Welshness. Ray charged twice the money poets wanted. Quoted membership of

Equity. Got it. Performed in the north many times. Always filled his venues. What you didn't get from this man was insight, nothing about where the poems really came from nor what they really were. All you got was Ray's personal take on where the poet might have been going. Ray did it well. Music Hall tradition. Dressed the part, smoking jacket, cravat. Delivered without script. Stood well, got his voice ringing all the way to the back. Poets always needed to read from bits of paper. Eye contact is less. Poets stumble. Audiences must want to learn something about who the versifiers actually are to really enjoy. Like going to see Elgar conduct his own *Dream of Gerontius*.

Poets can be different. R.S. standing before his audience in silence for five minutes as he untied the string holding his volumes together. J.P. Ward coming on wearing a donkey jacket and forgetting which poem to tackle next. John Idris Jones, flanked by twin harpists, spinning with the fairground horses at Barry Island. Paul Henry magically producing his guitar and singing a song mid-set. Mike Jenkins doing Captain Beefheart impersonations on a harmonica. Tom Earley losing his papers. Mike Horovitz reading for three hours without a break. All of this riddled with echoes of Dylan Thomas' booming declamations. Vowels stretched in the wrong places. Speaking voices forgotten. Weird elevation imposed on their verses. But listen to what they say before, catch the context. Maybe you can survive an hour without needing to start counting the spots on the wall paper.

I don't do this. I came up through the industrial academy of Raymond Garlick and Roland Mathias, where lightness has flown and reality is entirely in the verse. Then I added the way the Beats took belief by the throat and exploded it. Couldn't manage without wit. Added something of the sound poets bending their voices through their tape recorders.

I bang out half an hour of poetry, some talk, some contextualising, little explanation, the verse itself needs to do that. I breathe like I imagine John Coltrane would. Hunt around for some place where I can connect with the starry dynamo and, once I've got it, I just let the breath go. Look them in the eye, the audience. Go inside. My thirty or so applaud politely and several buy books. Dannie Abse taught me this. Never go anywhere without your suitcase of stock. A book in the hand is worth six on the shelf down the road in the distant Smiths. Talk afterwards, be friendly, smile, hang around and sign whatever they want. I rarely get this far north. For them I'm new. The books go well.

Readings are so singular, I've given thousands, a life-time's worth, and I still do not understand their mechanics. Alan Brownjohn once

headed deep into the Yorkshire Dales for a reading in another converted chapel, lonely in its country outpost. After a long drive he
found it, reaching the door in time. Met with the organiser and his
wife, sitting in the front row, awaiting him with wonder in their
breath. They spoke of how it is with crowds, how they never come
when you want them, how the weather can make all the difference (it
had been a sunny day), how the distance they have to travel can make
or break. Fifteen minutes went. Nothing. Half an hour passed. No
one showed. The organiser suggested then that he himself go on first
to "warm them up", stood, his wife introduced him, and he proceeded to read his indifferent poetry to his wife and to seated
Brownjohn, polite to the last. When the organiser had finished and
both Brownjohn and the organiser's wife had applauded quietly they
had a break. Twenty minutes. No coffee. Brownjohn asked if there
was a toilet. There was not. The organiser then announced that he
and his wife had to go and gave Brownjohn the chapel key, big, dark
metal, hung by string to a fob made from a chunk of wood, asked him
if he could lock up after he had finished reading and to push the key
back in through the letterbox. The organiser and his wife shook
hands, thanked the poet and then left. Brownjohn sat for a while,
bemused and silent. He opened his book and then shut it. Got up and
turned the lights off. The cheque, he had been assured, would be in
the post.

Ucheldre is nothing like this.

I stay overnight, out towards South Stack, with the centre director,
David Crystal, who if it were not for the beard could be mistaken for
Spike Milligan, both Irish, both with modified accents, one hilarious
the other much the same. Crystal has made his name as an compiler
of encyclopaedias, a writer on the fate of languages and a defender of
linguistic change. I likes doing this I does I thinks I do. Fate of the
world. His house is thick with networks of knowledge and data. One
in three of the world's population use English to some degree.
Dominance is inevitable. But on local terms. Crystal predicts ever
greater diversification as out there, beyond our tongue, the lishes take
hold. Singlish, Japlish, Chinglish, Wenglish, Spanglish. These are vari-
ations with their own vocabularies and structures. They often veer on
side of the unintelligible to speakers of the standard tongue. Will
minority languages fade and die? On the evidence of internet use,
Crystal thinks not. The web currently has more than 1500 languages
rattling its html and that number along with the total number of
pages in use is growing. We're a multilingual fractured universe. He

does an imitation of Bob Cobbing, the late sound text manipulator. Tan tandinare tan tanrita tanrota tan. The spell that transcends boundaries. Whatever the language it won't keep you out forever. Sut mae'ch cymraeg chi, David? Dim yn ddrwg.

In the morning there is mist. I see nothing of this holy place as I leave, less of Môn than I would have liked, follow the taillights of a bulk grain carrier, going back empty from Dublin. I turn south when I reach the mainland, climb again through the mountains, Ireland on the radio until the rocks of Wales bugger it. The CD this time is Chris Painter's *Clarinet Quartet*, hand-copied, elevating, innovative and, on this occasion so it seems, impossible to eject. I hear it right through three times before turning the player off somewhere near Carno. Silence. Ah yes.

NANT GWRTHEYRN

Up here on the Gwynedd clifftop, between Pistyll and Trefor, is a village that the maps seem uncertain about. Quarry. Hut circles. Contours. Symbol for a picnic table. A few black oblongs to represent buildings. No post code of its own. This is the Nant Gwrtheyrn Welsh Language and Heritage Centre. A reclaimed quarry village on a shelf of flat land at the foot of a precipitous cliff, well south of Anglesey, facing out into Caernarfon Bay. I'm here because I am curious. It's out of season, no course running, Caffi Meinir ar gau, a chubby waitress in regulation white blouse and black skirt idling across the tables with a J-cloth, two cars in the tiny car park. Over the green topped bund is a white slash of pebbles and the sound of the sea. But I am getting ahead of myself. I haven't got down yet and that's an experience in itself.

Nant Gwrtheyrn was a couple of farms until the quarries opened in 1850. Entrepreneurs all over Wales were looking for ways to cut up the land and sell it on. This was the industrial revolution. The time when the green world changed completely. If it wasn't iron ore then it was coal or slate. Up here on the coast next to the shining sea it was stone. Granite from which to build the roads and walls of rapidly expanding English cities. Quarries opened first at Trefor and at Penmaenmawr. The rock went out to Birkenhead, Liverpool and Manchester by ship from Nant Gwrtheyrn. Soon quarries were opened at the Nant itself. A jetty was built and houses erected. Holyhead View, a row of thirteen workers cottages, known locally as the Barics, were occupied by Irish itinerant workers. In 1878 more houses were added in L shaped rows. Three Nant quarries[6] were now at work, their produce loaded onto 200-ton ships at the jetty. There was a bakery and a shop and a large quarry manager's residence. The 1886 census showed two hundred people living in the village. Most of them Welsh[7] with a smattering of Scots and a few English. They built themselves a wooden school, and a chapel, Y Babell Goed, and then when God appeared to be needed more than ever to counter the ungodly feasting and drinking on the Sabbath, Capel Seilio from stone. Seilio is still there. Y Babell Goed went down in a storm.

The Nant has no tavern and there are tales of desperate workers rolling barrels down the precipitous track. Most, however, visited the Vic in Llithfaen, on the cliff top. Staggered home, stumbling and sprawling, fell from great heights to the sea, broke limbs on the raucous rock, froze to death in the winds blasting in from the icy north. Drunkenness no worse than now. Only the locations have changed.

Production peak was the First World War after which output faltered. Nant Quarry shut in 1915, reopened half-heartedly in the 1930s and then closed again along with all the others in 1939. The workers and their families left. Nant Gwrtheyrn filled with Llŷn tumbleweed and Gwynedd dust. A ghost town of lost dogs and sporadic squatters and, after 1959 a ghost town of no one at all.

The rebirth of the village as a centre for the learning of Welsh was the idea of Carl Clowes, a doctor from Manchester whose practice was in nearby Llanaelhaern and who wanted to ensure that his children were brought up speaking the language of the land he was now working in. Around him others had woken to the late twentieth century need for a new way to pass Welsh on. To do this for both those from afar who were losing their fluency and for those who had moved into the area and wanted to fit in. The idea for a centre was born, a committee formed, a trust fund established and a campaign launched. Like so many ventures in Welsh Wales Nant Gwrtheyrn became a cause close to the hearts of almost everyone who came into contact with its proponents. By 1978 enough money had been raised to buy the empty village and by 1982, despite a traditional Welsh lack of telephones, heat, light and running water, the first course was run. Ydych chi'n dysgu cymraeg? Ydw, ni gyd yma yn trio ein gorau glas. We are. Pob lwc a hwyl fawr. There is something about learning the language, this language, that makes you a trusting child again. Putting up with privation, mangling the consonants but getting the vowels to sing, glorying in the Welsh world.

As a centre the Nant has gone from strength to strength. New roofs, repointed walls, repainted, services restored. It now runs year round residential immersion courses for adults and offers holiday and conference accommodation. There is also a suggestion on the centre's website that you might like to get married here. Priodas go iawn. Diolch i'r nefoedd. In Wales the out of fashion masquerades as the new. We are distant and different. We have what they don't have in the cities – clear minds and pure air.

Getting down is no picnic. I look at the road falling away from me in what appears to be an almost vertical slide of hard-top and park the car in a lay by and walk. It takes a good half an hour of breath and care. You could drive, some do, but there's barely space for more than a handful of cars at the bottom. The Nant's official website advises visitors to leave their cars more or less where I did. "It will take a 20-30 minute walk to get down and a 40-50 minute walk to get back up". Casual drop-in is not a feature.

When it is in action the Nant buzzes. Attendees are here because they want to be and oh how they do. You take up the tongue, you enthuse, you enthuse further, you pay your money and then you travel a great distance to arrive and immerse yourself in the language of heaven. Grim, guttural, gorgeous. Where the world speaks slowly and everyone smiles. So convivial. Croeso mawr. Wales, land of warm welcome where no one cries. In this country English no longer cuts it. In this county did it ever. But if you are wearing a pink tracksuit or have a soft Suffolk accent then don't try bore da in the local taverns. And remember, if you are thinking of moving in, that this is the place where more than two hundred outsider cottages were burned to the ground and no perpetrator was ever caught. "We don't know who they are" – neighbourhood police. "These people must be stopped" – local politicians. "An Elsan culture threatens us" – R.S. Thomas. Wales, land of contradictions. Speak to us in our language and we will open our arms. But don't stay that long, we don't like you that much.

In Llŷn the accent has an adenoidal scream about it that recalls both Ireland and Liverpool but is ultimately a sound that can only be itself. The words come out slowly, hovering in the air above you but dive and squall the moment their meanings hook. "When the language is at the end of the headlands, / Where will they go, the gabblers of names / And at their lips the string of villages, / And all of Wales a song in their mouths?"[8] The impenetrability, perceived or real, is the very strength of the tongue that was, for most of the twentieth century, clearly dying. You don't impregnate this language and thin it to unreality. You take it on with effort, great effort, and you master what you can. You respect its age. It's older than English by hundreds of years. And at the end of the headlands where its land runs out you turn and walk back, filling the air with what you've learned. R.S. Thomas did this. Would you know that man, born to English parentage in English-speaking Cardiff, ended his life here on Llŷn, spoke out for the cottage burners and refused any language bar the one that came at him out of the rock upon which he stood. And if you are lucky enough for the language to be yours by birth, by first right, then you do nothing special. Just carry on.

Gwrtheyrn's history before the quarries is about as complex as anything dreamt by Tolkien. For three farms and a patch of pebbles next to a roaring sea the tales are disproportionately many. Castles, curses, marriages, armies, monks, magic. Vortigern[9] owned this spot and filled it with his mystic acts. Maybe the name *Gwrtheyrn* actually came from *Gor*, super, and *teyrn*, king. Brook of the super kings. River of power. Place of fantasy where druids rise from the deep soil to defeat all who strode here in the limpid air.

I've climbed Yr Eifl, highest point on the Llŷn, north of the Nant by a kilometre or two. There are three peaks here, Tre'r Ceiri, Garn Ganol and Garn Fawr, none of them higher than 564 meters, strung about with ancient tracks and the best example of an iron age hillfort I've seen anywhere. The peat has largely all been stripped from the surfaces by generations of Llŷn cottagers. The corkscrew road sinks below acid heather. Yr Eifl has been quarried extensively – granite for London, crystalline curling stones for the world Olympics. So much has gone that Garn Fawr's seaward face is almost exhausted of its stone. Abandoned now but for a microwave relay station and some disused wartime lookouts. Up here the language rides the thermals. I'm on them too. My enthusiasm is as hot as that in the quarry-worker class rooms of the Nant. But it is an enthusiasm not for the simple code of words, nor what they say baldly. It is not for their politics nor their geography but, instead, for what they do and where you can make them go. Why else write anything. Why speak in Welsh. Why speak in any tongue at all.

From here the Llŷn simmers off into the distance, another place of borders where something ends and something else, falteringly, begins. Wales behind me is huge, beyond me so small.

BANGOR

Entering Bangor is like entering a cave, like reaching Kamchatka in the Russian Far East, crossing into north Korea, entering the pure lands which you've never before seen. This was how I imagined it to be. Was it like that? No. In 1721 Bangor had seventy houses, plus one in Upper Bangor and one in Garth. Population 400[10]. But it had the church of the Celtic missionary, Deiniol, the great stone cathedral. A wooden shack with straw roof on fenced ground in 525. The fence was interwoven with branches. The style was called Bangor. So too the place.

It might have slept on through the centuries, too, in its soft miasma of Welsh belief. Might have done this if it hadn't been for the diversion of the post route to Ireland. This once went over the tidal Lafan Sands from where the crossing to Beaumaris was not easy. A ferry from Bangor to Porthaethwy was a safer bet. Bangor found itself on the main run from Dublin to London. When Richard Pennant opened his slate quarries at Bethesda and used Bangor as a port growth increased. Subsidiary industry arrived in Pennant's wake. A foundry was established. A sawmill opened. Shipbuilding began. A steam packet service to Liverpool started in 1822. Thomas Telford built his bridge across the Menai Straits in 1826. The railways arrived in 1848. Population leaped in bounds.

There was an isolation hospital at Minfford. A workhouse. An infirmary. Shops, banks, hotels. Seats of learning. Normal College in 1862, the University College in 1884 and St Mary's College in 1893. The pleasure pier opened in 1896. The Vaynol Estate[11] dating back to the Tudors was a home for the gentry. The BBC set up radio studios in the 1930s. During the second world war they transferred their entire light entertainment provision here from London. Bangor, nowhere more powerful in Gwynedd. Spiritual capital of the north. If not that then certainly its most important town. Bangor, Wales (avoid Bangor Maine, Bangor County Down, and *Didn't we have a lovely time, the day we went to Bangor* – folk song rumoured written about Rhyl, there's no seafront at Bangor, nearest brass band is Porthaethwy[12]). Population today around 12,500. Around 55% Welsh speaking. Feels like more.

I've driven north, across the distance. Been here before. Bangor, a river valley, slit in a land full of rivers. No coast that's obvious. I didn't realise the town sat on the Menai Straits with the salt waters washing by until I'd been here three times.

I'm here this time to give a talk for Ian Davidson and Zoe Skoulding at the University. Seventy students who all want to know what motivates me and how this affects my work. My hotel is a green painted, extension-addled ancient construct. It's on slightly raised ground, like a Siliwen house, above the pier. Hard to make out in the dark. It was opened for the tourist trade from English conurbations. Bar with chairs

that itch. Nylon mock-Wilton like the stuff in our house in 1948. Coffee served in small cups with ornate handles, silver tray, clattering catch of spoons and sugar basin. Your room is on the first floor, hard to get in there given the size of the furniture. Huge tallboy and giant dressing table. Put my case in the sink. Stand inside the wardrobe in order to get my jacket off. Poked in eye by bent dry-cleaners wire coat hanger.

Earlier I went looking for the River Adda. Hard to find. It's been culverted piecemeal fashion over the past 250 years, four kilometres through the city centre to outfall in Bangor Harbour. Periodically it fails and car parks flood, basements fill, streets seep. Work is ongoing to improve it. The city seems permanently damp.

Walk back from the college following the line of the culvert with Ian Gregson. Post-modernist, *Call Centre Lovesongs*, critic. Little connected with lit Wales. Poems of his should reach further. He tells me about the sons of Bangor. Those who've made this place. Empty streets tonight. No moon.

Who comes from Bangor? Thomas Parry, Alun Llywelyn-Williams, Aled Jones, A.O.H. Jarman, Brenda Chamberlain, Tony Conran, Tony Brown, Huw Wheldon. Hywel ab Owain Gwynedd buried near the cathedral's altar.

Before I climb back into my time machine of a hotel I take a look at the pier. Second longest in Wales. Victorian. Lead cupolas on its storm shelters. Restored. Almost invisible in the starlight. I'll go back in the morning light and take some photos. The following day, when I remember, I'm already roaring along the fast sloping A470 into Rhayadyr. Seafront long gone. Bangor still dark when I left it. Next time.

notes

1. Which roughly translates as: His gravestone, the grave of a man who was a hero to his people; Dwyfor is a beautiful watercolour, it constantly comforts the grave.
2. Sir Clough Williams Ellis, architect, 1883-1978.
3. Field of the speckled calf.
4. No staff are available to let guests in after midnight. No keys will be issued. Debate on this matter is discouraged.
5. William Wordsworth – *The Prelude*, 1850. Wordsworth first climbed Snowdon in 1791.
6. Cae'r Nant, Porth y Nant and Carreg y Llam (*History of Nant Gwrtheyrn*, Prof Bedwyr Lewis Jones & Elen Rhys – www.acen.co.uk).
7. Two out of three came from Pistyll and Edeyrn on the Llŷn peninsular, from Penmaenmawr in Arfon and from Anglesey farms.
8. Twm Morys – *Wrth Glywed Sais yn Siarad*, author's translation.
9. Vortigern, King of Britain after the Romans. His legend mixes with that of Arthur and flows through Wales like Merlin. Bedd Gwrtheyrn, Vortigern's Grave, is there, somewhere near the Nant. "In a wind-beaten valley of Snowdon, near the sea, that his dead body decked in green armour had a mound of earth and stones raised over it" said George Borrow in 1862.
10. Browne Willis: *A Survey of the Cathedral Church of Bangor*, 1721.
11. William de Hunton lived here in 1394. High Sheriff Thomas Wyn ap Willim (Thomas Williams) took ownership in 1572. At its height the estate covered over 35,000 acres of land stretching form the Menai Straits into Snowdonia and down into the Llyn Peninsula. Today it still runs to more than 1000. (BBC website).
12. "Do you recall the thrill of it all / As we walked along the seafront / Then on the sand we heard a brass band / That made a tiddly tum ta ra ra / Elsie and me had one cup of tea" – *Day Trip To Bangor* written by Debbie Cook, recorded by Fiddler's Dram (Fiddler's Dram, Dingles Records, 1980).

Dear contact@peterfinch.co.uk

http://ferangette.com

What is Exquisite Bangor store?

At Exquisite Replica, we specialize in the sales
of brand-name quality, luxury replicas at some
of the lowest prices possible.
With our large selection of products, you can be
sure to find that perfect gift for yourself or a
loved one.

Encyclopaedia, fish kettle, branded Bangor headscarf, pier replica,
miniature rs, oxymorgan.

Visit Exquisite Bangor Shop!
http://ferangette.com

Thanks
Buddug Anniston

contact@peterfinch.co.uk wrote:

SOLD OUT !Do you want Bangor or other brander
watch under 250?

MORE

A470

You can read about the A470 and anticipate its wonder. You can check its many miles at AA Routefinder[1] and hold that figure in your memory, weight it against other journeys you've made, flights to Jersey, rolls along the M4 to Swindon, trips to the coast at Dorset. You can savour this long road in its wicked diversity of dual carriage, overtaking lane, underpass and bridge. You can imagine the riot of colour alongside it, green, then grey green then more green. You can consider its inclines – the one near Merthyr at Aberfan where rising north it always starts to rain. You can relish its slopes and bends and anticipate with great bates in your breath the moment of starting.

Nothing, however, can prepare you for what it is mind-numbingly really like: featureless, dark, difficult, bend after bend of tractors, drizzle, rain, milk tankers, caravans, and lorries full of hay. No rest stops, few lay bys. A couple of burger vans across the Beacons, the Vulcan north of Newbridge, rain swept toilets and pull-in at Carno. The long A470, bare and blighted. The bastard prodigy of the mid twentieth century planners who wanted to link the unlinkable. Unreal and unconvincing, a road that drove all the way from Cardiff to Llandudno. It's almost two hundred miles, enough to get to Dublin or Norwich. Who loves it? The only thing we have in this country that truly links the north with the south. Like a line of sheep scuffling through the hills, a thread unravelling across the mountains as the world slowly turns.

Communication in Wales has always been difficult. First there's the language, an adenoidal northern variation that, on first encounter, sounds total alien from the clear tones emanating from the south. Or, put another way, there's a thin anglicised substitute for the language of heaven that fills the distant reaches of the southern valleys and which sounds so fake to the true sons of Wales in their northern Gwynedd haunts. Then there's television which, until the arrival of satellite, had so much trouble even making it from one valley to the next. Irish stations came in clearer to the folk of Pwllheli. And finally there's transport. No river we all own, north and south. Two Tafs, both in the wrong places, the Wye and the Dee not meeting and the Severn too English. Across the Cambrian Massif no canals are possible. The railways run brilliantly along the northern and southern coasts, taking Londoners swiftly to Fishguard and Dubliners, via the last redoubt of the druids on Anglesey, to the heart of England. There's a mid-Wales snake for tourists that single-tracks from

Swansea to Shrewsbury and a new-generation Arriva Trains two-car diesel clatter that goes right along the Wales-England border, Cardiff to Bangor, six hours, tea trolley passes your seat eight times, you eat too many crisps. Sometimes it gets stuck at junctions and takes nine hours. That leaves roads.

The Romans built Sarn Helen to take their troops from Neath[2] northwards. It crossed the Beacons in a straight line, parts of it are still in place, used by offroaders and horse riders. Further north the road from Osegontium (Caernarfon) to Mamicum (Manchester) can mostly be traced. And there are other fragments running near Newtown and Ruthin and Moridunum (Carmarthen) but nothing left that joins up and certainly nothing that ever attempted to cross Wales' great green centre. That was left to the Kite.

For the most part future raiders and invaders did not concern themselves with longitudinal travel. Wales north and Wales south were different countries. They could both be subdued by advances along the latitudes in from the Welsh marches, from Mercia, that place where Wales used to be, from England.

It took the industrial revolution to give Wales anything that could be considered even vaguely as a transport infrastructure and even then the new, hard-topped roads were built along the routes of earlier trails, tracks and paths. Green lanes capped and topped with stone and hot macadam, turned smooth, turned dark. Carriages acquired tyres and engines. Things got faster.

Over in England the London Parliament was busy classifying. Order is an English obsession. Roads were designated either A or B. The As, the important ones, got investment. The Bs languished. Around 1923, to reduce confusion, the whole system began to be numbered. Arterial roads were counted clockwise as they sped out from London. A1, A2, A3, A4, A5, A6. Less important roads were given higher numbers – A20, A18. As a rule of thumb the more digits the less important the road was considered. Most of the A roads in Wales have three or four – A483, A4161, A4067. None of these connected the north to the south. To manage this task you took out your AA Members Handbook and traced a many numbered way across its yellow pages. You set off and took several traffic-choked hours to reach Merthyr. There you languished on the town's dark streets, in queues of black cars and creaking pre-War, speed limited, wooden-cabbed lorries. You got lost at Brecon, took the wrong road at Llandrindod. Reached Newtown, found yourself south of Birmingham, then, unaccountably, Wolverhampton.

While working on the *Western Mail* in 1972 the journalist John Osmond came up with an idea which would, he imagined, help unite disparate Wales. Let's have a road that links us, a Welsh M1, but without the compulsory purchase and the expense of so many bridges and underpasses. Something we could love. The newspaper ran a campaign over several months, garnering support, and which eventually resulted in John appearing before the Welsh Office Roads Division at a meeting in Graham Buildings on Newport Road in Cardiff. Osmond was shown a great map of Wales. Where would you put this road, he was asked? John pointed.

The A470, our great Welsh connector, ended up being cobbled together from an array four-digit A roads that already latticed Wales[3]. Some small bits added. New signs. Much road marking. You can traverse it now. You can. You get in your car in Cardiff, or Llandudno, and take one road that goes all the way. But to do this requires determination, stamina, a head for heights and more hours than it takes to fly to Rome. Wales, one land under god. Feels like nationhood under muslin, fog and flying sticks. A place full of travelling hay and endless bends.

So began this relationship we all have with this road we love, it's ours, we have a literary magazine named after it, an online football fanzine, a road movie of photographs, lights and landscape and love. Kieron Lyons has digitally filmed the entire route from the front of his car, rain and licence holder, plays it back speeded up. There's a TV history and a forthcoming book. But how we hate it. The time lost, draining away through the footwell carpets of our cars, radio signal gone as we traverse the deserts of Caersws, Clatter, Dolgoch, Llanbrynmair, Commins Coch. Rté from Ireland coming in strong as we climb over Dinas Mawddwy. Only Radio One possible everywhere else. Listen to that one CD we've remembered to bring over and over again. Head full of passing trees and banks of thin faced sheep.

Those in power whose job it is to run this country see their lives lost in a haze of motorised weariness. Meetings are arranged on the principle of equal misery. Video conferencing is done when possible but it's never the same. Everyone travels. We meet in the centre. Llandrindod, Rhayadyr, Newtown. Hotels, motels, halls, bars. Everyone believes that it is they who have travelled the furthest. Starting from Cardiff, Newtown is in the far distant north. Starting from Bangor, Rhayadr is a million miles down in the sunny south. No one is right in this ungreen, fuel consuming, big carbon-footprinted activity. Nothing can be done. In the late 1990s the IWA (Institute for Welsh Affairs) under John Osmond commissioned a report into speeding up transportation[4]. Could the A470 be straightened? Could corners be flattened, could overtaking lanes be added, roundabouts filtered, lights changed. How fast could we make it? How much would this all cost? The result suggested that many millions might buy us a journey time of three hours rather than five. Get there in a morning and still have energy to speak. The Institute revived the idea in 2008. More listening but no action. In research labs at Bangor they are building a teleporter. In Cardiff they plan a matter transmitter. In the blues club at Merthyr Crippled Hard Armed Davies is singing, *Got them down and out A470 blues again*. Bottleneck rattling.

The A470 starts right by the barrage-enclosed fresh-water sea at Cardiff Bay. Here sits Harvey Hood's *Celtic Ring*, a great sculptured bronze hoop that marks the sea boundary of the Taff Trail. To its immediate north is the Flourish, the elongated drop-shaped twist of road which is as far south as the A470's tarmac goes. Once the artery ran north up Bute Street but Cardiff has built itself a dual-carriage wayed grand boulevard, Lloyd George Avenue, designated the A470. Bus lane from the word go. Straight as a die. Nothing else like it on the A470, anywhere. It ends near the pier at Llandudno. Retirees walking their dogs. Lifeguards. Punch and Judy. Northern water lapping the shore.

A470. Spanner size. Screw. Engine part. Transistor. Flight number. Diode. Additive. Food number. Designated area. Horizontal dimension. Transaction printer. Miniature ewer. Ink ribbon. Cash register interface. Thread. Registrar's home. Formulated beverage. Preamp. Jumper pattern. Hoop. Tyre. Star Cluster. Big Band. Impact Matrix. Holdings. Airbrush set. Hex. Diesel Loco. Road.

Orgs

Acas
Acme
ACW
Amgueddfa Cymru
BBC
Bedol
Biwro
Boda Cyf

CADW
Caflass
The Catholic Agency For Willies
Cymdeithas Hanes Pethau
Cyngor Cefn Gwlad
Decoy
ELWa
Fforwm
Ffynon
Glasu
Gonad
Grwp Grip
Haberdashers
Menter Iaith Ely Racecourse
Mewn
Minge
NACODS
NASUWT
NATFHE
NAWLIGNUM
NFERSCYa
NERFUS
NORNANMILER
Oriel Davies
PCS
Penarth Times
Planed
Planet
Punnet
Replica Watches!
Seren
Sgrîn
Sianco
Sosbanelli
Y Syfydliad Tart Cyhoeddus
Sustainable Stapling
Torfaen Tornado
Uned Public
USDAW
Vam
Welsh Council for Creision Tatws

CAPITAL OF THE NORTH

In the north of Wales the Celtic fog drifts eastwards across the border. Not that anyone here uses the word. Celtic is the sea where they fruitlessly explore for oil. Celtic is the heart of Catholic football in Glasgow. The Celtic Celts. With great coats and beards and loud non-English voices. With interlacing tattooed on their forearms. Do they still exist. Are they real or are they not?

Visiting Crosby sometime in the early 1990s I'd found myself in a time warp. In an upstairs pub room full of seeping conversation and the beepboop of guitars from somewhere below I faced an audience of new-agers, street walkers, locals, men in duffels and reefer jackets, women with piled yellow hair and giant hoop earrings, wearing black tights below white short dresses, smoking, drinking dark beers, and with docs and working boots doubling as town shoes below the cast iron tables. I began. It's great, I said, looking out through the window the rain-specked dark and buses passing and the street lights following the line of the Mersey estuary, to be here at last, Liverpool, capital of North Wales. Celtic silence. Could have said capital of Montenegro for all the connection I made. Nothing. Not a flicker.

Later, in those damp streets, I walked through some place that wasn't England. Walked to my digs at a converted seminary where nuns from Ireland helped Catholicism by putting up strangers for money. You're from Wales, the sister told me. In case I didn't know. She showed me to my cell with its giant crucifix on the wall above the bed. Wales as it might have been if it hadn't been for Henry and the bedrock of the Celtic Church. That word again.

Liverpool has much more than a passing Welsh connection. It's a city giant, by our standards, sitting there right on the northern border. It turns on its radio in the morning and blasts Liverpool at the whole of the north Wales coastal belt. Today it is the place you visit for big stores, for the M&S that Flint does not possess, for Gap and Next and Waterstones. For the buzz and the culture and then the clubs and bars and the dope and the drinking. The Welsh connection has been there as long as Liverpool has. Lliferpwll. Lerpwl.

Liverpool has a fair idea that it isn't quite England. The New York of Europe. The end of the line. The place where the north reaches Wales and Ireland almost simultaneously. Where the population is a rich mix of immigrant, so rich that native no longer exists, if they ever did. Everyone got to Liverpool from somewhere else. The city is not mentioned in the Domesday Book. King John founded the port in 1207 because he needed an independent dispatch point from which to send troops to Ireland. Before that there was nothing. An ox-bow made by the bending Mersey. Liuerpul. Dank creek. Pool of mud. A dog and two fishermen.

The Earl of Derby built a four-towered castle here in 1232. This lasted until 1726 when it was replaced by a series of subsiding churches. The site today is occupied by the Victorian Monument[5]. The place grew because of the ships. Ships that went to America and the West Indies. Cloth, coal and salt from the Liverpool hinterland exchanged for the twin poisons of the Western world: tobacco and sugar. Ships that carried slaves. Liverpool's black community began when the first dock was built in 1715. Older than Cardiff's, just. It was the industrial revolution that turned Liverpool from burgeoning port to dynamic world city. Made it famous everywhere. The world knew of Britain and they also knew of Liverpool. Population rose from 6000 to 80,000 in the eighteenth century. In Wales the largest conurbation at the time was tiny Carmarthen.

Trade expanded rapidly during the nineteenth century. Population ballooned. By 1851 around a quarter were Irish, fleeing the Great

Famine, looking for work, safety, life, salvation. Their mark as indelible as the local Welsh walking in across the leaky and ill-defined border. Liverpool was the leading port of the British Empire. The weight and residual Victorian power of its major buildings are strong reminders. Despite the hard and hoary hold of Imperial England Liverpool hosted the 1884, 1900 and 1929 National Eisteddfodau. Population was 850,000 by the time of 1930 depression. The post-industrial slide from that time on, accelerating towards the millennium was as bad in Liverpool as it was anywhere. Local unemployment rates in the 1980s were the highest in the UK. Tear gas subdued riots took place in Toxteth, the large working class walking suburb. Liverpool's Grangetown. A Welsh district and an Irish district but by the 1980s predominantly Asian and Afro-Caribbean black.

Liverpool's twentieth century downs were many. Worst bombed city in the UK during World War 2. Far Left Derek Hatton Militant take-over of local services in the 1980s. Ninety-six Liverpool football fans dead at Hillsborough. The James Bulger murder. The stealing of Welsh water by the building of the damn at Tryweryn and the drowning of the so-Welsh village of Capel Celyn near Bala in 1965. The half-hearted apology from the Council, forty years on, which mouldered on about earlier insensitivity and unintentional hurt and did little to refurbish Welsh pride.

The rebuild in progress when I visit in 2007 is in high gear. At the Albert Dock opposite the bus station, already looking like a part of Cloud City on the set of Star Wars, there are eighteen cranes in action redeveloping what looks like the entire of Liverpool 1. This is the Paradise Project – the redevelopment of 42 acres of prime city in time

for 2008, the year Liverpool takes on the hard won mantle of European Capital of Culture.

It's a dull day. I don't recall ever having been here when it hasn't been. The visitor attractions of the sleek and repointed Albert Dock, the Maritime Museum, Tate Liverpool, the WW2 amphibious landing craft, American D-Day Dukws painted bright yellow which plunge with their waterproofed

riders into the Salthouse Dock to shrieks and screams, they are all behind me. We go up the hill, along Duke Street, towards the Cathedral, one of them, the art college, Chinatown and the Georgian once-Bohemia of Canning Street, Liverpool 8. Brian Patten lived here, tiny flat from which he ran his poetry mag, *Underdog*, No 18. Stuart Sutcliffe, almost Beatle, lived at 83. Adrian Henri, spirit of the age for the city that was the epicentre of the 60s, lived at no 64. This was where Allen Ginsberg stayed when he swept into this place to pick up the vibes in 1965. "Liverpool is at the present moment the centre of consciousness of the human universe." Just along Princes Road at Windermere Terrace lived Roger McGough. The Liverpool Scene identified by the critic Edward Lucie-Smith and launched on the world by Penguin in their classic Modern Poets No 10 *The Mersey Sound* changed the way we did things. "I have seen Père UBU walking across Lime Street / And Alfred Jarry cycling down Elliott Street" "And Marcel Proust in the Kardomah eating Madeleine butties dipped in tea."[6] They're still here too. In Chinatown, just below the Anglican Cathedral on St James Mount, I ask an aged Chinese, Mao jacket, trainers, day-sack holding a flask of soup, to translate the words across the entrance arch. 歡迎到中國鎮 But what does it say? 歡迎到中國鎮 He tells me again, fluent Mandarin. I've picked the only Chinaman in a hundred yards who speaks no English. A visitor here, like me. Cornwallis Street has its nameplate in Roman script and below that in Chinese pictograms. In the Cathedral which looks as if it has stood for a thousand years but actually was only completed in 1978 after a century of build, I buy a postcard. *Liverpool Historic Pub Crawl*. Thumb nails of The Grapes, Mount Street, Ye Cracke, Rice Street, Crocodile, Harrington Street, The Philharmonic, Hope Street, Carnarvon Castle, Tarleton Street. Fifty more. God and the grape close together once again.

Along Hope Street where Henri would have walked is the Art College. He taught here. On the corner of Mount Street is John King's public sculpture, *A Case History*. Boxes, bags, and cases made

from concrete celebrating the
famous who once lived nearby.
Arthur Askey comedian,
Josephine Butler pioneer in
social welfare, Paul McCartney
Sir and singer, Stuart Sutcliffe
almost, Charles Dickens
writer, R.J. Lloyd promoter of
Esperanto, and a cast from a
box of books addressed to the
Liverpool Poets. Tourists have
their photos snapped standing
next to a case that might have
held John Lennon's guitar.

Henri looked like Toulouse-Lautrec would have if he'd had legs.
Beard, long dark hair, Buddy Holly glasses. He was the pop artist who
painted oils of red panties which faded to white in the sunlight. His
poems trod the same territory, engaging with the city he lived in and
stayed in even when his fellow poets, powered by fame, had left.
Henri was a dominant presence during the 60s. He was an instigator
of art happenings, a capturer of city-scapes, an organiser of readings
and events. He was an indefatigable generator of the avant garde who
made cut ups from Milton mixed with the *TV Times* and pushed into
high relief everyone from Charles Mingus to William Burroughs. If
you weren't you, who would you like to be? Paul McCartney, Gustav
Mahler, Danilo Dolci, Napoleon Solo, Adrian Mitchell and Marcel
Duchamp[7]. And a hundred others. Names of the age. People we'd all
like to be. None of them Welsh. Henri spent his childhood in Rhyl,
went to school there, worked the funfairs season on season, living in
a Welsh house with Welsh neighbours and Wales there all around him.
Not much stuck.

At the opposite end of Hope Street the Catholic Cathedral is brutalist concrete made soft by its need to point like a crown at Heaven.
It does not resemble the Anglican structure on St Stephens Mount
even though it was consecrated earlier. The Metropolitan Cathedral
of Christ The King, architect Frederick Gibberd, took five years to
realise and its two-thousand-three-hundred-seater cylindrical space
sits on top of a Lutyens 1933 crypt. This is the only part of the first
architect's pre-War grandiose design for the original cathedral to have
been realised. The building's stark modernism is moderated by bright
coloured light coming through John Piper's contemporary stained

glass. Inside the space is huge and open but somehow lacks awe, has little gravitas, lacks a sense of history. The crypt, the cathedral's one genuine connection with the past, hosts an annual CAMRA Beer festival. God and hops again. Couldn't happen deep in non-conformist Wales.

In Waterstones on Bold Street Liverpool's connection with its poetic past is self-evident. Not one Henri title anywhere bar a reprint of the now ancient Penguin. Someone in the history section is taking digital snaps of the index to a giant history of the city. Beats paying. The shop assistants take no notice. I find a loose pound coin on the settee installed to encourage browsers. I'll put it in the blind box. Can't find one. Back at the Tate is a wall map which shows Liverpool's position as the centre of most things. Echo and the Bunnymen at Erics. Brian Epstein and the Beatles. Jeff Nuttall, Maurice Cockrill and Keith Arnatt at Liverpool College of Art. Yoko Ono and Mike McGear somewhere between Poetry and Music. The Boyle Family at the Docks. Le Corbusier at the Walker Art Gallery. A map of names and arrows and photos of places in squares. Beyond this I stumble on Henri's greatest painting *The Entry of Christ into Liverpool 1962-4*. Oil on Hessian. 68"x95". Père Ubu in his white suit with a black spiral on front. George Melly. Patten. McGough. The whole larger Liverpool cultural presence standing arrayed below a banner reading 'Long Live Socialism', next to an advert for Colmans Mustard, and then one for Guinness. The figures stand in line waiting to be recognised. If you were there then you'd be painted. Centre of the Creative Universe.

Following the Welsh connection I visit the Welsh Streets in Toxteth.

Walking distance from everywhere, boarded up, wrecked, abandoned. Enid Street. Geraint Street. Merlin Street. Dovey Street. Powis Street. Gwydir Street. Teilo Street. Ringo Starr was born here in clapped out Madryn. No plaque. The Merseyside Bangladesh Association building stands in faded green paint, maroon coloured chipboard windows, deserted. All Items Of Value Have Been Removed

From These Premises. A squat-
ter hangs on, flowers in baskets
hanging outside the only one
of five hundred houses where
anyone still lives. Flattening is
days away. The council prom-
ise to rebuild Ringo's house as
a tourist attraction, brick by
brick, somewhere else. Would
they be the same bricks? Same
colour scheme on the restruc-
tured plaster inside? Will it cost
£13 to visit as it does to the
National Trust run terrace at

20 Forthlyn Road where Paul McCartney once lived? Beatle music
no longer leaks from the radios. There are none. All grey silence.
Liverpool changing again.

I roar through the Mersey Tunnel back to the Wirral and then on
to where Wales, on the political map, begins again. Queensferry. The
TV aerials, like they all do from here to Wrexham, point resolutely at
English transmitters. The one-time Arts Minister Alun Pugh told me
that when he lived with his future wife in Chester it came as a sign of
the strengthening of their relationship when she had her aerial turned
west so that he could pick up news of Ruthin and Caernarfon instead
of Wolverhampton and Cheadle Hulme. This is the first one I've ever
had to change to point at Wales, the aerial engineer told him. Glyndŵr
come back. But maybe it's too late.

CODA

Like the sheep and the poor the question is still with us. In Wales do
we know who we are? Was there ever a time when we did? This is a
linguistic matter, they'll tell you, out there in the green fields, the
green distance, beyond the hills, in the green crags where cymrecti-
tude never sleeps.

Wales *is* these places, say the ones who are in them. A Wales of
small and scattered populations, who are all certain of who they are,
and where doubt is a quality that none possess.

Before 1979, according to the historian Gwyn Alf Williams, two
hundred years of industrial history had bonded the Welsh intelligentsia

with its people. The cultures of the Welsh and English in Wales had begun to draw together. The national consciousness of the race was being articulated. You could sense it arriving. Dragons on tote bags, *Penguin Modern Poets No 27* featuring John Ormond, John Tripp and Emyr Humphreys, the rise of the myth of Richard Burton. Welsh music in the pubs of Swansea. Welsh language on the streets of Cardiff. This, despite Radio England next door across the border, broadcasting itself at 8000 decibels, knocking the very birds out of the high Welsh air. England, rarely Britain, England standing for us all. The food of England, the roads of England, England's empire vanished in the sand, I'm flying back to England, the Act of Union – Scotland and England. No mention of Wales. Not the same kingdom. Queen of England, Bank of England, World Cup England, England vs. West Indies, the *Book of English Manners*, the English rose, English brogues, an Englishman abroad, his English home is his English castle, Aberystwyth on England's western shore.

When the referendum came in 1979 to decide if the Welsh wanted to establish its first elected Assembly since 1404 – the London Welsh came back on their 125 Diesels in droves and drummed up a PR storm. Made no difference. Do you want the provisions of the Wales Act 1978 to be put into effect? That was the question. Only 58% of the electorate actually bothered to answer it. A mere 12% said yes. Defeat was depression on a grand scale for the free thinkers and the ones whose consciousness at last had risen above the parapet. It took another twenty years in the winding, devastated Welsh wilderness for things to change. But we've made the leap now. Some may not care. But an increasing number do.

In the cities, where most of us live, the density of the population is such that the matter of dispersed and regional Wales becomes just so much air. Wales of the scattered communities, straws in the western wind. In the public services, providers may meet in Ludlow, Llandrindod, Shrewsbury or Newtown. But the real action is still on the coast where the transport runs and the glistening clubs hold thousands. Are they building superstores in Llanfairfechan? They are not.

We live our lives under street lamps, in places where the fields don't reach, where the sky can be avoided if needs be, where temperatures stay even and where there's everything that anyone could ever need. Buy it since you've earned it. Take it if you have not. Screw yourself on dope if your intellect won't support you. If you've nothing then just stand around for a while and the arms of authority will reach out and help. Wales, once the cauldron of the industrial revolution, is now a cotton-wool nation, full of football and big-brother slim-screen television. 62% of us have contempt for the law[8]. What bearing has the history of Welshness on this all?

Where that history does matter is where high-rise has yet to happen. Where the blood of the past is in the land and still marks the soil when it's turned. Out there is the hinterland – the Wales of legend, with its myths and celtic crosses, its

old ways and ancient language, its compactness, its streak of separateness, its air of difference, its love of rain and sky and its way of circling itself with its own arms, like Ioan Gruffudd in the *Fantastic Four*. That Wales – so small amid the three million – hangs onto something that in a world of federal enormity, linguistic dictatorships and oil-powered multi-national commercial empire, is almost forgotten. Small is beautiful. So said E.F. Schumacher in 1973. True then, even more so now. Growth is not necessarily good. Bigger is not necessarily better. Mass production should be replaced by production by the masses. Assets are not ultimately expendable. Scale should be reduced, resources renewed. Now the coal is gone and the oil will never be found this is what Wales can excel at. Wales can do it. In that short gap of demographic time before the cities finally grow together. Before they make an anonymous land where geography holds no sway and universal hedonism begins to matter more than the real. These things could work. Welsh windfarms and Welsh tidal power, Welsh cottage production linked by wifi and cheese with strange names filling the restaurants of the world. But, given the lumpen down there in the vertical drinkeries of Newport and Cardiff and Swansea, hope is thin. Fantasy. Small nations are good at that.

Out there in the land of governance and provision, the Welsh Assembly Government is busy dispersing Wales to the regions. A political process which is as unloved as it is ungreen. At the old Hotpoint Factory in Llandudno Junction they are establishing a new North Wales office to house eleven departments[9]. Moving six hundred reluctant southerners to the rain belts of the north won't hack it. The carbon footprint of the project will take fifty years to repay.

Walking down the corridor will be replaced by a five hour drive the entire length of the A470. Five in a Toyota Prius might not lose us a whole acre of rainforest but it will still spoil a lot of air. Llandudno Junction – does the government not know what image that name can conjure. Built in the age of steam and rich with Victoriana. Welsh Assembly PR department on gardening leave.

Where does Wales go? Is this simply a matter of education? Fight the mind-emptying apolitical numbness of the cities with winning Welsh reportage, bright Welsh news read by passionate new presenters? Our media are in terminal shrinkage. Fewer than a third of the people living in Wales consume Welsh daily news and it's getting worse (Lee Waters)[10].

In the face of advancing globalism there may be no answers at all. Post-modernism has been preaching diversity and the pre-eminence of the fringes since the mid-eighties and still the centre holds. In the twenty-first century Wales has no solution beyond the one it has always had: the rain, the rocks, the difficulty of the Welsh landscape and the remoteness of the west and the north. Or it's the future – a place the world will want to emulate with its carefully planned disparate communities, its cared-for landscape, its world-level new media zap of *Dr Who, Torchwood, Gavin and Stacey*, Katherine Jenkins, the Stereophonics, Ioan Gruffudd, Guto Harri, Owen Sheers and Michael Ball, its permanently stern independence of spirit and its endless joy of being alive.

Which way will the land run? Red dragon soaring or a slow drift to stagnation? Global sea levels may rise but Wales has mountains. Climb them. On top you are nearer heaven.

notes

1. www.theaa.com 185.21 miles. 4 hours 27 minutes.
2. Nidum to Y Caer known. Beyond that lost.
3. Peter Thomas, Secretary of State for Wales, designated the route between Cardiff and Llandudno as the A470 in November, 1972. Prior to this the A470 ran only as far north as Llangurig. The complete route north to south was also served by eleven other trunk roads (Agenda, summer 2008).
4. *Uniting the Nation*, Institute of Welsh Affairs, 1999.
5. Monument to Queen Victoria, Derby Square, built 1902, intended to represent the spirit of patriotism of Liverpool's citizens, as well as the national self-confidence that Victoria's long reign had engendered.
6. From Adrian Henri's 'Liverpool Poems', *Tonight at Noon*, Rapp & Whiting, 1968.
7. From 'Me', Henri's name-drop poem from *The Mersey Sound*.
8. Poll conducted by Professor Suzanna Karstedt at Centre for Crime and Justice Studies at

King's College, London, 2007.
9.   Due to open 2009.
10. As quoted in *Agenda*, summer 2007. The total number of viewers for news programmes on all TV channels combined amounts to fewer than 400,000. Combined circulation of the five highest selling Welsh-based newspapers adds up to fewer that 250,000. The loss of analogue TV to a total reliance on digital in 2009 is expected to make matters worse.

THE PHOTOGRAPHS

WORKS CONSULTED

Did You Know? 100 Interesting Facts You Might Not Have Known About Merthyr – Merthyr Central Library, 2006

Aris, Mary – *Historic Landscapes of the Great Orme* – Gwasg Carreg Gwalch, 1996

Aspden, Bryan – *News Of The Changes* – Poetry Wales Press, 1984

Bick, David – *Waller's Description of the Mines In Cardiganshire* – Black Dwarf Publications, 2004

Bowen, E.G. – *Britain and the Western Seaways* – Thames & Hudson, 1972

Bowen, E.G. (ed) – *Wales – A Physical, Historical and Regional Geography* – Methuen, 1957

Buswick, Judy & Ted – *Slate Of Hand – Stone For Fine Art & Folk Art* – Trafford Publishing, 2007

Catalog Swyddogol Y Sioe / Official Show Catalogue – Royal Welsh Show Llanelwedd, 2006

David, Christopher – *St Winefride's Well – a history and guide* – Gomer, 1969

Davis, Paul – *Sacred Springs – In Search Of The Holy Wells And Spas Of Wales* – Blorenge Books, 2003

Davies, Peter B.S. – *Forgotten Mines* – Merrivale, 1995

Draper, Christopher – *Walks From Llandudno* – Gwasg Carreg Gwalch, 1999

Evans, Aled Lewis – *Y Caffi* - Gwasg Pantycelyn, 2002

Ford, Rebecca – *Footprint Wales* – Footprint, 2005

Gardner, W.H. – *Gerard Manley Hopkins – A Selection of his Poems and Prose* – Penguin, 1953

Green, John – *Afon Ystwyth – The Story Of A River* – Artery Publications, 2006

Grunenberg, Chrisoph & Knifton, Robert (editors) – *Centre of the Creative Universe: Liverpool & the Avant-Garde* – Liverpool University Press, 2007

Harries, George – *A Squint at St David's – Some Impressions of Early Days* – Merrivale, 2003

Heaton, Robert – *Elihu Yale the Great Welsh American* – Wrexham Area Civic Society, 1991

Henri, Adrian, McGough, Roger, & Patten, Brian – *Penguin Modern Poets 10 – The Mersey Sound* - Penguin Books, 1967

Howell, Raymond – *A History of Gwent* – Gomer 1988

Hughes, T.J. – *Wales's Best One Hundred Churches* – Seren, 2007

Jenkins, Elis – *Neath and District: A Symposium* – Elis Jenkins, 1974

Jenkins, Nigel – *Writers of Wales – John Tripp* – University of Wales Press, 1989

John, Brian – *National Trail Guides – Pembrokeshire Coast Path* – Aurum Press, 2004

John, Brian – *Presely Hills* – Pembrokeshire Coast National Park, 1981

John, Brian – *Walking In The Presely Hills* - Pembrokeshire Coast National Park, 1989

Kerouac, Jack – *Big Sur* – Four Square, 1965

Kidner, R.W. – *The Rhymney Railway* – Oakwood Press, 1995

Knightly, Dr Charles – *Sacred Places The North Wales Borderlands – A Closer Look* – Denbighshire County Council Tourism Unit, 2002

Lewis, W.J. – *A Fashionable Watering Place – Aberystwyth* – Cambrian News

Mason, Edmund J. – *Portrait of the Brecon Beacons* – Robert Hale, 1975

Melly, George – *Adrian Henri – Art of the Sixties* – Whitford Fine Art 1997

Miles, Dillwyn – *The Ancient Borough of Newport In Pembrokeshire* – Cemais Publications, 1995

Morgan, Gerald – *Ceredigion – A Wealth Of History* - Gomer, 2005

Newman, John – *The Buildings of Wales – Glamorgan* – Penguin, 1995

Ormond, John – *Definition of a Waterfall* – OUP, 1975

Osmond, John (editor) – *The Preseli Papers* – Plaid Cymru, 2007

Parker, Mike & Whitfield, Paul – *The Rough Guide To Wales* – Rough Guides, 2006

Pierce, Gwynedd O. – *Place Names In Glamorgan* – Merton Priory Press, 2002

Pryce, Malcolm – *Aberystwyth Mon Amour* – Bloomsbury, 2001

Renn, Derek and Avent, Richard – *Flint Castle Ewloe Castle* –CADW, 1995

Richards, Alun John – *The Slate Quarries of Pembrokeshire* – Gwasg Carreg Gwalch. 1998

Roberts, Dewi & Roberts, Pamela – *The Teatime Guide – Afternoon Tea Venues In North Wales* – Gwasg Carreg Gwalch, 1995

Roberts, Tony – *St Davids* – Abercastle Publications.

Senior, Michael – *Llandudno's Story* – Gwasg Carreg Gwalch, 1996

Sim, Jacki – *St Davids Peninsula* – Pebbles Books, 1999

Stephens, Meic (editor) – *The Oxford Companion To The Literature of Wales* – OUP, 1986

Stephens, Meic – *The Literary Pilgrim In Wales* – Gwasg Carreg Gwalch, 2000

Thomas, Roger – *The Brecon Beacons National Park* – Michael Joseph, 1987

Tilney, Chrystal – *The Archive Photographs Series – Dinas Powys, St Andrews Major and Michaelston-Le-Pit* – Chalford Publishing 1996

Underwood, Terry – *The City of Newport – The Gateway to Wales* – Rompdown Ltd, 2005

Williams, W. Alister – *The Encyclopaedia of Wrexham* – Bridge Books, 2001

Williams, W. Alister – *The Parish Church of St Giles, Wrexham* – Parish Church of St Giles, 2000

Williams, Glanmor (ed) – *Swansea An Illustrated History* - Christopher Davies, 1990

Williams, Gwyn A. – *When Was Wales?* – Pelican Books, 1985

INDEX

THANKS AND ACKNOWLEDGEMENTS

As much of this book comes from the memory of visits as it does from the making of new ones. I need to thank Sue who stuck with it as we dragged ourselves across water-filled fields, up the sides of mountains, along railways, through lost industrial complexes and around towns we'd never normally find the excuse to spend time in. All in the name of research. Wales is bigger than you think.

A good many people have helped, knowingly and not, in conversation and in answering my queries. These include Sally Baker, John Barnie, Julie Bibby, Norman Burns, Tom Davies, George Brinley Evans, Grahame Davies, Christopher Draper, Byron Jones, Teona Dorien-Smith, Morgan Francis, Elis Gwyn Jones, Halcyon Hinde, John L'Aiguille, John Osmond, John Pikoulis, Childe Roland, Lesley Smith, Meic Stephens, George & Jane Tremlett, Elin Williams, John Williams. There are others and if I've unwittingly left you out of this roll call then I apologise.

I should thank also Mick Felton and the staff at Seren Books who have helped turn my original *Real Cardiff* into the Wales-wide successful series that it now is.

Earlier versions of some of the pieces in *Real Wales* have appeared in *Planet*, and *Cambria*. They have also provided the inspiration for my introductions to *Real Aberystwyth*, *Real Swansea* and *Real Wrexham*, all published by Seren.

THE AUTHOR

Peter Finch is a writer who lives in Cardiff. He's written poetry for as long as he can remember and his many books include *Useful, Poems for Ghosts* and *Food* from Seren, *Antibodies* from Stride and *The Welsh Poems* from Shearsman. His *Selected Later Poems* was brought out by Seren at the end of 2007. A selection of his work appeared in Hungarian translation as *Vizet* in 2003. He has written a number of books on the business of writing including *How to Publish Yourself* (Allinson & Busby) and *The Poetry Business* (Seren). For many years he compiled the poetry section for Macmillan's annual *Writer's Handbook*. His extensive website can be found at www.peterfinch.co.uk. A former publisher and for many years a bookseller, he is currently the Chief Executive of Academi, the Welsh National Literature Promotion Agency and Society of Writers.

His psychogeography, alternative handbook and sporadic history of the capital of Wales, *Real Cardiff* appeared in 2002. This spawned a whole Seren series of books on the conurbations of Wales which Finch now edits. His *Real Cardiff Two* appeared in 2004. A volume three is in preparation.